The Disciple Dilemma

ENDORSEMENTS

I'm known for books, lectures and debates focusing on Intelligent Design, and its antithesis - naturalistic Darwinism. So it caught my eye that *The Disciple Dilemma* claims discipleship is being diverted away from its Designer's intent, devolving downward, into a morass of spiritual entropy. Could this be true? Dennis Allen argues that Christianity's altered discipling "DNA" brings in an ominous dilemma. Get ready for a few jolts as Allen shows us how the historical Church, corporate America and today's Christian culture struggle with the discipleship mandate. You might find yourself laughing, recoiling or pushing back as you read *The Disciple Dilemma*, but I am quite sure it will change the way you think about your role in the quest to recover Christ's discipling for us all.

–Tom Woodward

Executive Director of the C.S. Lewis Society, Tampa, FL

Research Professor, Trinity College

Author of the award-winning book *Doubts About Darwin*

The Disciple Dilemma is a must read for those who desire to comprehend the tie between true leadership and discipleship grounded in the Lordship of Christ. It effectively sets before the reader the dilemma faced by Christians today: whether to follow the shallow 'easy-believism' of our Modern Western church and business traditions, or to comprehend and take on the costly service of following Christ in sound leadership and discipleship.

–Tom Harvey

Academic Dean of the Oxford Centre for Mission Studies, Oxford UK

Missionary and Seminary Professor to Asia

Author of *Acquainted With Grief: Wang Mingdao's Stand for the Persecuted Church in China*

I am an entrepreneur, investor and a global apologist. The two common links in all those roles are people and leadership. *The Disciple Dilemma* is making the case that leaders in all vocations and roles serving Christ must understand and tackle the dilemma we now face. If we are to restore committed and surrendered disciples to go into the watching world, we must understand these issues. If you lead one or more people in work, ministry or family this book is useful for you. Be ready for intrigue, provocation, perhaps even laughter, but above all be ready to be changed.

–Andy Moore
Entrepreneur and Apologist, Oxford UK
Managing Director at Chorus Network
Director at ADF International (UK)
Founder of Living Telos blog

If discipleship could be likened to the operating software for followers of Christ, then *The Disciple Dilemma* is making the case that some of our software has been hacked! *The Disciple Dilemma* brings to light peculiar symptoms infesting the contemporary Christian community generally, and disciples specifically. But it doesn't stop there. Dennis caught my interest when he began to connect ancient history, corporate practices and church traditions to our present-day challenges. And he's made a case that this trojan-horse code is infecting commercial, civic and societal outcomes as well as Christian discipleship. *The Disciple Dilemma* urges Christian leaders to reformat discipleship back to Version 1.0, Christ's way. This is a vital read for leaders!

–Mike Hardin
Provost and Vice President, Samford University, Birmingham, Alabama
Professor of Quantitative Analysis
Formerly, Dean of the University of Alabama Culverhouse College of Business
Author and Ordained Minister

With candid insight that is as unapologetic as it is refreshing, *The Disciple Dilemma* locates the Western church in a place of spiritual anemia and exposes the ancient path of fast-held traditions that brought us here. Allen doesn't pave an easy road of sanitized solutions or cookie-cutter fixes, but instead calls us to seek out the wilder, messier, costlier road that Christ Himself journeyed on His mission to make disciples. As a leader in ministry and business, I encourage Christians to take the iconoclastic challenges found in these pages seriously... and then summon the audacity to do something about it.

–Kara Kennedy

Executive Director, ClearTrust LLC, Lutz, Florida

Entrepreneur and Apologist

Board Member, the Securities Transfer Association and the C.S. Lewis Society

Author of *Supper, Reflections from our Table*

One of the greatest challenges for me serving as a senior executive has always been people. Specifically, finding, recruiting, motivating and retaining great people to do what they are called to do. As a leader in the Christian community, you're facing that same problem, serving and coaching your people in discipleship. Allen takes us on a challenging walk through Biblical, corporate and church history to show us the divergence of Western discipling from Christ's way of doing things. If you are a leader in Christian community, and I am not only speaking to Pastors, the responsibility is on you to get discipleship with your people fully aligned with Christ's ways. This book is a strategic and Biblical workout that Christian leadership needs to consider with all our hearts, minds and strength."

–Dave Engelhardt

President of the C.S. Lewis Society, Tampa, Florida

President of CertainTeed Gypsum (Retired)

Formerly, President ThyssenKrupp Elevator

Why are millennials leaving the church in droves? Why do pastors and staff members work themselves to exhaustion while most church members warm the pews? Why do believers war with one another instead of pulling together? Why has society stopped listening to the concerns of Christians? Using humor and incisive insight, Allen presents an historic case for re-thinking the way we do discipling. I recommend *The Disciple Dilemma* for any leaders who wonder what's going on in the ranks of disciples.

–Dixie Hunke
IMB Missionary to China and Africa
Birmingham, Alabama

The Disciple Dilemma makes the audacious claim that since the second century the Christian community has been attempting to clone, instead of make disciples. What's the problem with that? Just as biological embryo cloning is fraught with high failure rates and subtle, life-threatening risks, discipleship cloning, which is another way to say mass-producing disciples, is not Jesus' way, and a low yield endeavor. Bluntly, cloning is not working well for the disciples nor Jesus' Church. Leaders, ranging from Pastors to teachers to personal disciplers need to read *The Disciple Dilemma*!

–Tim Bertram
CEO ProKidney, Raleigh, North Carolina
DVM; Board Certified Toxicologist

My life's work is discipleship, on the mission fields of Southeastern Europe, the U.S. and Latin America. *The Disciple Dilemma* aims at the world of disciples and missions. If you lead or disciple one, two or a thousand people you need to read this book. You may not agree with everything written, but you will feel like Allen has been looking over your shoulder, as the book takes you through the things that hamper disciples, and what we, as leaders, need to do to regain the fuller way of Christ in making disciples. Read the book!

–Josip Debeljuh
Serving as a Missionary, Zagreb Croatia
Global Outreach International & The Church at Brook Hills
DMin Candidate in Missions, Midwestern Baptist Theological Seminary

Where was this book when I began my pastoral ministry? Discipleship is something we pastors assume we are very familiar with, but are we actually on mission making disciples as Jesus has called us? Are we forging reproductive disciples or just multiplying 'Christianized' spectators? Dennis Allen challenges us to understand discipling properly and engage it effectively. We would like a simple three or four point guide, but Allen tells us we must do a lot more thinking through what is needed biblically. We can't simply copy what others are doing. You may not like everything Allen says, but I believe his book will help you be a better disciple maker.

–John Grossmann

Senior Pastor

Grace Evangelical Free Church, Cincinnati, OH

A must-read for leaders in every facet of Christian community. As a leader and global missionary with Campus Outreach I am convinced that being a disciple and making disciples are our calling, regardless of gender, vocation, age or location. And I believe discipleship is under siege today in many Christian communities. *The Disciple Dilemma* raises haunting questions as it forces us to hold our traditions of discipleship up to the looking glass of Jesus' model of discipleship. Whether you lead one or thousands, this book is a candid, clever and thought-provoking wake-up call to the disciple-making dilemma that sits before us!

–Melanie Rogers

International Ministry Strategy Director, Campus Outreach SERVE

Birmingham, AL

THE
DISCIPLE
DILEMMA

Rethinking and Reforming How
The Church Does Discipleship

DENNIS ALLEN

NEW YORK

LONDON • NASHVILLE • MELBOURNE • VANCOUVER

THE DISCIPLE DILEMMA

Rethinking and Reforming How the Church Does Discipleship

Published in New York, New York, by Morgan James Publishing. Morgan James is a trademark of Morgan James, LLC. www.MorganJamesPublishing.com

All Scripture quotations, unless otherwise indicated, are taken from the Holy Bible, New International Version®, NIV®. Copyright ©1973, 1978, 1984, 2011 by Biblica, Inc.™ Used by permission of Zondervan. All rights reserved worldwide. www.zondervan.com. The "NIV" and "New International Version" are trademarks registered in the United States Patent and Trademark Office by Biblica, Inc.™

Scripture quotations marked ESV are taken from the ESV® Bible (The Holy Bible, English Standard Version®). Copyright © 2001 by Crossway, a publishing ministry of Good News Publishers. Used by permission. All rights reserved.

A FREE ebook edition is available for you or a friend with the purchase of this print book.

CLEARLY SIGN YOUR NAME ABOVE

Instructions to claim your free ebook edition:
1. Visit MorganJamesBOGO.com
2. Sign your name CLEARLY in the space above
3. Complete the form and submit a photo of this entire page
4. You or your friend can download the ebook to your preferred device

ISBN 9781631957826 paperback
ISBN 9781631957833 ebook
Library of Congress Control Number: 2021947677

Cover Design by:
Megan Dillon
megan@creativeninjadesigns.com

Interior Design by:
Chris Treccani
www.3dogcreative.net

Morgan James is a proud partner of Habitat for Humanity Peninsula and Greater Williamsburg. Partners in building since 2006.

Get involved today! Visit MorganJamesPublishing.com/giving-back

For Calvin & Barbara Miller, Mickey & Carol Dalrymple,
and Wilson & Charline Henderson.

WITH IMMENSE GRATITUDE

To my beloved, Karen, my coach, counselor and friend. She really did try to clean up my tpyos.

To Newton & Vivian (Dad & Mom), Raymond, Brent, Ken, Dixie, Melanie, Meredith, Josip, Marko, Libby and Matt for your support and help in this project.

To the faculty and class of BP 2019 at OCCA, The Oxford Centre for Christian Apologetics. Especially David Lloyd and Os Guinness. This is your fault.

To the team at Morgan James Publishing, Chris, Emily, Amber, Jim, Wes, Tom and of course David, who tirelessly coached, counseled and kept us on track.

To Thomas Womack's insightful editing, and Lisa Grimenstein's precise proofreading, such that the fears of my grammar teachers were not yet again realized.

Reston, Virginia
Spring 2022

CONTENTS

See to it that no one takes you captive through hollow and deceptive philosophy,
which depends on human tradition and the elemental spiritual forces
of this world rather than on Christ.
COLOSSIANS 2:8

This Lifes dim Windows of the Soul / Distorts the Heavens from Pole to Pole /
And leads you to Believe a Lie / When you see with not thro the Eye
WILLIAM BLAKE "*THE EVERLASTING GOSPEL*"

INTRODUCTION

Jesus designed and directed the deployment of an operating system (O/S) that he said was to be taken to all the world. You probably know that an operating system is the software allowing computers, spaceships and your cell phones to perform their complex tasks. Christ's O/S is equipped with a communications app, capable of transmitting life-changing information to people. The O/S is designed to be networked, as it is optimized for teamed action, versus going-it-alone. It is globally deployable. The system is fault-tolerant, able to be fully restored by its developer after internally-induced failures. It is a learning O/S, structured to absorb increasing knowledge about its developer and his other creations throughout its lifespan. Jesus's O/S is written to relate to, to care for, console and comfort people living in a fallen world's isolation, despair, violence, oppression, disease, poverty and divisiveness, just to name a few. The O/S exists to be Christ's building blocks for his Kingdom.

The system is literally, the flesh and bones of missions, ministries, fellowship, study, prayer and worship. This amazing O/S from Christ is designed to operate reliably and winsomely in corrosive environments including hatred, cancel and skepticism—and it is capable, emphasis on the word capable, of operating in graciousness, without fear or anger, even if the individual system itself faces abuse or destruction in doing its job. And, dare we suggest it, the O/S is intended to exemplify and spread peace in the polarities of local, national and global anger and chaos. It is an O/S designed to interact with all sorts of people: neighbors and alien alike, coworkers, professors, artists, the military, business people, the media, family. Maybe even politicians...

But there's a problem.

The operating system has been compromised by a centuries-old malicious link that introduces a subtle, destructive, replicating virus in the system. The result? Symptoms like these: Functions run slower. The system freezes up sporadically. The virus mutes the system's communications feature, or disables its restoration and replication features. Increasingly, the virus causes the system to simply shut down.

In other words, the operating system has been hacked! And we may not even suspect anything is wrong. What is the system? What do we mean by hacked? What should we do? Welcome to *The Disciple Dilemma*.

Canaries and Traditions

If you think about it, those symptoms we just mentioned are like coal mine canaries. Canaries were used as an early warning system for low oxygen levels in coal mines. When the canary swooned, it meant that something needed to be done, and fast, or big problems were in store for the miners. Modern electronic oxygen monitors in coal mines are traditionally yellow today in honor of their winged forerunners.

Like a canary in a coal mine, the symptoms are telling us that oxygen is running low on discipleship in Western Christianity. Problem is, for discipleship in many Christian communities, there's a tradition to put the canary in a dark corner, covered and out of sight, and go on expecting all to run well.

A tradition is a customary thing. It hangs on, stays put, pulls thinking and habits into its orbit—regardless of whether that tradition is worthwhile. Some traditions have been hanging on our cultural walls for centuries, framing what's to be taken as good and right. Many traditions we follow today, like the yellow-colored oxygen monitors are good things. But some of the traditions we are immersed in, for disciples, are neither good nor right.

Traditions can be hard routines to overturn, because the roots run so deep in their environment. There was, and may still be, a chant about traditions in one Catholic seminary in New York:

> It's tradition, it's tradition, it's a very, very, very old tradi-
> tion!
> You can ask the Roman Rota; it won't help you one iota!
> For no amount of wishin', no, no amount of wishin'
> can ever change or hope to change a very old tradition.[1]

How's the canary looking right now? Do we even want to pull out the canary cage and see? If that bird is conked there will be panic! Some people will want to run away. Some don't want to know about the canary at all, preferring to stay quiet, and keep on keepin' on. Still others think all this fuss about a stupid bird will just embarrass us and interfere with what we're doing. Don't ask, don't tell, and for heaven's sake don't yell about the bird. We just don't, traditionally, want to worry with the bird. We'd be mad if anyone hinted that the bird wasn't ok. What to do? It's a dilemma.

My mentors over the years taught me that corporate America has its own version of a dilemma. What is it? Business usually does a poor job developing employee purpose, dedication, execution and retention—in a sense, making poor commercial disciples. History demonstrates that addressing these kinds of people dilemmas require leaders who will change the traditions that don't work. Christian communities are facing similar people problems. Here are two introductory examples, with more to fol-low: One, a majority (over 60%) of believers are abandoning their faith, and not coming back. Two, the remnant minority of believers in Christian-ity are largely going mute on their faith outside the walls of their churches. The canary is swooning! Christianity faces the urgent task to reform the way it develops conviction, courage, and execution among the followers of Christ—in being disciples and making disciples. Looking to Scripture, we can see how discipling was intended to be done, and by touring the failings and foibles of business and even the historical Church's treatment of disciples we can see the best of the worst ways to *not* do it.

My business resume reads like an attention-deficit-disorder diagnosis: electronics, energy, building materials, healthcare, defense, aviation, software, and conglomerates. I've been a CEO six times. I've worked for several Wall Street powerhouses to help their distressed midsized corporate holdings get back on their feet. And over those years I've (perhaps like you) participated in leadership roles outside business. For me that was in mega, medium-sized, and small churches, serving on boards and in ministries and charities. If you've been a CEO or served in any top leadership roles, you know all about having that ringside seat, experiencing the best and worst in organizations. You get to witness things that drive intended results, and other things that stall them out. You see traditions that serve a mission well, and other traditions and cultures that bog things down to a full stop.

Now you and I both serve Christ as his disciples. All the things that go with being an individual disciple apply to us. Plus something else. You lead people. It may be one person, it may be a family, it may be dozens or thousands as a leader. Here's where it gets personal. Dealing with this dilemma we're about to look into is on you and on me to grasp, to address and to change.

There are ominous symptoms showing up in Christianity's people— in disciples. Symptoms like younger generations within the Church, in numbers approaching six in ten walking off from Christianity, calling it arrogant, evil, or just irrelevant. The minority—those remaining in their faith, at a rate of nine out of ten—say they're unable or unwilling to discuss their faith with anyone outside the walls of their church. These symptoms are just headlines. We have many more discipleship trends like this to talk about.

Is it possible the symptoms impacting discipleship are just passing fads? Misrepresented perhaps, or blown out of proportion? Will they fade out on their own? The studies we'll discuss say the frequency and mutations of these symptoms are growing, the clamor to fix things increasing. A tipping point—or a ripping point is arriving. But what kind of tip/rip?

Some trend watchers suggest our people need to return to the way things used to be, back to the basics, whatever those basics were. Others push for pulling up the drawbridge, to live out faith isolated from modernity's baggage. Some press for better programs to right the symptoms, some that we just throw the bums out and move-on-dot-org. And there are those who demand that we wake up, modern up and cater to society's whims and fads to reverse the declines. It may be that none of those are biblically appropriate.

These approaches point in different directions to cure things, yet they are together in saying that Western Christianity is truly caught up in a dilemma for the soul of its community. That soul would be disciples. And if the dilemma about disciples is real, then to Christian leadership comes the responsibility to recognize where we are—and crucially then, to act on what ought to be done about the dilemma itself.

An Iceberg

The dilemma could be compared to an iceberg. The symptoms lie on the surface, the things we can observe and notice about contemporary disciples. It's easy to track and talk about those observable things. But just like an iceberg, what you see above the waterline is only the result of much larger things below the surface. Eliminating symptoms doesn't eliminate the problem any better than blowing your nose eliminates a cold. Beneath the surface, hidden under the waterline, are the bigger issues, the causes. The larger morass are old traditions in the Christian world that cause the symptoms. Though by operating as traditions, they do their work hidden in plain sight. The traditions are stealthy but massive replication engines, generating the symptoms that make for fragile or failed disciples.

We should be skeptical about claims like this. Surely somebody on staff would have clamored about these traditions already, right? Or someone, someday, will write a book on them and about what we should do—

won't they? Maybe we can just sit it out, let somebody else deal with things like this.

But if the disciple dilemma is real, the dysfunctional machinery will keep replicating the symptoms. That means the dilemma will embed problems in today's disciples. Which means the disciples coming along today, brought up in the dilemma are passing the virus, so to speak, of the dilemma along to the next round (or generations) of disciples, if they are even making disciples at all. In other words, the next generation of disciples may not be coming along at all given the net losses and the rapid declines in making disciples. And because those that do come along are likely to be replicates of the dilemma itself. The dilemma is replication failure, so when disciples cannot or will not make new disciples, the multiplication of the church becomes subtraction and division, which is to say a decreasing number.

Do we stick to our traditions in the Western world of post-apostolic discipling? Or is it possible that Christ's way and ours are not aligned?

This disciple dilemma is a fog that's clouding much of Western Christian culture while masquerading as blue-sky truth. The dilemma means there's little salt, little light, and much discord among the majority of Christ's disciples. The followers of Christ nowadays look pretty much like everyone else in society—lone wolves, politically angry listing "left" or "right," bewildered about why everyone else doesn't get it. Except on Sunday. On Sundays, people tribe up and hang with the traditional people like them. This kind of bunker tribalism and segregation doesn't go unnoticed by the watching world.

Deep pathologies in Western religious culture are at work here, luring people to fade out, or become spectator-believers, conforming to modernity instead of Christ. The traditions drive competition between churches and disunity among believers. That hostility spills over into society, politics, nations and into our children. The societal baggage of affluence, apparent success, and fame among Christ followers makes us hunger for significance, and weighs us down as a timid people that clique up and tune out. That withdrawal cedes the terrain disciples should be walking on away, abandoning business, government, the academies, the arts, and the media to the darkness, to the narcolepsy of wokeness.

Just Relax?

We might want to just keep calm and evangel along, expecting everything to eventually sort itself out. After all, God wouldn't let his people walk off some traditions-cliff into a spiritual abyss, right? Judah and Israel took that bet on several occasions—and lost.

The lure of traditions is a very old, familiar, comforting, complex, and consequential problem. Complex in centuries of well-intentioned but impotent traditions seen by many as the good and right way, which makes change of any sort very tough to bring about. And the dilemma is consequential because these traditions are reinforcing dissipation and passivity in their mass-production underdiscipling.

Interestingly, with only minor semantic tweaks, a similar dilemma lurks in businesses just as it does in Christian community. Not specifically spiritual things mind you, but things that dissipate the motivation and passion of employees in businesses to function well. We've been living with these kinds of people problems throughout business and religious history. Leaders trying to snatch failure from the jaws of victory, using a script of traditions and accommodation instead of going after the root causes.

In this book, we'll go over how much damage all this has caused over the years in the church—and in businesses. We'll aim for clarity on what the dilemma is (in chapters 1–7), what its effects are (chapters 8–9), then explore principles for moving forward on a better path (chapters 10–14). The first half of *The Disciple Dilemma* is an attempt to make visible the long running, complex, and subtle demise of discipleship. Then, with these challenges on the table, the second half is a leadership path forward, hopefully one you'll consider as a path to reform discipleship as Christ intended.

A lot of people object that Christianity isn't business, so don't run it that way. Okay, fair point. This is *not* an attempt to say you need to deploy the latest Wall Street ideas in your church. Folks tried that already and proved it doesn't work. There will be some funny and provocative examples about people trying to do that, to make disciples in some bizarre ways alongside equally odd attempts by businesses to produce dedicated and effective employees. Understand, ponder, think, and hopefully even laugh a little—then consider how these traditions may be influencing Christianity more than you might have realized. Consider how forms of crisis or opportunism in Christianity resulted in edicts, mandates, and get-by choices that became cultural norms, and then morphed into long-standing traditions, deeply wounding discipleship.

And in case you were hoping that time heals all such wounds, both Christian history and commercial practice demonstrate that these issues do not self-eliminate over the years. They morph, contaminate and replicate in the spiritual body of Christ's people as efficiently as any virus in our mortal frames.

Understand the Times

In 1 Chronicles 12:32, we find this description of certain leaders in Israel: "from Issachar, men who understood the times and knew what Israel should do." That word *times* implies the social symptoms, causes, consequences, and the way forward. Leaders must understand *our times* and know what to do regarding discipleship.

The times today? We instinctively sense that winsome, passionate disciples are increasingly rare. We see fewer disciples influencing others locally, regionally, nationally, globally. There's an eerie silence among most believers in the working world, in communities and thought centers.

No technique, sermon or program offers a panacea for a dilemma like this. This is where leaders must check in. The reason this book is for leaders is that only leaders can get at the root cause of the dilemma. Because to address the dilemma, it's leadership that will have to make the call to change the way things are. Show the way. Lead the way.

Otherwise, the system and its traditions will keep reproducing, because that's all the existing process is capable of producing.

What This Book Is and Isn't

This book is not an attack on any church, ministry, or denomination, nor any particular size of Christian community, big or small. It is not an inference that God's plans could be wrecked if not for you and me saving the day. Lastly, the book is not an attempt to list do's and don'ts of being disciples.

Now to the "is" of things. The book is written to leaders, leaders discipling one, two, or thousands. Leaders meaning pastors, parents, elders, missionaries, teachers, deacons, trustees, bishops, business folks, secretaries and scoutmasters. It's especially for leaders, women and men alike who are concerned about the trajectory of discipleship.

This experience may be something of a strategy scrimmage for you. Much like when a board of directors asks provocative questions to probe things, to gauge performance, to up the game—to see if these assertions and questions have merit, and if so, to explore what's to be done. But there's not much time.

Of course, our ultimate hope lies in the sovereign and Trinitarian God who moves among us and in history. He has indeed spoken about his expectations for discipleship. Especially to leaders. To do discipleship his way. That's where things get interesting.

Do we realize where we are? The journey needs to begin now. With you. This journey will be long, challenging, perhaps uncomfortable. But leaders are called by God to serve in humility and with courage in these situations.

May this book result in a strategic change of direction. A change that will see the dilemma for what it is and what it has done to disciples, so that these and subsequent disciples might flourish biblically—lest we continue to replicate a traditionally timid, distracted and brittle Christianity into future generations, producing believers less and less willing to speak of their true hope, less equipped to serve a watching world. We're all called to the better way, a surrendered life as a disciple, out there among the world, pointing people to the risen Christ.

Part One
What *Is* the Dilemma?

Ironically, the conditions that caused the demise of disciple building and lay ministry in those times [second and third centuries] are recurring in the modern church and pose the same threats.

Carl Wilson, *With Christ in the School of Disciple Building*

The problem isn't that we don't have enough Christians.
The problem is Christ doesn't have enough disciples.

Pastor Tony Evans, "Making Kingdom Disciples"

1

Is Something Amiss?

Statistically speaking, your community of believers is probably infected. Most everyone in your small groups, teams, committees, youth groups, worship gatherings, mission trips and ministry operations. Odds are 99 to 1 that they're infected. But not with a virus. It's a dilemma. You might be one of the fortunate communities where the ancients, contemporary society and organizational culture exempted you from the dilemma, but you would be a rarity to be without any of the consequences. Let's set up the problem and get this dilemma out into the light.

Here are four different situations posing a common question:

1. There's a "Check Engine" light flashing when you drive your car, and a bizarre noise under the hood.
2. Your young children and their friends have been upstairs, quiet for far too long.
3. Your boss says she wants to meet with you and the HR director on Friday about your career.
4. The doctor tells you the heart scan needs to be run again, right away.

The common question would be: "Is something amiss?"

Take a look at the bullet points in this chapter. After you skim them, if I were to ask you that same question "Is something amiss?" you would be justified to reply: "It's the disciples, stupid!"[2] So let's talk about the symptoms that drive that common question looking at Christian communities—churches, small groups, ministries, mission agencies and parachurch organizations. People have been telling us for a long time there's a discipleship problem. For example, "Ironically, the conditions that caused the demise of disciple building and lay ministry in those times [second and third centuries] are recurring in the modern church and pose the same threats." was the jolt for me from Carl Smith in his seminal book *With Christ in the School of Disciple Building.*[3] And Tony Evans: "The problem isn't that we don't have enough Christians. The problem is Christ doesn't have enough disciples."[4]

Some symptoms surrounding disciples are good. But others indicate that something's badly amiss, and these symptoms center on disciples. Not all disciples. But even if, as a leader, you're sure your own people are ok, you still might have nagging doubts about those other Christians out there, looking around your part of the world. Facts to back up that nagging sense of unease are not hard to find. Just as an opener, consider these Pew Research Center findings:[5]

- Eternal life is not exclusive to Christianity, according to six out of ten Christians.
- Absolute truth does not exist for 40 percent of Christians.
- Talking about faith is "not my job" for 35 percent of Christians.

And toss in a few findings from some other credible research houses:
- 92 percent of Christians do not believe sharing faith is important[6]
- 65 percent of Christians say living out faith is better than talking about it[7]
- The average tithe today is 2.5 percent and declining. It was 3.3 percent during the Great Depression.[8]

Pew Research's "Religious Landscape Study" tells us that the Protestant census breaks into two-thirds conservative evangelical and one-third liberal/mainline. In other words, evangelicals—the ones who should be the most likely to ascribe to a high view of Scripture and a high view of the person and work of Christ—account for 66 percent of the people in Protestant Christianity. The minority, the 34 percent frequently hew toward looser/lesser views on the reality and resurrection of Jesus, skepticism toward biblical accuracy and inspiration, tending to see truth as an unknowable, and that salvation cannot simply be exclusively in Christ. Yet it's a majority of Protestants who claim that God would not make Jesus the only way to heaven, and that truth, in the classic sense of the biblical narrative, does not exist.

How does a Frankensteinian worldview like this get sewn together in a society? It may be, we think, those Republican right-wingers holding us back, or the social justice lefty progressives. Some say it's due to our academies, that they're the ones polluting minds. Bad politicians are another scapegoat, wrecking morals and principles, or perhaps it's the olders, or the youngers, or movies, music, morals, conservatives, liberals, racists, cis-genders, nationalism, marxism and the beat goes on. Whatever it might be, the symptoms flourish right here amongst us, the believers, in the minds, hearts and social media of the so-called faithful, who are otherwise known as disciples.[9]

What symptoms should we expect of disciples raised with an anemic, spiritually speaking, framework to take to college, or off to the workplace, off to the military, the media, or the universities? (*Off* may in fact be the operative word to use.) What we should expect is a fragile disciple. The New Testament says disciples must be readied with a living and active personal faith, not a bequeathed tradition, lest they become fair game "taken captive by philosophy and empty deceit, according to human tradition, according to the elemental spirits of the world, and not according to Christ." Colossians 2:8 [ESV]

Now it would be one thing to take one or two numbers in a few research studies to force a dire conclusion about discipleship. But there's more to discuss. Let's read on. What do these numbers suggest to you?

- 65 percent of the US population identify as Christian, which suggests there are around 200 million believers. Less than a quarter of those Christians—about 50 million—attend a church.[10]
- In Great Britain, 60 percent of the UK's 60 million people (about 38 million) claim Christianity. Of those 38 million Christians, 8 percent—about three and a half million—actually attend a church somewhere.[11]
- 82 percent of US Christians surveyed say they have no Bible study, no faith community, no mentor.[12]
- 80 percent of Christians say they lack the skills or relationships to feel okay to talk about their faith.[13]

This means that eight of every ten Christians have, at best, little or no association with a community of believers, no developmental life in Christ aside from an occasional sermon. These followers run stealthy about their life in Christ outside their churches, first because most claim not to know how to discuss their belief, or alternatively, believe that to talk about their beliefs is not ethical. And a great many, in increasing numbers are walking off the grid altogether, having been abandoned in their questions, life and belief system. This is anemic discipleship for anybody else watching and listening.

Are these discipling problems being solved by the traditional methods common to modern Christian community—small groups, discipling classes, mission trips and top-notch facilities? Well, there are studies for all that too, with consistently somber findings like these, from the Barna Research Group: [14]

- 41 percent of believers attending church say spiritual growth is an entirely private matter.
- 33 percent of believers say going it alone in spiritual growth is right for them.

- 52 percent of Protestant church leaders say small groups are the key to discipleship.
- 74 percent of Christians say that they're satisfied, or almost where they want to be, spiritually.
- 65 percent of congregants think discipling at their church is good
- Yet only 1 percent of pastors believe discipleship is good in their churches.

Who's right? These trends paint a very Western portrait about disciples: the lone wolf, needin' nothin' from nobody.

People abandoning their faith is not a new thing, but it is uniquely on the rise today. Youthful departures from church have been a problem for centuries. Especially so in the US since the World Wars. But the academics tell us that as the pre-1980's parents raised children of their own, they typically came back to church. Not so any longer.

- 59 percent of millennials drop out of church, and having kids does not bring them back.[15]
- From 1990 to 2016, "Nones" (no religious affiliation) quadrupled from 4 percent to 17 percent.[16]
- "Nones" are 17 percent of the boomer generation (born 1946-1964), but for millennials (born 1981-1994) the rate more than doubles to 36 percent.[17]
- US church membership is down 17 percent from 1999 to 2016. Protestant headcount trends are down 8 percent from 2007 to 2019, and accelerating downward. And for the Roman Catholic Church, for every person who comes in, six leave.[18]
- Beginning with the Gen Xr's (born 1965-1976) most church groups have begun to shrink, a new trend compared to the two hundred preceding years.[19]

If discipling is going well, what gives with these studies? William Wilberforce, the great British politician and emancipator, warned in 1797 about the risk of traditions versus religious commitment. In the opening pages of his book *A Practical View of Christianity*, he discussed traditions ensnaring the typical child growing up at that time:

> He was born in a Christian country, of course he is a Christian; His father was a member of the Church of England, so is he. When such is the hereditary religion handed down from generation to generation, it cannot surprise us to observe young men of sense and spirit beginning to doubt altogether the truth of the system in which they have been brought up, ready to abandon a station which they are unable to defend. Knowing Christianity chiefly in the difficulties which it contains, and in the impossibilities which are falsely imputed to it, they fall perhaps into the company of infidels; and, as might be expected, are shaken by frivolous objections and profane cavil's, which, had they been grounded and bottomed in reason and argument, passed by them, as "the idle wind," and scarcely have seemed worthy of serious notice.[20]

In other words, being brought up in a religion—or simply associating with groups of people involved in it—does not make for enduring disciples.

A lot of people are writing thoughtfully about the whys underlying the challenges in Christianity and in Western society generally. Some, like Rod Dreher say families and sexuality have been wrecked—and if we can get that sorted, we'll be heading in a better way.[21] Others, like R.R. Reno, point to populism, politics, and nationalism as the real problem.[22] Here in the populists, they say, are the roots of the problems in Christian community and society. From another angle, Jonathan Wilson Hartgrove's work strongly suggests the problems of racism, slavery, and the tragedies of oppression in the Western world are the root cause.[23] Or we can look to authors like Sherry Weddell, a Southern Baptist-turned-Catholic scholar, who has published a number of books on discipleship's trends, problems, and better traits, her most famous book being *Forming Intentional Disciples*, where she thoughtfully lays out her case of cause and effect, and a program to set things to rights.[24] Is any of that getting at the problem? Are those things together the problem? Sexuality, politics, racism, program deficiencies? We should consider the possibility that those kinds of issues, rightly describing real impacts on disciples are in fact more societal symptoms of a much larger dilemma infesting the community and the individual people of Christ. Each of these excellent authors' works are well-researched, valid descriptors and superb background. Yet they are the symptoms, not the cause of the disciple dilemma. This means we must find a way to locate the real cause, and then bridge the obvious question of "what someone ought to do" and "what the Church should do," nationally, locally, personally. There must be a beginning to a national, perhaps a global reset for Christian community. A beginning to get us all back to the centerline of what we each do in addressing the disciple dilemma. And that personal first responder must be you. As leaders.

If you've been in a leadership role in the Christian community, you've probably had the feeling that something in the spiritual DNA of many believers isn't quite right. Like a spring winding down in an old clock, a slowing tempo in what we were intended to be. We know that *agape*, surrender, commitment, and endurance were supposed to be prime strands of our new DNA in Christ. Nowadays that DNA seems kind of scarce. But the symptoms are there, evident to almost everyone.

These facts and figures point to corrosive trends that are accelerating among Christian believers of all stripes and types. Usually when this subject comes up with people a common question is "What's the answer to it all?" The problem is, the problem isn't even on the table yet.

Then and Now

Os Guinness has a helpful phrase he uses in seeing the bigger picture: "Contrast is the mother of clarity."[25] Let's lean on that wisdom here. Consider these contrasts between modern-day discipleship and what we can observe from the New Testament period:

- In today's world, the modern thinks of disciples as Christians who upgrade—the premium version, so to speak, of a believer. The New Testament believer knew that every Christian was a disciple.
- The modern sees discipling as possible only if one is a believer. In contrast, New Testament discipling began with people as skeptics or scoffers.
- The modern may, occasionally, be inclined to try to "save" people, but prefers operating from within the safety of groups—such as mission trips and inviting people to church.
- If someone does come to Christ, the modern is inclined to get a convert to sign on, to join somewhere, then the modern can move on to the next prospect. In contrast, the disciples of the New Testament period were inviting people—often relatives, neighbors or recent acquaintances—to "come and see" (and evaluate) Jesus the Christ.
- The modern thinks about discipling as group activity (>3) gatherings, memberships and programs because that's what Christians do—if the cause is right, and the friendships are interesting. The New Testament disciple was mentored, teamed in close proximity to a very few others, and to live with one another as disciples.
- The modern sees lordship as a cost-capped option, if at all. That Jesus will not ask for more than one is willing to give and he will not be unhappy if we opt out of the lord part. For New Testament Christians, it was full and unconditional surrender.
- For the modern, Christianity often is about improving a quality of life, pursuing world causes and right thinking to validate discipleship. For the New Testament disciple, it meant literally setting their life aside and pursuing their Master.
- Moderns embrace identity, uniqueness and individualism. New Testament disciples sought to lose their identity and devote their life, skills and energy in service to God and the people around them.

- The modern seeks solutions with recurring challenges such as sex, money, career or meaning. For New Testament disciples—to fall short is human and grace would prevail.
- The modern disciple is self-made, autonomous, independent. For the New Testament believer, it was never a solo act.
- The modern has an exit ramp, a mission accomplished milestone—it might mean being a good example until the kids have grown up, or taking that big mission trip, or maybe hitting age sixty-five when somebody else ought to step in. Yet, for the New Testament disciple, it never ended. Continuous improvement—sanctification—discipleship was lifelong. There was never any retiring as a disciple.
- For the modern, failure to live up to biblical standards means that something's wrong with the biblical standards. For the New Testament disciple, such failures simply confirmed what was already known: something's wrong with us as human beings.

While not comprehensive, these contrasts highlight symptoms in discipling—symptoms of optional commitment, faith abandonment, spectatorship versus followership, and gospel muteness—all corrosive to a disciple. Is something amiss?

Abandonment

How excited would you be to dine in a restaurant if you encountered pages of internet rants by unhappy customers and disgruntled staff?

That's a good picture of today's Western church. About six in ten millennial disciples (born 1970's to mid-90's) have walked away from Christ,[26] and unlike the generations before them, the millennials are not coming back to their faith when their own kids are born. Meanwhile the boomers (born 1946-1964), who've stuck around a little better are graying out, and the Gen Zers (born after 1996) are opting out in numbers larger than millennials. The walkaways—often referred to as "Nones" or

"Dones"—are telling people, just like that restaurant illustration, that their former religion is antiquated, ignorant, intolerant, irrelevant, or evil.

Other symptoms: "What happened to the guys?" There's a gender gap on the mission field. A mere two generations earlier, single men represented half the mission force, but today single women outnumber single men on the mission field more than two to one.[27] If you include married couples, single men now constitute only about three percent of field team headcounts.[28] Seminary applicants are declining: According to one study focusing on the Midwest, candidates are entering seminary at half the rate that pastoral retirees are leaving.[29] If you've been involved in any pastoral search committee work lately, you know the Midwest is not alone in such scarcity.

What would you think if you found out that key executives were dumping their stock shares in a company you were heavily invested in? Using that illustration, financial support of the church keeps declining in younger generations. Even discounting for age and income, trends point to millennials tithing at only half the rate of people in their same age group during the Great Depression.[30]

How much confidence would you place in a doctor who told you that by using his treatments for your illness you could expect the same recovery rate as people who got no treatments at all? Why should outsiders embrace Christianity when marital infidelity, divorce and surrender to philosophical ambiguity now ensnare between half and three-quarters of regular church attenders and staff, right in line with the modern secular community?[31] That doesn't imply we're getting more enlightened these days. Christian community fares no better with abortion rates, unwed cohabitation, and views of "fluidity," whether poly, trans, or gay that would make Caligula blush.

Mere Spectators and Mutes

Suppose you went into a hardware store to pick up a part to repair a faucet, and the employees said, "We aren't here to help; you'll need to meet with the boss if you want something. And by the way, she's too busy to talk to you." Would you stick around long in that store?

Discipling can be like that inside churches. Few people know how to talk about the hope they have, nor do they have a significant inclination to do so.[32] And how about the foundation of many disciples' faith today? The surveys and studies suggest that religious knowledge for many claiming Christianity is "something they just know or feel"[33], a rerun on the take-it-on-faith (don't sweat the details) thinking that diluted much Christian thinking in the 1970's. If the casual Christian is questioned to any degree—by their kids or friends or coworkers—they go for a lifeline with someone else, like a pastor, leader or the theological profundity of Google.

If you're a leader in a church, you may already sense the passivity—people as audience, content to be spectators, sitting through a service and watching the pros perform. Meanwhile about nine in ten believers in churches say they feel unable or unwilling to discuss what they believe with people outside their church walls.[34]

Today only one in three churchgoers holds to a biblical worldview (the life, teachings and resurrection of Christ, the reality of the biblical God, and the innate fallenness of each human being), even as the number of churchgoers keeps declining. For example, church attendance is only half of what it was in the 1990s.[35] Eight in ten adults in churches today have no Christian development outside of a sermon—meaning no personal Bible study, no Christian peer relationships and little or no prayer life.[36] For most believers, spiritual life is a private endeavor, with no spiritual interaction, period. Yet most Christians in these studies also report that their spiritual situation is doing just fine.[37]

There's also a growing shopping mentality—believers floating from church to church.[38] If what you want isn't available at one church, head over to another. Unfortunately, we can be very picky and coddled disciples.

Size Matters

The demographics are telling us a story. Most churches are shrinking. More than half of the fifty-two million worshipers in the US will attend services at ten percent of the churches open this week. Several hundred churches will host over ten thousand. In business, the Federal Trade Commission would consider these kinds of big organizations as monopolies. In Christianity they're known as mega and giga churches. And intentional or not, their facilities, broad programming, customer service features, and popular personalities siphon members out of smaller churches.

If you participate in one of those kinds of churches, please do not take this as an attack on your church or its size. But size must be a leadership concern, or size will become a god. To push the issue a bit, here's a haunting question: Is the primary source of headcount growth in that church from unbelievers who are coming to faith in Christ, or is it largely pilgrims coming from other nearby churches? A follow-up question for discipleship trails close behind: How does a group of that size try to live out Christ's model of personal discipling outside of worship? If "small groups" is the quick answer (and it usually is), the chapters ahead will make for very interesting reading.

Complications abound for discipling in churches of every size, from the getting-biggers to the small and the stagnant. In a business growth is absolutely necessary to survive. That may or may not be true of any given church situation. But growth always brings baggage. Budgets and member services must grow, or decline ensues. To keep growing, modern churches often look to Harvard Business School's best ideas in branding, budget, concierge services (we do everything for you), and professional programming, just like businesses do to attract market share. Numbers and programs become predominant. And this impacts discipling. Discipleship the way Jesus modeled it can be extremely challenging as size and scale of groups swell.

What about the medium-sized and smaller churches, those having fewer than five hundred attending on a Sunday? Some use me-too tactics to retain people—similar programs and worship venues and facility offerings. Attendance might be steady or ticking up a bit. But Christians transferring in appear to be the main source of growth for these gatherings too—not new believers, and not non-believers. Some churches in the medium/small size bracket struggle as congregations gray out, staff becomes tough to recruit, and there's pressure to be more attractional, like the big guys. The point here is that all sizes and styles of Christian community face challenges in effective discipleship.

If you go to Europe, you can see the trailer for the movie of the larger Western world. My wife Karen and I went to Edinburgh, Scotland in 2017. A vibrant church that I'd visited as a young boy there in the 1970s has been converted into a trendy nightclub called "Sin". Two other church buildings there, still frescoed in wonderful Christian artistry, are flea markets.

Churches are fading out in Europe, as members die off or leave, and the capital required exceeds cash flow. The churches in Europe that continue, even the beautiful cathedrals, will be nearly vacant on Sundays. They're winding down. Yes, there are many exceptions. But too often the church buildings are becoming relics or historical monuments. Christianity has become, to use Hugh Hewitt's term, a "quaint and charming lunacy"[39] in the Western landscape, as discipleship morphs into membership, and then to just shipped out. The last century's trends in Europe are now becoming ours.

Beyond Symptoms

The symptoms aren't the root cause. The symptoms only divert us from the roots. Snuffing the symptoms won't cure the problem, though symptoms always get the attention. Resulting in little net gain for disciples. The symptoms can only be addressed by attacking the roots, which are nestled in the culture of a Christian community.

If you have any experience in attempting a culture change somewhere, you understand how tough, how tedious, and how unglamorous this can be for a microwave society expecting instant results and little cost. A culture change is much more like growing an oak tree. It takes time. It consumes resources. And yet such massive change in thinking and life is essential to reform every disciple to the ways of Christ (Matthew 10:34-39). Leaders—usually for decent reasons—follow tradition to get through the day or through the problems of the moment. It worked before, didn't it? Gotta solve this problem now—right? And people, being busy and all, traditionally, follow their leaders on the well-worn paths. Because in busy worlds—whether in riots, religion, or retail—the traditional thing to do is to rely on the traditions. And those traditional routes become ruts, unbreakable habits, and this-is-the-way-it's-done. Effective? Well, that's another thing.

It's important here not to confuse bad traditions with the core tenets and principles of our faith, such as the creeds, or the inspiration and veracity of Scripture. Those are traditions built on truth, evidence, history, and reality. Those are traditions we must hold fast to. They're not only truth, but Traditions with a capital *T*. This book's message is not about messing with those capital *T* theological bulwarks.

The less worthy traditions emerged from reactionary and expedient choices dating all the way back to the days after the apostles. Yet today they're alive and well among us, with a slightly updated veneer. These historic but flawed traditions in Christian culture wreck disciples and threaten any leader who dares challenge their preeminence.

Addressing the disciple dilemma means tackling the humanly-crafted choices that converted short-term fixes into long-standing traditional practices. This isn't a question of rejecting good principles and truths. It's about being trapped in bad habits.

Six Not-Good Traditions

And what exactly would they be—those old habits, those old traditions?

Here are six not-good traditions for us to consider together. While there are certainly other traditions that could be discussed, perhaps ought to be discussed, these six are crucial in order to grasp the breadth, depth and tenure of the dilemma. We'll take a separate chapter for each tradition:

1. Making the lordship of Christ an option in a disciple's thinking.
2. Catching converts and then releasing them, hoping things work out for them as disciples.
3. Letting influence and power disrupt discipleship cultures.
4. Saddling leaders with sole responsibility for discipleship.

5. Expecting discipleship to happen by herding God's people together.

6. Leaders making the *not* main things the main things.

It can all seem backward. The obvious symptoms of a broken world and struggling Christians are over there on one side of the ledger, needing attention now! But we're over here on this side of the ledger talking about traditions and icebergs and such.

Surely a more direct route exists. We tend to think that what will get this thing fixed is a sermon, or a seminar, or a program or a Bible study. Maybe even dust off the mission statement, wherever it is we put it, and tune it up to display. Those are the common kinds of plays for busy leadership. But snap fixes won't endure. Root causes will require digging out. It will take even more time to plant a new culture, to have it take, to have it grow. This will be a greenhouse timeline, not an Instacart pickup. Working on culture change requires consistent personal effort by leaders, regular and frequent, over a long period. It takes time to get the better way, truth, and life into people's muscle memory and lifestyles.

For discipleship to be right in the community of Christ, leaders will have to rebuild the fabric of the community. And because the challenge to set discipling right is unique to each community and the process is tangled and consequential, leaders will find that untangling this dilemma from that fabric of their community is tough. But it is our mission, and it is Christ's expectation.

Here is the dilemma: Do leaders leave alone these old traditions and hope for better results and fewer symptoms with disciples? Or do we go a different way, and take responsibility for needed changes and outcomes? Church folk don't like change, you know.

The core questions become:

1. Is there really a problem?
2. Can we get at the causes?
3. What's the right path out of this?

What Leaders Owe Their People

Most Christians operate under a far-less-than-complete grasp of discipleship. A grasp which, if unchanged, keeps replicating the symptoms we've described.

If you lead people of any number and in any way in Christ, this situation is yours to address, no matter how new you are to your role as a leader, no matter how old the roots of the traditions, no matter how small or large your community. Leaders owe their people a culture and clear path for discipleship to flourish.

The admonition to lead is summarized well in this statement from Paul to the Ephesians:

> So Christ himself gave the apostles, the prophets, the evangelists, the pastors and teachers, to equip his people for works of service, so that the body of Christ may be built up until we all reach unity in the faith and in the knowledge of the Son of God and become mature, attaining to the whole measure of the fullness of Christ. (Ephesians 4:11–13)

There's no short-term fix for the disciple dilemma. Institutions cannot make disciples. Sermons do not make disciples. Men and women's groups won't make disciples. Headcount and amazing facilities and programs do not make disciples. Which means leaders cannot look to traditional answers to solve the dilemma's challenges in discipleship. So this book is not about programs to fix discipleship. Nor is it a checklist on how to be a good disciple. It's a book for leaders, to help you see the need for change in your traditional culture, so that flourishing and vibrant disciples make more disciples—which is the entrance to the exit away from the disciple dilemma.

This may well be your calling. "And who knows whether you have not come to the kingdom for such a time as this?" (ESV) Esther 4:14. You are now entering The Disciple Dilemma.

All authority in heaven and on earth has been given to me.
Therefore go and make disciples of all nations,
baptizing them in the name of the Father and of the Son and of the Holy Spirit,
and teaching them to obey everything I have commanded you.
Jesus, in Matthew 28:18–20

Whoever wants to be my disciple must deny themselves
and take up their cross and follow me.
Jesus, in Matthew 16:24

Even while these people were worshiping the Lord, they were serving their idols.
To this day their children and grandchildren continue to do as their ancestors did.
2 Kings 17:41

People enjoy being a "fan" of Jesus,
but not so much the "disciple" part.
Sam Allberry, "Discipleship ≠ Following Christ Your Way"

2

Christian Tradition:
Salvation Is Free, Lordship Is Optional

Business Tradition:
I'm Here for the Benefits

Rome, AD 310: The new pope, Eusebius, was facing a gnarly personnel problem. His chairman of the board, Emperor Maxentius of Rome, was not happy with the way this Holy CEO was handling the business. The emperor would not risk his own standing among the powerful over these quirky people. Nor would Maxentius tolerate any appearance of being soft. That image might embolden his enemies. Enemies like his archrival, that other emperor off in the East, Constantine. Maxentius demanded that Pope Eusebius quash, and quash fast, the howls of these whining exiles from Eusebius's flock. The problem had erupted out of the direst of circumstances—immediate threat of life and limb for self and kin of these now marginalized people.

On and off for three centuries, the Roman Empire had been systematically persecuting the Christian faithful. The terror escalated in the middle of the third century under Emperor Decius, then intensified even more under Diocletian at the beginning of the fourth century. The martyred were many, and a host of Christians suffered greatly from imprisonment, torture, or went into hiding.

But a large number of others, to escape the horrific Roman persecution, had "lapsed" by renouncing their Christianity. They became known as *lapsi*. Some of them, compromised by fear for their lives and their families' lives, publicly participated in pagan worship, distasteful though it was to gain relief. Others drafted written statements of their intention to offer such worship, which in some places was enough to satisfy local authorities. Some simply lied to the authorities, which occasionally did the trick. More seriously, some handed over copies of Scripture to be burned, or treacherously revealed to authorities the names of believers so the betrayers could ingratiate themselves with the persecution police.

When the Roman government's pogroms would finally ebb enough for the church to regather in relative peace, many lapsi lobbied for immediate restoration of their church rights. Some among the enduring faithful didn't see things that way and demanded permanent excommunication of the whole lot of the lapsi. Church leaders prescribed various layers of penance that the lapsi could follow in order to be restored, but for some of the lapsi, penance was unthinkable, insulting, humiliating.

This throbbing headache for church leaders became a political hot potato as well, as the imperial government began to frown on the mounting disorderliness in this particular segment of the population. A pernicious fracture had opened in the Christian community—a fracture between those who'd paid a high price in refusing to worship Caesar and those who saw that price of faithfulness as being too much to ask. For the lapsi, the lordship of the forgiving Christ could be optioned off when truly necessary. And optioned back when things calmed down.

Optional lordship. Was it a problem only during Roman persecution?

Hardly. History from the Hebrews until the here and now is full of examples where Christ's lordship gets treated like a sketchy stock tip. You may have bought in at first, but you can sell out when trouble looms, and short back in when you want to. You can read about it even while

Jesus was physically walking among his own, when "many of his disciples turned back and no longer followed him" (John 6:66).

Christ told us about this kind of sellout ahead of time as he laid out the parable of the seeds, the weeds, and the rocks (Mark 4:13–19)— affirming that some will fade out when things get tough.

Jump ahead another six hundred years. From the sixth through the tenth centuries, pagan chieftains and their followers came to profess Christianity as their new religion. Yet lordship—the exclusivity of Christ above all others and through all circumstances—was often put on layaway. The old idols, demon worship, and pagan rituals were frequently blended in with the gospel. This kind of pluralism became all the rage, sponsored by local trend-setting elites.[40]

There are so many examples of lordship opt-outs across history. In the twentieth century, many in the church in Nazi Germany bailed on the lordship of Christ, buying in to the Führer's theology of the Final Solution.[41] Many of these Germanic lapsi would argue that their pledges under duress were only words, meaningless phrases to avoid personal catastrophe.

"People enjoy being a "fan" of Jesus, but not so much the "disciple" part."[42] In our twenty-first century, we see similar fractures between lordship and lifestyle as believers are intimidated or enraptured by the rages of the woke, the correct politic, or seduced by the trendy happiness-and-wealth prosperity cults. An example of this kind of contemporary optionality is found in a popular church in Pasadena, California. Their website and mission statement make it plain that all people are welcome, which is beautiful. Then we read endorsements from local groups, saying that this church gets top marks for inclusivity, in celebrating and affirming practicing gay ordinands and gay marriages.[43] Now every church overlooks some things while emphasizing other things. But when it comes to options being exercised, are followers of Christ to toss out the jots and keep the tittles? Is biblical context in the challenging passages optional? This kind of thinking is a modern example of the old tradition of opting out of the hard stuff.

While I disagree with this particular church's stance on LGBTQA+ dogma, that isn't the core of the discipleship issue. Our concern here is how the leaders of a church are advocating an opt-out life when the biblical content doesn't match society. When leaders opt out, or torture the text to attempt to say the Bible's hard stuff is too costly, or too cruel, or too oppressive, then usually their disciples opt out too. And the replication engine of underdiscipled believers churns on. Churches should be open arms to many who desperately need Christ and may feel belittled or excluded as individuals. Good for those churches in that kind of inclusion. Yet in closing their arms to Scripture, leadership strips out the real answer for a social cause. Opting instead for a cause which will not deliver on its promises of setting things right. Leaders who promote a lordship-lite quest over discipleship will not protect their people for long from the ever-changing social conformity demands of the new, woke, canceling, progressive world—a world which, by the way, will not tolerate optionality from its doctrines in any form.

Words matter in discipleship. So a first-order challenge leaders face today in every organization—especially in Christianity—is to establish meaning and comprehension around words that matter, in order to establish what is true. Words like *lordship* and *repentance* have deep and compelling implications for life circumstances—for tragedy, difficulty, threats, and especially discipling. Lordship matters, infinitely for God's design. Yet the fad today is ambiguity, not truth affirming a definitive purpose. We are societies and sadly also disciples veering away from purpose toward scientific mysticism or simply personal preferences. For example, consider the irony when a prominent scholar and naturalist like Richard Dawkins assures us there's no meaning to be found anywhere in life:

> The universe we observe has precisely the properties we should expect if there is, at bottom, no design, no purpose, no evil and no good, nothing but blind, pitiless indifference. As that unhappy poet A. E. Housman put it, "For Nature, heartless, witless Nature, will neither care

nor know." DNA neither cares nor knows. DNA just is.
And we dance to its music.[44]

This is a prominent scientist and author making either a meaningless claim or a mystical statement. If there is "no purpose" then his words are random utterings without any more significance than navel lint, or alternatively he has been granted a cosmic waiver, somehow, such that his words and his alone grasp the profundity that all thought, matter, and life is just a slosh of randomness. Likewise, for options-minded disciples, how can the conflicted and evolving tide of personal preferences and causes and emotions today be the better way for a disciple?

Modern society abhors being stuck with meaning and the implications of words. We want options! Personal preference is one of the rare rigidly fixed touchstones for meaning today, whatever "rigid" means and whatever "preference" implies.

Problem is, it doesn't work that way. For an example of the impact when words become optional (lose their meaning), read Genesis 11, the story of the tower of Babel. Here was a stunning example of arrogant leadership putting up a fist to God, telling people to press on in their highfalutin ways. In what would be the first recorded commercial real estate liquidation in history, the slurred and changing meaning of words resulted in complete mission collapse. When no one knew what the other guy's words meant, words that used to matter no longer did. Which meant that nothing mattered. Cultural pandemonium set in across the lands.

A quick read of Jesus's words in the Gospels will convince the most casual reader that it isn't possible to remain a disciple unless you've surrendered (given up—enslaved, out of options, devoid of freedom) to lordship, a costly lordship of self-denial, derision, persecution, torture, death.

The essence of the word *disciple* goes like this: Christians are just another nickname for disciples of Christ. Opting out of lordship actually means, according to Christ, to not be his follower.[45] Not a disciple, not a believer. There's no optional lordship.

Today's defection rates among Christians as Nones and Dones seem to echo the behavior of German believers in World War II who turned to the Final Solution version of religion. Jesus as a Savior is fine. But lordship? Well now, that's going to need to be negotiated. Surely Christ didn't intend me to lose friends who get unhinged about my allegiance to him, right? Certainly he did not intend me having to become a social outcast against the trending diktats. You could get canceled for that. If Christ's lordship means I'm on the wrong end of tolerance with friends and their causes when wokeness flip-flops on the next thing, then no thanks. I'll just be saved, and we can discuss lordship next week. Optionally.

Is Optional Lordship Possible?

Every significant event in life demands a full commitment. Citizenship is granted only with a pledge of complete loyalty. Marriage demands renouncement of all other romantic and erotic relationships. Professional athletes have to forsake years of individual freedoms to make it on the pro circuit. Other worldviews are no different. The Islamic states and their Islamist proxies demand servile allegiance to Allah. Communist regimes such as North Korea and China require craven commitment to the mother country and leaders, even requiring that people betray family and friends for the sake of the government's ultimacy. Even the tolerance crowd today is intolerant of the intolerant.

And then there's Christ—who tells us we must exclusively follow him, without regard to cost, without regard to consequences, and with the assurance of hardship and maybe early death (Luke 9:62; 14:26-34). We're given assurance that this commitment will divide families and friends (Luke 12:53). And Jesus expects this exclusivity to rise above all these other competing claims.

There's no exit clause in discipleship. No bailout options in commitment to Christ, the Most-High God. This should not be confused with a distortion of Lordship prevalent in "Christendom culture thinking" whereby some believe that non-believers must conform to the lifestyles of Christians. Biblically that's ridiculous—first because the culture sees

Christ's ways as foolishness, and secondly, the whole point of a disciple is to go reason and invite non-believers to observe their lives, to see Christ and to consider his ways.

It may seem cruel to harass the lapsi, especially from the cushy Monday-morning-quarterback seats we sit in today. After all, how would *you* behave if your family was under a death threat for your religious practices? Peter choked when Jesus was on trial, right?

Yet there's more than meets the eye here. The recanting by the lapsi was only the tip of that traditions iceberg. Let's look below the surface, because there's more to the story, more that relates to discipleship.

Once the coast was clear of government oppression, the deconverted reconverters protested loudly and politically. They entreated the government to coerce the church's pontiff. Their demand: "Reinstate our standing in the church *now*—no apologies, no preconditions!" The lapsi believed they'd done nothing wrong; that they'd simply dodged a personal bullet with a few choice words or perhaps a bad decision or two. The lapsi demanded to be taken back without even so much as "sorry" to those who stayed the course, many of whom were imprisoned, tortured, or killed, just for being followers of Christ.

Was the lapsi's failure simply the fault of Rome's coercive power of persecution? Hardly. What was going on? In a word: a disciple's commitment. Jesus's haunting words about understanding the cost ahead of discipleship ring out here:

> If anyone comes to me and does not hate father and mother, wife and children, brothers and sisters—yes, even their own life—such a person cannot be my disciple. And whoever does not carry their cross and follow me cannot be my disciple. Suppose one of you wants to build a tower. Won't you first sit down and estimate the cost to see if you have enough money to complete it? For if you lay the foundation and are not able to finish it, everyone who sees it will ridicule you, saying, "This person began to build

and wasn't able to finish." Or suppose a king is about to go to war against another king. Won't he first sit down and consider whether he is able with ten thousand men to oppose the one coming against him with twenty thousand? If he is not able, he will send a delegation while the other is still a long way off and will ask for terms of peace. In the same way, those of you who do not give up everything you have cannot be my disciples. (Luke 14:26–33)

Jesus is telling us to make our choice with the prophetic fact that it will cost many of us dearly. No optionality is offered. We may buckle from the pressures, but we cannot in good conscience claim an exemption that lordship is somehow temporary or optional.

Is it realistic to expect Christians to perform flawlessly all the time, even under these kinds of awful situations? Of course not. People will always fall short. And grace has to be part of the church's regimen when people do fail. But in our failures, we as individuals are bluntly commanded in Scripture to practice repentance, humility, and reunification. To stand back up and push on—that's the character of a disciple.

Commitment is a lofty virtue. And it's crucial to any worthy endeavor. If you're in an organization where personal commitment is optional—well then, you're in a Soviet gulag. Or a dying organization.

One of the most challenging, never-ending, and under-appreciated jobs of leaders is to convince, teach, coach, and motivate people to realize that without personal commitment, they're just mercenaries. They'll be no better than a clump of people who come for convenience of the moment, then flit away. People who'll take off for the next better offer, or who'll bail out at the first sign of trouble, who will not serve a calling.

How is it possible to even nuance "optional lordship"? Would it be something like "I am forever giving my eternal existence over to Jesus, who is God—unless I get scared, or I get some better offer from some other god"? If God is actually the sovereign Creator, then Jesus's lordship—from the start, and forever—is not open for discussion. (See Isaiah 29:13; Matthew 7:21; 15:8; Mark 7:6; Luke 6:46).

Leaders Are Implicated

What should leaders conclude? Leaders cannot force individuals to be committed to anything. People ultimately make their own choices. But the individual's decision is not what we need to focus on. It's the duty of leaders to deploy a mission and establish a culture for disciples to flourish—a mission and culture allowing disciples to understand that God expects them to surrender to his lordship as well as to enjoy salvation. Leaders owe their people this comprehension of lordship, and the mandate to live in lifelong, unmitigated surrender to Christ as his disciples.

The damage of a misguided mission and the lure of a faulty culture are the genesis of heresies such as optional lordship. Why is there so much desertion in the churches today? Why so much silence about faith from believers in the communities? When people in the trenches, factories, and pews see their role as small cogs in a big machine, where their job is to just keep quiet and keep on keeping on, then purpose and meaning die. That's when people go quiet, people get fragile, apathetic, despairing, and people just leave.

The hope of achieving anything through disciples living in such optionality is, at best, a crapshoot. Only in the fullness of Christ's way, unvarnished, can any person really see their own purpose, and experience their crucial and unique role in communities and in their vocation. Only in discipling people as Christ did, without ditching lordship can anyone truly own their faith, rather than rent Jesus as a Savior from personal experiences at church or from family expectations. Renting that kind of optioned faith only to ditch it when their emotional lease runs out, or the popular view shifts.

The focus in this chapter has been on an old tradition—of optional lordship impairing the individual disciple. Unless each disciple fully comprehends their surrender and commitment to Christ—what it means and implies to be a disciple and to make disciples—then apathy, desertion, silence, and irrelevance will be common symptoms. Consider this sobering passage about believers responding to Jesus:

At the same time many even among the leaders believed in him. But because of the Pharisees they would not openly acknowledge their faith for fear they would be put out of the synagogue; for they loved human praise more than praise from God. (John 12:42-43)

Society, it seems, does often resent the lordship of disciples. And it even affected disciples who were face-to-face with Christ himself.

Permit me to dazzle you with my death grip on the obvious: If you're saved in Christ, you're saved. Salvation is conferred completely by Christ's work on the cross for a person. But a follower who isn't following is not a follower. Follow me? And likewise, a disciple who isn't being discipled is not being a disciple. Jesus said that plainly. The non-follower is inert. To say it another way, you are still a parent, whether or not you're doing anything of value as a father or mother. And you remain under the saving blood of Christ's atonement whether or not you're obedient. Personal sins will not negate Christ's work on the cross for his people. But discipleship is a journey. You cannot travel unless you're traveling.

A disciple is someone on a journey of following Christ. A disciple is not someone who isn't following Christ as Lord. Disciples will fail, disciples will get back up, disciples have lapses, but they're actively following their Lord, however imperfectly.

Notice that the optional lordship scenario first surfaced, as we mentioned, in John 6:66. Jesus, God incarnate, was face-to-face among them and some still chose to stop following! They chose to *not* be a disciple. Disciples, per Christ, are not static. Disciples are underway on a journey: Whoever wants to be my disciple must deny themselves and take up their cross and follow me (Matthew 16:24). Not actively following? Not a disciple.

Well-meaning organizations enable opt-out distractions too. How do they do this? The fog of the traditions is driving it. We can see this in two similar messages often being transmitted by Christian communities: "Get saved, join us, and you're good"; and its works-based twin message: "Discipleship is achieved by being in our small groups, Sunday school, mission trips and weekly programs." If you're a sincere, converted, busy churchgoing believer—well then, you must be a disciple.

There can be no optionality in this surrender for disciples and leaders must see to it that the core of their community leads with such truth. This lordship will naturally encompass worship, prayer, learning, ministries, reaching out. But ahead of all that, the first step is how leaders create that atmosphere of surrender, that inclination toward lordship for disciples. Otherwise, the tradition of optional or overlooked lordship will produce risk-averse day traders ready to jump ship at a moment's notice.

And so this chapter makes a case that an optional lordship tradition has thrived from the Caesars to the modern day—a tradition of marginally committed believers, a tradition of leaving lordship off the base package so to speak. This tradition would be embedded into Christianity not as a glaring defect, but rather as a cherished technique of not making the deal too daunting. "Don't worry about giving away your life. Just pray the sinner's prayer and start the membership classes." We want them saved, seated in the pews, sending in money, signed up for small groups. Surrender? Maybe another day.

* * *

At the end of the next five chapters, we'll recap the traditions we've covered to help reinforce the historic trends impacting discipling. Thus far we've looked at one of the six traditions:

- Optional lordship degrades discipleship.

Next up, we explore the traditional means of making Christians: catch, convert, and release. It sounds humane—being a catcher and releaser of men, turning them loose to be themselves. It's actually a fishy tale of abandonment.

The Christian life comes to mean nothing more
than living in the world and as the world, in being no different from the world,
in fact, in being prohibited from being different from the world
for the sake of grace. The upshot of it all is that my only duty as a Christian
is to leave the world for an hour or so on a Sunday morning and go to church
to be assured that my sins are all forgiven. I need no longer try to follow Christ,
for cheap grace, the bitterest foe of discipleship,
which true discipleship must loathe and detest,
has freed me from that.

Dietrich Bonhoeffer, *The Cost of Discipleship*

There is no longer a Christian mind.

Harry Blamires, *The Christian Mind: How Should a Christian Think?*

A gospel which is only about the moment of conversion
but does not extend to every moment of life in Christ
is too small. A gospel that gets your sins forgiven
but offers no power for transformation is too small.

Fred Sanders, *The Deep Things of God*

3

Christian Tradition:
Catch and Release—Underdiscipled Converts

Business Tradition:
Hire Faster! The Last Ones We Didn't Train Are Leaving

He was the Billy Graham of his day—a powerful evangelist in the fifth century AD. Thousands flocked to hear him preach about Christ, and many of those listening turned to the gospel.[46]

Ironically, this son of a shepherd was, from age sixteen until his death, an introvert. After becoming a monk, he was heckled and labeled a fanatic by his austere monastic brethren for his passion to pray and seek God. So he struck out on his own.

For twenty-five years he pursued solitude, prayer, and meditation, solo. He holed up in caves and remote huts where he fasted and prayed. He was often hounded by the curious and by the needy, who sought advice and intercessory favor from this quirky ascetic. In his quest to put some distance between his unwanted celebrity status and the incessant masses, he came up with a brilliant plan. He would raise his standard of living.

He literally raised it. He was a pillar saint. His last thirty-seven years were spent perched atop a pillar near Aleppo in northern Syria.

He is Simeon (or Symeon) the Stylite elder.[47] This odd man has been celebrated in poetry by Sir Alfred Tennyson and venerated to sainthood by Eastern and Western churches. How does this Simeon fit into a discussion about leaders and their effect on discipleship? Simeon had a knack for making converts. Lots of them.

But somehow things didn't seem to stick among his redeemed listeners, who were largely Bedouins.[48] It started out well enough, to be sure. Under Simeon (literally *under* him), clan leaders known as *shayks* pledged themselves and their families to God. As a member of the shayk's clan, you did what the shayk told you to do. And for a convert to the Stylite guy's religion, there was a lot to do: busting up idols, knocking off ancestor worship, and shunning the sketchy diets of camels and wild donkeys. Even chastity took hold, converts giving up the old ecstasy rituals for the man-God Jesus. But somehow things just weren't…right. Murderous intertribal raids kept flaring up, pitting converts against one another. And the idols, after vanishing for a while, would reappear.

"A gospel which is only about the moment of conversion but does not extend to every moment of life in Christ is too small. A gospel that gets your sins forgiven but offers no power for transformation is too small."[49] There was conversion going on everywhere around Simeon. But growth among the converts? Sanctification? That was sparse. For example, Bishop Theodoret, Simeon's biographer, was nearly savaged while visiting new converts at the pillar. Theodoret was trying to celebrate communion with the new congregants, and his beard was nearly plucked in the rush. He became mosh in the pit of the tribesmen diving for the free hors d'oeuvres—the communion goblets and bread. Theodoret thought it was his curtain call, until Simeon's shouts from the pillar compelled the Bedouin chieftains to get their people to back off.

Historians tell us many converted Bedouin tribesmen didn't even understand the Stylite saint's own language, much less grasp the meaning of Theodoret's sacramental feast. These clansmen were just doing the tribal thing. If you're a member of the clan, you don't ask questions. If the shayk says we're Christians, then by the gods, we're Christians! For this week, anyway. Pass the wild donkey pâté please.

Conversion of the Bedouins was a big thing for the guy on the pillar. For the Bedouins, not so much. It was a little like sport fishing: catch them, release them, and hope it goes well for them.

Utter Mission Failure

The episode of Simeon and his converts points to another church tradition alive and well today. It's the notion that getting someone to accept Jesus is the do-all and end-all of Christianity. Once converted, they'll surely live happily ever after. That notion is close kin to one of the classic leadership failures in business: recruiting people, failing to develop them, and being surprised at the results.

My reading of Scripture has convinced me that getting people saved is not the mission Christ gave us. Yes, we should preach the gospel, and yes, we should want people to meet Christ. But to stop there, thinking we have no further role in that convert's life, is utter mission failure.

Here's where we encounter a massive root of the disciple dilemma: going after the wrong mission—in this case a mission built on a tradition of making converts rather than disciples. This lines up with the thinking of Dietrich Bonhoeffer, the German theologian in World War II: "The Christian life comes to mean nothing more than living in the world and as the world, in being no different from the world, in fact, in being prohibited from being different from the world for the sake of grace. The upshot of it all is that my only duty as a Christian is to leave the world for an hour or so on a Sunday morning and go to church to be assured that my sins are all forgiven. I need no longer try to follow Christ, for cheap grace, the bitterest foe of discipleship, which true discipleship must loathe and detest, has freed me from that."[50] When converts become the mission, the imperative is getting the next convert, not developing the existing disciples. And like Simeon's followers, converts have no grounding to sustain their new faith. Just like in business, these underdeveloped people will most likely pretend, or guess at understanding their roles, usually poorly. Or become silent and passive, unable to support the mission. Or just leave.

Let's pretend that for your next New Year's resolution, you decide to clean up your supersized eating habits and become the image of a Greek god/goddess. To realize this objective, you decide to surrender your gluttonous ways to a life of karate. You resolve to go to the local karate studio and ask the sensei to teach you the ways of Chuck Norris. Upon your arrival, the sensei hears your confession, and he's thrilled. After receiving your generous donation for training, he motions and says, "Come with me!" You enter a locker room, where he gives you a karate uniform and a little white belt. He tells you that these are the outward signs of a new student. You put them on, and he says he'll now help you begin your journey. You're in!

He motions you to follow him into another building. There's a lot going on there—people doing peculiar gyrations with their bodies—arms, fists, feet. There are bells and smells. All pretty strange! Somebody in the corner is nursing a bloody nose. Hmm...tripped over something maybe?

The sensei takes you onto a platform he calls "the ring," which is actually square, with ropes around the edges. The sensei introduces you to others gathered just outside the ropes. They crowd up to you with high fives, cheering your arrival. This is pretty cool.

You notice a very large guy standing within the ring on the other side, dressed in an outfit kinda like yours, but black. His name is Terminator. You know his name is Terminator because it's tattooed across his massive chest in giant red gothic letters. He points at you and smiles. Or is that a growl?

The sensei waves at Terminator, and they both laugh. How nice, you think; they must be dear friends.

Terminator yells in your direction about something. Really loud. It's as if he's yelling *at* you. Something about "I'll feed your flesh to the birds and the wild animals!" Gosh, that sounds just like what Goliath said to Dav....nah, can't be. People near the ring are starting to look at you and cringe. Why is that little girl shaking her head and looking down? And money is furiously changing hands. How odd.

A gong clangs somewhere nearby. Terminator is coming straight toward you. You look at the sensei, who tosses you a book and says, "Congratulations on your decision to turn your life over to karate. That book has everything you need to know. Good luck—you're gonna need it!" He bows and quickly walks off as Terminator extends the right hand of—

Fade to black.

Is this a great way to start your journey into karate, or what? Making converts can be like that. "Welcome, glad you're here. Here's a Bible, there's the website. See ya next Sunday." Some may say that churches are never that callous, and many converts do just fine after their conversion. Yes, many churches are not that callous; and yes, some converts do just fine maturing in their faith, more or less alone. But the question here is should conversion be the objective, or the beginning of a journey?

Here's a true story from the business world that makes a similar point.

Los Angeles, September 2016: The new CEO arrives to take over a failing manufacturing corporation, a private equity buyout gone very wrong. The board lays out the situation. Two years earlier, the company was growing and profitable. Now, losses are trending into the millions of dollars. Sales are down 30 percent year on year, and market share is shrinking, even while the overall industry is growing. Multiple worker injuries occur every week. Complaints about product quality are at record levels, and customers are switching out the brand for competitors.

And another thing really stands out. Turnover. Employees are voluntarily leaving the company. The rate is 35 percent. Every month! That's 420 percent a year, which means you have to replace the entire workforce in the factories more than four times a year.

So the new CEO sneaks out to the production lines—unannounced, and wearing a factory uniform—to pick up on the real story from the regular folks. Not knowing it's the CEO, people talk freely. "We showed up, we got hired the same day. They'll hire anybody. You can even flake out and not show up and they'll rehire you in a few days. They put a wrench in your hands and send you out to work. But we don't know what we're doing. We don't even know why we do it. We're just bodies. Sure, we have work teams. We say hi, we all act happy, but everybody's just getting by, faking it, you know? Oh, and they pay minimum wage here. We said something to the bosses about how hard it is to get by on that, and they told us to get back to work. Somebody just mentioned another factory in town that's hiring—big sign-on bonus, and more pay. A bunch of us are outta here next week." This was a classic case of working hard to convert people into employees without any "discipling" to help them develop and flourish.

Another example: MassMutual—the Massachusetts Mutual Life Insurance Company—is listed by Payscale.com in 2021 as the most turnover-intensive corporation in the US. Their employees average nine months before they leave.[51]

Reasons for high turnover will always vary, but in business they tend to be less about pay and more about poor development and training:

1. Managers take little or no responsibility for personally mentoring and developing new individuals.
2. New hires are left in the dark about the bigger picture, their role in that picture, and their opportunity.
3. New hires have no comprehension of the corporate mission, and leaders usually have low comprehension of their people's conditions, developmental needs, and thinking.
4. Employees feel alone, with little or no close camaraderie to keep each other motivated and safe.
5. The above factors result in boredom, apathy—and turnover.

These top five retention-killers are what leaders must address. These kinds of facts reinforce a reality in Christianity as well as in business: You cannot simply bring people in (convert them) and hope all goes well. People need to grasp how vital it is to be mentored, and know how to not only hire people, but how to develop people. It means people walking closely alongside other people, daily. Not catch, convert, and release, but invite them in and disciple. Those traits in business sound mighty close to the conversion stories in Christian culture today:

- People come because of family or friends. Owning their faith, instead of the moments of their conversion? That's a crapshoot.
- Converts get saved and enrolled, then are left mostly alone to figure out what's next.
- Members dieting on one or two helpings of sermons or Sunday School a month, a common mythology confused with real discipleship.
- Unrealistic small group expectations are assumed—something akin to hoping coffee breaks and a weekly staff meeting equal good personal development.
- Followers and employees, frustrated over lack of personal development, meaning and mission, shut down or walk off.

Why Only Converts?

The word *convert* isn't common in English translations of Scripture, but making converts is a deeply held tradition—the central mission for many churches. Of course, we want to bring in new people, but why would we ever want to stop with their arrival?

In Acts 14:21 we see that great preaching brought many people to faith: "They preached the gospel in that city and won a large number of disciples." A lot of people make the mistake that the term "won" means that making converts is the do-all-end-all for Christianity. But the context doesn't support that assumption. Conversion is convincing someone to believe something they didn't formerly believe. In other words, to switch their thinking from this to that. A careful read of the rest of that Acts passage and on into verse 22 shows that regular iteration and development of individuals was the fuller process. This is discipleship—the journey onward, once the mental grasp has taken. This passage in Acts portrays the journey of new disciples becoming more mature disciples, disciples developing in relationships with one another, to build up disciples and make disciples.

Conversion is a flaky resting place. In business, customers "convert" all the time from brand X to brand Y. It's a tenuous victory. As soon as the next better deal comes along, guess what? Your convert deconverts. Bart Ehrman, a religion professor at Duke University, was a Christian convert who then converted to agnosticism. Joshua Harris—author of the bestseller *I Kissed Dating Goodbye*, and later a megachurch pastor—was a convert into and then out of Christianity. Scores of similar convert stories await your next Google search under "de-converted Christians".

In chapter 1 we talked about the surveys suggesting that most millennials are converting away from being believers to Nones and Dones. Most of those dearly departed are not expected back.[52] Conversion's tenuous footing is evident in the stories you'll read online and in the survey findings about the Nones and Dones, that these Christians have no significant community with other disciples, nor any personal spiritual development. Conversion has been Western Christianity's bragging rights for years, yet for most converts there's no sense of what comes next—such as personal surrender, how to actually study the wonder of Scripture, what prayer is about, how sanctification works and especially how to just go through life as a believer. Rarely does the convert get any help in learning from others, grasping what it means to be giving away their own life for Christ's purposes. In other words, converted people without personal disciplers alongside them are at great risk of becoming those Nones and Dones. Evangelizing people without discipleship is akin to trading out the engines on a plane so more passenger seats can be installed. You get a bigger headcount aboard for sure, but the reason you got on board is now a lost cause! And the cost of trying to use an organization as the engine of discipling in the West is astonishing. If you want some sticker shock, run the monetized cost per convert in the Western churches. Before someone objects about trying put a price on souls saved, realize that I'm leading up to point—to a more biblical way than monetizing or capitalizing souls.

What should matter to leaders is not headcount, nor baptisms, nor even the number saved. Those metrics are lagging indicators. Meaning that unless your objective is to worry, these statistics come in too late for it to matter anyway. Lagging signs of underdiscipled people already exploited by whatever's next in life that distracts from Christ. And what's next nowadays is statistically not a good thing. Like a dodgy used car sale, the convert deal is done without full disclosure. Much fast talk about salvation, fixing wrongs, mission tripping, or getting the material blessings due the convert upon conversion. But the lordship part gets a hyper-speed ad monologue, if it gets raised at all. We keep pushing the free gift, lest the prospect balk and we lose out on closing the convert deal.

The idea that leading another person to become a convert to Christ without discipleship, without expecting them to thrive spiritually, is insanity. Many presume that sermons, church membership, mission trips, and small groups carry the freight for effective discipleship. Paul made it plain in Ephesians 4:11 that such things are vital in equipping believers. Like a form of spiritual vitamins. Vitamins are good things, but vitamins alone won't sustain discipleship. These traditional activities and events can be valuable aids to discipleship, but they are not a disciple's real nourishment, not his daily life and not the transformational discipling journey we are called to. We must acknowledge what Bill Hull of the Navigators said: "Realize that some will always be spectators."[53] Spectators, where some even as converts personally choose to skip out on being a disciple, some for the rest of their lives. Aware, but uncommitted.

William Wilberforce, speaking about human slavery, ridiculed such spectator sentiment: "You may choose to look the other way, but you can never again say you did not know."[54] Likewise, we've been forewarned, there are no Christian spectators. Disciples are surrendered, sent out, serving, becoming (more) sanctified and not solo.

Like a slowly spinning top, a new or underdiscipled believer can be wobbly. They've not had time and experience with other disciples to allow for personal, developmental discipleship, as Jesus provided his disciples. Paul warned about the risks in assuming too much from new believers in 1 Timothy 3:6: "He must not be a recent convert [Greek *neophuton*, a "neophyte" or "novice"] or he may become conceited and fall under the same judgment as the devil." And that can mean trouble on three fronts—two are personal, but one of them is vexing to the broader Christian community.

First, Paul tells us that the underdiscipled novice is at risk of becoming arrogant while picking up leadership titles or status. Second, people have a tendency to become impatient with the development process Christ prescribed; wanting greater control, they may walk away from the longer process. This is especially true of those who think they "get it" before they really get it. This results in an ill-prepared person facing responsibilities, situations, and questions they aren't yet ready to biblically answer. Third—and very challenging to a Christian community—the underdiscipled can multiply quickly, and these hordes of partially equipped believers can swamp a church. The underdiscipled become a majority, with poor or partially formed worldviews and expectations amuck.

The implications of an underdiscipled life toward God can be seen in Old and New Testament warnings: "Everyone did as they saw fit" (ESV), also translated as "what was right in their own eyes" (NIV) Judges 17:6; 21:25; "They have an unhealthy interest in controversies and quarrels about words that result in envy, strife, malicious talk, evil suspicions and constant friction between people" (NIV) 1 Timothy 6:4–5.

In underdiscipling, we're mass-producing fragile converts rather than following the directions and example of Christ. This is another way of saying that people who aren't personally discipled by another disciple are at risk for getting their faith tangled up in whimsical notions or Googleized theology. Being underdiscipled can lead to really weird and flaky thinking. (Read Judges 17 and its bizarre story about Micah to see just one example.)

When I talk to people who walked out on faith in Christ, I usually hear about two issues. One is some injustice or affront, two is their early conversion expectation—and it's usually about Jesus saving them from bad things, sometimes even talk about them being rescued from hell. But I rarely hear meaningful comprehension early on in their faith about their commitment, of Christ's lordship, of their personally embedded commitment—their discipleship. Very often I hear about anger against someone in the Christian community who let them down, or behaved badly—as if human brokenness was supposed to get washed off at conversion like our guilt. Just as often I hear the Nones and Dones say things like, "God isn't nice", or "God wasn't fair"—another indicator of a convert lacking a grasp of the real nature of mankind and the fragility of their discipling journey.

This context isn't an evaluation of someone's salvation. It's pointing to a tradition of underdiscipled converts. Converts fished for (as Jesus said we're to fish), and converts caught—but then released back into the wild of life, which is not as Jesus taught.

Few churches today design their culture beyond conversion to develop deep relational discipling. The usual menu for discipleship is membership and activities, a buffet of Bible studies, small groups, or Sunday school, kids' events, mission trips, and Sunday services. The thinking in modern Christianity goes something like this: She was converted, so she's saved. Therefore, since she's good to go on that one big thing, she can go back to regular life with a few new Christian activities merged in. One more group to socialize with. The convert trap is sprung. Discipleship without any personal, relational coaching begins a downward arc, as confusion and often isolation set back in.

We *should* celebrate salvation. What an unfathomable gift! Salvation is part and parcel of what comes in surrendering our lives to Christ. Yet asking Christ to save and rule and own us as the Lord of our lives must be the start, not the finish. And it's up to the people who started the conversation and journey with that person to start and stay alongside them, versus convert and walk off. It's leaders who bear the responsibility for teaching such guardianship to all good news bearers in Christian community.

Can a convert instinctively grasp the depth of discipleship on a solo journey? What could we expect if that person is a spiritual orphan, abandoned after conversion, or is never introduced at a personal, exemplary and relational level to the splendor of the hope we have in Christ? Should we be surprised if these orphaned believers go heretical, or suffocate or flee from the deafening silence?

Just as with Simeon's Bedouins, there are consequences in making converts without any real follow-through in discipleship. If discipleship—developing people in full surrender and fealty to Christ—is opted out of the good news, aren't we then encountering the old news, not the good news?

The Lausanne Conference of 1974—officially the International Congress on World Evangelization—would change the way many Protestant Christians thought about our mission as Christians. The famous covenant from the conference was signed by a virtual who's who in Christianity: names like Billy Graham, Ralph Winter, Donald McGavran, and John Stott. The declaration would tweak, in a beguiling way, the aim of Western Christians in going forward. In the last of its fifteen sections, one particuarly noteworthy line stated that the promise of Jesus Christ's return "is a further spur to our evangelism, for we remember his words that the gospel must first be preached to all nations." This key phrase incorporates Jesus's words in Mark 13:10 (see also Matthew 24:14). Meanwhile, in the covenant's introduction, the signers assert their belief in the gospel as "God's good news for the whole world," while they declare that "we are determined by his grace to obey Christ's commission to proclaim it to all mankind and to make disciples of every nation"—thus quoting Jesus's words in Matthew 28:19.

But the document is far more about simply evangelizing all nations rather than making disciples of all nations. And that emphasis would stick. Go convert. Everywhere. The notion of going to all nations would become a travel agent's fantasy. According to some scholars, Lausanne whiffed a bit on that word *nations* in the context of Matthew 28 by interpreting the Greek word *ethne* to mean "ethnolinguistic people groups" (as defined by modern anthropology) rather than the broader concept of "nations" as understood by the Bible's original writers and readers, especially in reference to God's promise to Abraham to bring blessing through him to "all nations."[55] This shift in meaning would result in a missions focus on getting converts in "unreached" people groups rather than making disciples where doing so is most strategic and fruitful. It meant going globe-trotting on conversionistic "all nations" tours. There's so much that's right and beautiful in globe-trotting for the gospel, but that cannot run unfettered from discipleship as the core mission.

Do leaders stick to the tradition of conversion as the mission? Or should we reconsider the intent of the words of Christ in Matthew 28.19, where making true disciples is the mission? This becomes personal for each one of our people. Ephesians 4.11 teaches that some, but not all of us, are called to be evangelists. But Jesus made it plain that everyone following him is expected to be a disciple and to make disciples. That's the essential fabric leaders own in a Christian culture, the fabric that motivates everyone to be disciples, as Christ intended disciples. Everything else in the Christian culture—including evangelism, addressing poverty, and righting injustice—depends entirely on those disciples maturing up, getting out into the world, inviting other individuals in the world to come and see.

Do the math on costs. Add up a church's asset value, plus the annual recurring budget dollars spent over the past ten years. Add up the new believers gained over that same timeline. Not simply new members, and not children raised inside the church, but new believers who came to Christ in the past ten years in that church. Subtract from that same headcount the number of people who abandoned their faith while in that church. (Few churches have any awareness of that number.) Then divide the dollars by the heads. You'll be stunned by the cost. Fifty thousand dollars per new believer would be cheap. Many churches would run north of a quarter million dollars per convert. And according to pastor and journalist John Dickerson in his book *The Great Evangelical Recession*, churches in Western Christianity will not be able to sustain that kind of cost past about 2030[56].

Yes, it sounds crass to quantify a cost for getting people saved. But conversion thinking is crazy costly as a strategy, it has sketchy support biblically, and it has a lousy depreciation schedule. Its track record today of losing converts is a lesson in basic leadership gross negligence. Underdiscipled converts are the result of mass-produced and often over-capitalized discipling, and Christianity owes disciples better than a tradition claiming that throwing money, edginess or crowds at discipleship is the answer.

Crazy Smart

On the other hand, making disciples as Jesus taught—by one disciple inviting others to come and see, to become surrendered followers walking alongside another—is crazy smart. Jesus wasn't offering an exchange, nor conversion, nor a repurposing. Jesus was bringing dead people to life and owning them fully as his rightful servants, and heirs. Jesus took people who were spiritually dead and secularly alive, reversing that proposition to be spiritually alive and untugged by the gravity of societies. Jim Elliot's famous saying comes to mind: "He is no fool who gives what he cannot keep to gain that which he cannot lose."[57] That kind of liberated disciple can speak into communities and commerce (and make other disciples) without concern for contingent costs, or elaborate capital investment, or even their own mortality. That's freedom: disciples who are shed of the frets of fate, shed of the "slavery by their fear of death" (Hebrews 2:15). Disciples who are Jesus's live manifestation of *agape* in a fractious world. Disciples are the only way to deploy unity and love. That kind of freedom and fruitfulness is unfathomable to the typical convert today.

John Piper is more expansive defining conversion: "Christian conversion involves *turning the heart* toward the true God away from wrong ideas about God and wrong affections for what is not God."[58] Piper infers far more than simply being saved here. He talks about a turning heart, a following of Christ in a way that suggests that sanctification is present tense. He's saying that spiritual disciplines are engaging, personal sanctification is taking root. In that context, a convert sounds just like a disciple.

Conversion as most of us think about it is the first regenerative step in making a disciple. Yet without development, these converts are left on their own. They may make their best efforts, trying to figure out how to live life as a disciple of Christ. Or they may be absorbed back into the environment around them. The cultural momentum in the West lauds the lone wolf. The iconic spirit of Americans is "I can do this on my own," and "I am the master of my fate." It's also the definition of dysfunctional discipleship. If a new believer—or for that matter, any believer—doesn't continuously develop and sustain their life alongside others in discipleship, the odds stack against them. Scripture bets against them.

Apollos in the book of Acts was an example of an underdiscipled follower who was close but not quite right about Christ. Simon the sorcerer in Acts 8 was off course too. Two different outcomes. Apollos gets discipled well. Simon asks for a do-over but disappears from any further Scripture reference. Like the Bedouins with Simeon the Stylite, Simon the sorcerer fades away. Converted, they were all left to figure it out on their own.

The damage isn't just the failure to mature these people in Christ. That's bad enough. The replication of bad thinking quickly multiplies. The underdiscipled are often enthusiastic newcomers. What they lack in understanding about Christ, they make up for in energy to get their new experience out loud and proud. And time only makes them more anxious to dig in on partially understood beliefs and to pass around partial truth or really bad variants of the gospel.

Defective discipleship can be like problems in manufacturing and production. Once bad (quality of) production is happening, it takes a lot of time, people, and effort to bring things back to rights. In manufacturing, a common metric is that fixing a bad product costs seven to twenty times more than doing it right to begin with on the production line. What must be the cost in time, relationships, and spiritual damage to help an underdiscipled believer to reverse course on some idea they've been clinging to? Being underdiscipled puts people at high risk for cult exploitation too, as believers without solid mentors and development fall victim to half-truths and silly thinking—cults like Jonestown, Mormonism, Jehovah's Witnesses, or the prosperity shams.

Have you ever wondered why so many splinter groups and cults slough off from the Christian faith? The repeated story is that underdiscipled people had only a peripheral relationship with a church, and left to their own devices, ran off on feelings and specious opinions about life, justice, and ambition. They developed epiphanies and visions that were horrid distortions of biblical reality. Examples like Mary Baker Eddy, Joseph

Smith, Joseph Stalin, and Sun Myung Moon come to mind as grossly underdiscipled people.

If we want to get more biblical, think about the Amorites, Amalekites, Sodomites, Egyptians, all descendants of Noah, all children of people on the ark, all coming from the same family that worshiped God. But in brief time their descendants drifted. Their fathers' God was no longer *their* God. Over generations, some incrementally faded away, while others chose not to pursue God the very day they left home. In meager discipleship, people dream up their own fantasies about how they see things in their religion, and the drift begins.

One of the best outcomes for underdiscipled believers is found in Acts 18:24–19:4. Here we meet a cluster of John the Baptist's disciples—theologically in the ditch, but preaching and teaching nonetheless, sowing chaos as they go. There's also a globe-trotting Egyptian known as Apollos—enthusiastic, but his story wasn't right either. Fortunately, the Bible story about these misfits has a happy ending. Aquilla and Priscilla intercept Apollos, and by their discipling relationship with him, transform Apollos into a winsome, bold, and persuasive preacher, straight now in his proclamation of Christ. And Aquilla and Priscilla send Apollos into a relationship with other solid believers where he'll go help preach the real stuff of Christ. These believers would continue to help develop and disciple the enthusiastic apologist. This is a terrific example of real discipleship.

What about John's other guys? Paul runs into other disciples of John when he's in Ephesus. He comes in really close, pouring on truth and introducing them to the Holy Spirit so they can effectively serve Christ.

In both cases, these disciplers—Priscilla and Aquilla, and Paul—acted as disciples should. They invited, and they got personal with younger, less mature believers. And through that relationship with those people, disciples developed into mature servants for Christ.

I would have bet that if anybody would get it right, it was disciples following John the Baptizer. And yet John's followers didn't seem to understand baptism, the signature event featuring John and Jesus. They seemed to have forgotten how they should be living out their lives as disciples.

These guys were with John when Jesus was alive. They might have even been present when Jesus was baptized! How could it possibly be that of all people, *they* didn't understand the gospel?

Think about this: there was a discipler (John), and there were his disciples. Then the discipler was gone. John was imprisoned and executed. And his disciples flaked out. We too often think that anybody in a church like ours is good to go, once converted. Biblical history tells another story: Be a disciple, live among disciples, or expect to fade out.

Think about the nation of the Egyptians. Underdiscipled for only a few generations, they would drift far away to multiple gods. The ancestors of the Egyptians got off the same ark that the ancestors of the Hebrews did. Yet they took off after their own wants, their own versions of bizarre gods. Where were their godly mentors? Where was the "remembering" brought up so often in Scripture, as in Deuteronomy 6? Discipleship—as in surrender, lordship, mentoring, and walking alongside others—matters. People without disciplers—like the prosperity gospel gang, the Mormons, the Egyptian cultists, and persons who actually like ambrosia—get off course fast.

In Our Christian Communities

How many believers have a personal (not group) discipleship mentor? How many have spiritual peers living life alongside them each week? How many are personally inviting and perhaps discipling someone else? Don't include small groups with five or more in that answer. Think three or less. Christ discipled twelve, and he intensely focused on three.

A Barna report declares that 82 percent of Christians who attend church regularly claim they have no active discipleship, no Bible study, no learning system, no group, no mentor.[59] So even inside churches and Christian organizations, the dearth of real relationships looks bleak. This is not to say small groups and Sunday school groups cannot provide rich interconnectedness. The point is that real discipleship for any one person by participating in groups (greater than three) is a rare thing.

Contrast that passivity and solitude with Paul's directive that by "speaking the truth in love, we will grow to become in every respect *the mature body* of him who is the head, that is, Christ. From him the whole body, joined and held together by *every supporting ligament*, grows and builds itself up in love, *as each part does its work*" (Ephesians 4:15–16, emphasis added). This is a call for leaders to build a community of people who can and do build people in discipleship. This implies that relationships must have a supporting structure to flourish. It means being organized as a community so that discipling is basic DNA—so that the culture reinforces your people in knowing how to disciple, wanting to disciple, and expecting people in the community to disciple. Culture motivates everyone to participate—not in some dictatorial or cultic way, but in the way, the truth, and the life of Christ, which is upbeat and hopeful, not oppressive.

Don't be surprised if those who are merely spectators refuse the journey. Old habits are hard to break. Yet leaders must initiate and create a culture that mandates the true way of believers. Don't shy away from mandates. You impose them all the time in your own life—either your service providers serve, or they get kicked to the curb. Either your restaurants provide delicious food, or they don't see you again. Christian community must likewise mandate how believers as disciples are to behave—surrendered, serving, growing, teaming.

It's an oft-used quote, and it's beautiful: "Iron sharpens iron" (Proverbs 27:17). It speaks of the power of believers together in life. This true way of personal and relational discipleship, which is separate from the larger gatherings and activities of most Christian organizations, has been a missing link for most believers over the centuries. Leaders who understand this separation and who organize to develop that kind of discipling are very rare.

"There is no longer a Christian mind." Harry Blamires was one of C. S. Lewis's protégés, and that sentence was the opening line in his 2005 book *The Christian Mind: How Should a Christian Think?*[60] He lamented the collapse of Christian thought, saying that in his experience most Christians were unable to think critically about their faith, or to engage conversationally with other worldviews—and therefore unable to live among nonbelievers as disciples, or to make disciples.

History tells us that convert traditions have been humming along just fine through the centuries, and still are. Their record of resiliency is not so good. Recall not only our look at Simeon the Stylite's Bedouins, but also the lapsi of the third and fourth centuries described in chapter 2. We could also point to Roman converts of the fourth century who came and went, or mass in/out conversions of Germanics, Saxons, and Slavs in the fifth to ninth centuries, or Russians forced to convert under Vladimir the Great in the tenth century, or populations in Asia, Latin America, and Africa who were Christianized (in connection with colonialism) beginning in the fifteenth century only to syncretize out. And we can certainly point to the Nones and Dones of today.

This is not intended to doubt whether getting people to come to Christ is important, or if we should spread the gospel into our societies. Absolutely yes to both. But back to the theme of this book—leaders are responsible to address the tradition of abandoned converts, the underdiscipling that has damaged countless believers for centuries.

I hope a rough image of the disciple dilemma is emerging for you, as we've looked at the tradition of underdiscipled converts, some of them opting out of Christ as our Lord. Underdiscipling is so deeply embedded in many Christian communities that it's hard to recognize—but very easy to trip over. Do we stay on this path?

Underdiscipled is the tradition in Western Christianity. It's so traditional to not know what discipleship looks like that we actually believe being part of a church or participating in a small group means all is good for us. Yet Jesus intended our lives to develop alongside people who follow God with all their hearts, minds, and strength. This forms the wellhead of a disciple's life of love and serving.

There were teachers and programs in biblical times (just like today) designed to drive mass-production disciples. Unless your family was committed to training you up in a whole-hearted pursuit of God's ways, you were likely only a social or political Jew, and not the all-of-my-heart follower God called you to be. Ironically, big discipleship production offers little hope for making or sustaining disciples.

An Iranian Christian woman speaking of her time living in exile in the West among believers called her experience "a Satanic lullaby."[61] The lullaby chorus being a Christianity where faith is private, internal, out of sight, contrasted with life in her home country where her life was public and on the line every day because of her transparent faith. The discipling chorus in the West is *diminuendo* (diminishing, quieting) about the personal cost, about the challenges required of the disciple. The lullaby's refrain exchanges the call of inviting people and making disciples and substitutes a passivated blending in around work and town. The chorus of the Western lullaby induces spiritual narcolepsy, where churchgoers, convinced the pros own the task of talking about hope, doze off spiritually. And in their dozing, they lose hope and thrash loudly about in their populist or political nightmares.

Convert Christianity is a mirage that looks and feels good, but doesn't survive outside the church walls. Outside those walls, people see little difference between the supposedly discipled and all the rest of the world, and they conclude that churches are irrelevant religious clubs. That suspicion is confirmed as outsiders hear little from timid disciples, or the clashing and unloving banter from the not-so-quiet divisions erupting inside the churches and on the headlines of the world.

Outside the church walls (as well as inside those walls, for a growing number) is where real people, often in their anger or despair, are longing for the very things Jesus's disciples were told to deliver: salt, light, life, love. As a standalone event, the convert mirage promises people living water, but leads to a dry well. Likened to lukewarm water in Revelation 3:16.

* * *

There are six traditions to think about in order to understand the disciple dilemma in its full context. So far, we've looked at two:

- Optional lordship degrades discipleship.
- A catch-and-release, converts-only focus will dilute discipleship.

The next tradition we'll explore is the idea that power is the key to Christian success. It will turn out to be a locked door.

Most people can bear adversity;
but if you wish to know what a man really is, give him power.
Robert G. Ingersoll, "True Greatness Exemplified in Abraham Lincoln"

The church must be reminded that it is not the master or the servant of the state,
but rather the conscience of the state. It must be the guide and the critic of the state,
and never its tool. If the church does not recapture its prophetic zeal,
it will become an irrelevant social club without moral or spiritual authority.
Martin Luther King Jr., "A Knock at Midnight"

4

Christian Tradition:
Power Makes Everything Better

Business Tradition:
Kiss the Ring

In October of 1999 pro golfer Payne Stewart chartered a Learjet in Orlando to fly to Dallas. The flight would be at an altitude of 39,000 feet. Something happened to the oxygen supply on the jet that day. Up that high, without pressurized oxygen, there is not enough atmosphere to keep you alive, and a condition known as hypoxia (oxygen deprivation) sets in. Hypoxia works like this: unless you act fast to regain oxygen under pressure, in seconds you'll fall into a coma, paralyzed. Air Force fighters would intercept the unresponsive and straying jet. Flying only feet away, the interceptors could see inside the Learjet cockpit and passenger windows. Everyone in the Learjet was comatose. The fighters were unable to rouse anyone on board and the Learjet crashed, at a steep angle and at a high speed into the South Dakota plains.[62] Hypoxia is "insidious". Insidious means hard to recognize, yet consequential. Traditions of power can be like that. Insidious. Hard to recognize. And bad things start happening if action isn't taken.

"Most people can bear adversity; but if you wish to know what a man really is, give him power."[63] I used to buy in to the old saying that only two things are certain in life—death and taxes. Over time I came to realize that one more certainty exists. It is Lord John Acton's famous observation that power tends to corrupt, and absolute power corrupts absolutely. Acton was telling us that morality and purpose will fray when leaders (and their organizations) are distracted from a healthy sense of purpose to the insidious diversion of power as control, sheer bureaucracy, entitlement or popularity.

You've likely experienced some event where people or organizations you believed in were warped or wrecked by scandals of power. Good people, wonderful organizations overcome by scandals involving inattention, or arrogance, or money or just old-fashioned abuse. The real mission gets lost in such times, and reputations are ruined. For leaders, the gravitational pull of power often manifests itself in arrogance or class separation, perhaps some form of "it's my turn in the limelight" or just being told by everyone how great they have become. And quite frequently, the people loyal to these victims of power become a duped shield, insulating and defending the power broker(s) and their practices, blind to the reality of the moment. And it usually is only moments. Power isolates a leader and their organization from the clarity and counsel that disciples are meant to offer to one another. The outcomes of this insular bubble are rarely good.

In business a common theme recurs in organizations that suffer from power problems. You can't ask questions and you cannot challenge ideas and decisions from the top. Or else. The overt or covert rule is to agree, and do not rile the potentates. But the polarity can get reversed and to no better outcome when members, employees or volunteers threaten leadership efforts to challenge status quo. That's power run amok as well, coming from (usually a vocal minority in) the pews. And all these power plays are destructive to discipling.

Dysfunctional power often creeps in unannounced, like hypoxia. It renders leaders unapproachable and tone-deaf as they become overwhelmed with the burdens, bills, big (or crisis-bound) organizational things. Power can likewise mesmerize leaders caught up in the glare of newfound popularity, or their expansive authority. Caught up with adoring fans telling them they're always right. And the tendency of such power poisoning is to pull control in close and away from others, and reject oversight and accountability. Power may seduce people to act with hubris or malice, since they have "become as gods". Power problems manifest in many ways, but for our purposes, thinking about discipleship, such power promotes unattached solo living and exchanges personal development for group expediency. And exploitation often follows. Exploitive power is the ability to change behaviors in individuals, with or without an individual's consent.[64] Stockholm syndrome (hostages bonding emotionally with their captors) is an example of exploitive power over a victim, just like robbery, rape and extortion. Hitler's book burnings on the other hand, are examples of coercive and negative influence subjugating an entire society against its own good.

Power as entitlement, coercion or busyness can paralyze or corrupt leaders as much as they victimize targeted individuals and communities. If power is subject to a mission, it serves that mission. Power taken outside a mission consumes the mission. It's a zero-sum game: either mission controls power, or power takes over the mission. There's only one winner.

Power is hard to recognize when it's your own. After all, there's a lot going on, so much to be done. People. Adulation. Compliments. And a power-saturated fall can come in a blink. It's insidious. Think of the rise and fall of ancient nations such as Greece and Rome. Corporate giants like WorldCom, Enron, and Bear Stearns. Or a person with a god-complex like Hitler, or Fidel Castro, Saddam Hussein, Jeffrey Epstein, Bernie Madoff. Or in a more subtle context, leaders trying to do well, trying to keep up with the circumstantial grind of life in a business or church or ministry. An organization's popularity, size, success, or "new vision" can smother the very purpose it was meant to serve as these things over-power mission.

Whether unintentional or malicious, power and influence unhinged from mission will consume everything else. Eventually, as Lord Acton recognized, human power (or its twin of social influence) will turn on its host, ironically leaving behind powerlessness. And usually not far behind it, disgrace, chaos, and dissipation.

Power and influence has coursed through Christianity's DNA going all the way back to the Hebrews, the apostles and up to the present day. But one example of power, often thought of as "the good guys win" involves an emperor with a culture-changing, religion-altering move forced in place by sheer power.

By AD 313, Emperor Constantine had defeated most of his rivals and was boss across the Roman Empire, east and west. Persecution of the church stopped almost instantly. Within four months of the overthrow, Christianity was open-air legit. Constantine claimed to have had a dream from God guaranteeing him victory over his rival *if* his forces were warring under the sign of the cross. They did. He won. Freedom of religion became a new normal.

The pope at the time (as bishop of Rome) was Miltiades, who was over-the-top happy about Constantine. Who wouldn't be? Persecution was gone. What had been up until now small gatherings, mostly house churches, went public—viral. As one scholar describes it, "Bitter persecution and the almost complete disorganization of worship which it brought about were replaced by imperial patronage and state provision for worship in the space of much less than a decade."[65]

Imagine it! Constantine wanted to do a deal with the church. A merger. Church and empire, empire and church. The implications boggle the mind: Tax exemptions. Patronage. Land grants. Monogrammed togas. Pensions. Joint policy reviews. Government authority bestowed on the Holy See. Everything you could hope for when big brother has your back. Heads will roll, literally. Budgets to die for. Unimaginable offices. And revenue! We can use El Jefe's clout to "motivate" the people to cough up the bling. The rich and famous will be with us now, if they like being with the "in" crowd. Chariots rolling in from miles around, all to be part of the God squad. Bring your wallets, by the way. We'll build basilicas. Buy lots of paintings and kitschy gothic furniture. Statues. Property uptown.

Communion lines like Disney World. No more foursomes and fivesomes huddled in some hovel or pigsty.

The sudden legitimacy for the church was unexpected, refreshing, exciting. And as is so often the case in rapid ascents of popularity, the church was the new rage. People clambered to sign up. Who actually came to be a follower of Christ? Who came only for the fire insurance? Who came only for the Constantine effect? Didn't matter. People wanted into churches. Let them declare their faith as new converts. Ante up their tithes, usher them in, sort the rest out later.

What had been a persecuted and marginalized religious oddity was suddenly the legit and respected cohort of a powerful and cruel government. Member rosters exploded. What's not to love about government sanctioned Christianity? Power and influence had arrived for the church.

Power's Price

And yet—for whatever benefits power promises—power demands a high price. It may present itself as a subtle change in the character of a person, or an almost-unnoticeable altered purpose in an organization. Or it may overwhelm the core things, ironically robbing a person or organization of the very reasons that brought power and influence to the scene in the first place (see Revelation 2:4).

Another real world example of power and its effects: In 1991 the chairman of Kmart decided it was time to flex the retailer's muscle and confront their chief rival, an emerging upstart called Walmart. Plotting to get ahead of the Bentonville boys on earnings, the aggressive CEO's hubris to transform the company was spelled out on the cover of Kmart's 1991 annual report: "Kmart has changed. We've changed the way we look, feel, think, and act." Well, they changed alright. Veering away from their core mission as a family-friendly retail merchandiser, Kmart kicked off their power play by launching a line of pornographic paperbacks in their Waldenbooks subsidiaries, along with the Kmart retail stores. It was a textbook power disaster, trading Kmart's family-friendly reputation for a move to ramp up profits. Kmart's perception of its power led it to believe customers and cooler heads were powerless to stop them. Customers who felt otherwise were irrelevant.

It wasn't as if the leadership wasn't warned. Wall Street and Church Street spoke up clearly ahead of the move imploring the retailer not to start down such a different path. The hicks were scorned and dismissed by corporate illuminati. Kmart's profitability started an immediate slide while the CEO fumed about "the fundamentalists" who were stirring up trouble against the chain's risqué books. Doubling down as the protests rose up, Kmart tried unsuccessfully to sue family advocacy groups in 1994 for encouraging Kmart boycotts.[66] The company began its long and costly descent into irrelevance. From a profitable market giant of almost 2,500 stores worldwide in 1990, Kmart today has less than fifty stores, and that number continues to drop.[67] Power can be a weak horse to ride when you trade your mission in.

Another power diversion example—this one less overt, more nuanced: The Garden Grove Community Church was founded in the 1950s by the Reverend Robert Schuller. Schuller sought to co-opt California's car craze by opening up services in a drive-in movie theater, to preach the gospel over the car speaker boxes, as the young evangelist stood atop the roof of the snack shack. It was a big hit. The church later moved from the drive-in theater to a retro building in Riverside, featuring an indoor sanctuary with a massive patio and sliding glass wall for simultaneous indoor and outdoor preaching to the drive-in car slots. The church was on a roll—on a roll in growth. The quest to sustain that growth meant rolling from the biblical gospel toward a different theology.

Schuller decided he needed to give people more of what they liked to hear. The popular pastor would look to his hero—Norman Vincent Peale and Peale's Christian Positivism—to scratch those itching ears, as Paul would say in 2 Timothy 4:3. Peale's positivism made happiness the ultimate thing. And the ultimate thing meant *You do you*, whatever that means. So stop worrying and feel really good about you. God will be happy with that. People will be happy with that. Your church can become bigger and more influential when you make people happy like that. The "Hour of Power" had arrived.

What do you do when you discover yourself to be the epicenter of such a popular wave? Do you stay lashed to that old well-worn mission, or lean into the excitement of the power surge? This wasn't a hard question to answer. This was a scratchable social itch that meant connections, books, television, fame.

Schuller, being no wallflower, opted to go with power and influence—power in brand recognition, and influence in the public square as people flocked to hear and sync up with this powerful, happening place. Influence and power had become the new Garden Grove mission.

In 1980, Garden Grove Church built its Crystal Cathedral at a price tag of $18 million ($60 million in 2021 dollars). It was a stunning venue. The church seated more than two thousand worshipers and became one of the first televised megachurches, with an estimated twenty million viewers for the *Hour of Power* television syndication.[68] Early on, Schuller's work had an endorsement from Billy Graham, when Schuller brought the gospel to Southern California in that drive-in theater outreach ministry. But the power of fame lured the message away from amazing grace toward "If it's going to be, it's up to me."

Schuller became a forerunner of what would come to be known as therapeutic moralistic deism: "God loves you and wants you to be happy—whatever that means to you, whatever you need that to mean for God."[69] Movie stars and celebrities bedecked the cathedral's stage every week, drawing curious and congregants alike to positivism's allure. Books flew off the store shelves. Pews were packed. Public appearances and weekly services on network TV swelled the ratings. The calendar for Schuller was booked out for years. Garden Grove Church had arrived. Influence was now spelled Garden Grove Community Church.

Convinced of the church's enduring future—*Success Is Never Ending: Failure Is Never Final* was even the title of one of Schuller's books—Garden Grove went for broke. Literally broke. Betting on big donors, the spectacle of the Cathedral, and the prominence of its motivational star

Reverend Schuller, the church hit up the bank for fifty million dollars in debt to keep things climbing. But as the eighties became the nineties, people began to tire of pop-psychology dressed in thin religious robes. By the early 2000s, with receipts insufficient to service the loans, time ran out. Bankruptcy had arrived. Garden Grove's leadership fractured, and the church imploded.

A recent demonstration of power's corrosive effects on Christian unity: In October 2019, a prominent American pastor, in a conference held at his home church, agreed to give two-to-three-word answers to rapid-fire topics. It was a format used over several years. In the 2019 session, the name of a well-known female Christian speaker who recently taught in a church was teed up by the moderator. The pastor is known for his vocal stance against any teaching by women to men. His two-word rejoinder for the female speaker's name, "Go home." generated laughter in the audience and a cacophony of echoes and retorts, both pro and con across news and social media outlets. Nothing was ever resolved, many were frustrated. No apologies ensued.

This next line may be a candidate for "The Understatement of the Year" award: there are differing doctrinal opinions on women teaching men in churches.[70] Steer away from that glaring distraction for a moment. Rather, consider how power—in this case a popular leader's retort—only produced quarrels and divisiveness without ever personally reaching out or confronting the other person. Power used in such ways is cancel culture—seeking to stifle or evict someone from their role by means of public shaming prior to any personal attempt at peace or understanding.

And the result? Divisiveness and social rants among disciples. This example is not meant to criticize a pastor for his theological convictions, nor to advocate a particular viewpoint. The point is that power plays do not result in conformity, but rather, in divisiveness. Power seduces anger among followers of such a discipler, teaches power over reasoning. And it burns credibility in front of a watching world.

Let's assume for the moment that one side is right in this kind of dis-agreement and the other is just wrong about it. But both affirm the resurrection and reality of Christ. Philippians 1:15–18 suggests that yes, some may not preach all the things Paul would, and maybe even some with bad motives. But they did preach Christ, which he says is actually good.

> Some indeed preach Christ from envy and rivalry, but others from good will. The latter do it out of love, knowing that I am put here for the defense of the gospel. The former proclaim Christ out of selfish ambition, not sincerely but thinking to afflict me in my imprisonment. What then? Only that in every way, whether in pretense or in truth, Christ is proclaimed, and in that I rejoice. (ESV)

Martin Luther King Jr. reframes the conversation about culture, Christians and power like this: "The church must be reminded that it is not the master or the servant of the state, but rather the conscience of the state. It must be the guide and the critic of the state, and never its tool. If the church does not recapture its prophetic zeal, it will become an irrelevant social club without moral or spiritual authority."[71] If we use cultural comedic tools to manipulate conformity, where then does our credibility lie? It is in vested power, not Christ's form of love. Why do so many popular Christians practice acidic social media put-downs, the kind perfected by politicians and late-night comedians desperate for better ratings? Why do so many Christians echo the use of such intimidation or derision thinking it will pass for "the reason for the hope" we have in Christ?

Power, used to embarrass, whether it's reactive or premeditated is simply not effective. Ironically, Paul in 2 Timothy 2:23 would categorize such behavior as the opposite: foolish and stupid divisiveness. Divisiveness disunifies, whether it's politics, commerce or Christianity. Disunity disses discipleship. Now it is true that prophets were given very clear statements from God to deliver to nations, kings and key people. Some of those statements were pretty tough. Yet even the tough statements were preceded with personal warm-up messaging, giving the offending people plenty of warning ahead of the prophet's wrath.

But we are not those prophets. We are disciples. Anger, arrogance and power are not our venue. Lose the power and reach for 1st Corinthians 1.20-31. Humility, meekness, weakness (not power), reasoning, listening and foolishness (not conforming to social tactics)—those are the tools of the disciple. So we encounter yet another tradition that infests and complicates discipleship, as power confiscates unity in its wake. Power and discipleship simply do not mix well. It is a hard and counter-intuitive play for us to shed. Muscle memory is tough to retrain.

There's a challenge when it comes to power seeping in to a church. The challenge is that power does not usually look bad. To most leaders power and its twin, influence, don't even look like a problem; they're just the way things are supposed to be. The good guys are supposed to be really powerful, to come out on top, to win. The outcome and rightful trappings of being on God's side must prevail in might, right? Here we should introduce another power trend known as "Christian Nationalism or Christian Populism." Christian Nationalism is employing political views and power to force religious conformity in society to the things associated with Christianity. "Christendom", the legally dictated religion of the Romans under Theodosius in AD 380 would be such an example. A government power structure supporting the culture of a religion.

Devout Muslims will tell you they serve a populist political religion. To serve Islamic Nationalism, Islamic discipleship demands national subjugation to its rules, retribution for social ills perceived and political sway over local laws. That Nationalistic drumbeat varies a bit from Shia to Sunni to Wahabi, but the point is that Sharia law demands conformance by means of power. Conform to the power of the Quranic law or face the consequences. In other words, the power is in the regulations and behavior on the outside, not the heart, the inside of the individual. Christian Nationalism tracks closely with a Sharia worldview. Find powerful allies, appropriate the power, pass laws, demand (external) conformance. The morality of the power source is a secondary concern, if at all, and perversely, the very thing a disciple should be about, meaning a heart change, is not necessary for conformity.

The problem is not in Christian citizens seeking to influence a culture. That's why we're here! The problem is not in using significant influence to work policies that degrade people and societies. All that is fair use of resources. The problem is in Christians seeking to appropriate control over individual people using amoral machinery to leverage non-conformists toward religious moral diktats.[72] These kinds of plays, imitating the French Revolution's penchant for power, conquest and entitlement have not fared well for Christian discipleship, and as Paul mentioned a few centuries back, they never will. (1st Corinthians 1.27) Christianity functions poorly using power that way, and discipleship dies under such coercion. If that kind of power strategy sounds like a trip back to Constantine, you're tracking with me. Power, ironically, is a weak play in the hearts of men. Why? Consider John Adams about power and morality: "We have no Government armed with Power capable of contending with human Passions unbridled by morality and Religion."[73] And then there's Paul's words we just hinted about found in 1 Corinthians 1:26–31:

> "For consider your calling, brothers: not many of you were wise according to worldly standards, not many were powerful, not many were of noble birth. But God chose what is foolish in the world to shame the wise; God chose what is weak in the world to shame the strong; God chose what is low and despised in the world, even things that are not, to bring to nothing things that are, so that no human being might boast in the presence of God. And because of him you are in Christ Jesus, who became to us wisdom from God, righteousness and sanctification and redemption, so that, as it is written, "Let the one who boasts, boast in the Lord." (ESV)

God's kingdom does not advance by co-opting political or social power. It does not advance demanding moral fealty by non-believers. It advances by disciples making and developing other disciples. And usually, the more that power and influence thrive in a church, the more leaders will be tone deaf to discipling, and will take offense at anything other than what they want to hear.

Power feels right looking at it from the leader's chair. Truth and satisfaction get to reign. Or so it seems. But from the pews, and for the public at large, power looks oppressive, harsh, hypocritical against Christ's message.

Before Constantine, the early churches fostered intimate life relationships. They knew each other well. Most churches were just a few people living alongside one another in small house gatherings, often in agrarian settings. Death and prison were ever-present realities for the faithful. Then things were suddenly different. Radically different. A new emperor conquers, and he likes you! Who saw that coming?

Deference and preference toward Christians entered the picture almost the moment Constantine endorsed Christianity in AD 313 with the Edict of Milan. The persecuted became the popular, and darlings of the emperor. Christian gatherings, which had been minuscule and fragmented clusters of religious oddballs—most of them expecting or even welcoming oppression and martyrdom—were now occasions for rock stars. From the fourth century onward, the way believers did Christianity would be redefined. Now it meant scaling up the churches to absorb the new faithful (as well as the curious), mixed with the spoils of revenue, authority, and social relevance. Particularly in the West.

It was a powerful moment.

Recognizing Influence and Power

Influence exercised outside the charter of a mission wreaks havoc on any society or any organization, in the same way that power damages individuals. Negative influence and power has impacted Christian history time and again, mangling the work and reputation of churches, and stifling disciples. And it might just be running in the operating system of your organization right now. If that is true and left unaddressed, discipleship will drown in the quicksand of power and influence.

Let's think about a church in its various forms, its modes to illustrate how organizations can be corrupted by power. The word *church* has so many different meanings in Western societies. For example, it can mean all global Christians—that's the Church, often spelled with a capital *C*. More often the word refers to a local gathering. And, church is about people. Yes, they're part of the global Church. There may be more than one campus or gathering for that church. But a local church is not the global and universal Church. It's less than the Church, and it's more than just a building, more than just an organization or a meeting.

Here's where leaders influence four aspects or facets of their organization. These four things profoundly affect a community—the way people think and behave. Each facet demands leadership's time, energy, commitment, and continuous truing up, lest mission loss begin, lest discipling collapse under an avalanche of other distractions, like power or influence traps.

1. *Gathering:* This is the spiritual assembling of believers in holy worship, praise, and prayer. This is the most people-intense facet, and it's often mistaken for discipling. Discipleship, as Christ modeled it, is aided here in equipping believers in corporate worship, sermons, or Sunday school. Larger group and community gatherings are crucial, of course, but the close life relationships needed for discipling rarely start or develop in such numbers. The trap is that influence and power will often attach in gatherings, as individuals in leadership or speaking roles gain prominence or fame, or simply hold stature as "the person upfront." The disciple fades into the crowded blur. Leaders must guard against allowing gatherings to substitute or eclipse discipleship.

2. *Operating:* This is the human staffing and administrative facet of a church. Organization is a given for any Christian group, small or large. (If you're a house church, this may be a very small institution with no staff and few administrative burdens.) In the institution, all the humanly observable functions and activities reside here: from org charts, policies, accounting, and websites to fixing toilets, paying bills, staff roles, ministries, and mission events. This can be a major time-sink for leaders who work the so-called administrative and business sides of things every day.

Other leaders may be only lightly involved for accountability or occasional signoffs on all the machinations in the institutional church. Power can easily become a significant dysfunction in this area of many churches since authority and decision-making happen here. One of the most common traps in corporate and Christian organizations is a myopic focus on the staff or the organization's brand, at the expense of developing individuals in the organization—in this case, disciples.

3. *Managing Assets:* The physical facility and resources of a church are another facet. A campus may be a small plot, or a multi-acre site, or several campuses. Assets include all the furniture and equipment as well as buildings and land. Assets can be intangibles, like "brand"—the way the church seeks to be different from others and attract/serve/convert more people through its unique style, personalities and teaching. But intangibles require attention and time to develop and defend. Leaders are expected to plan, finance, and acquire assets for a church, usually based on perceived needs. Power can be insidious in church facilities, budgets, property, and related assets. One extreme of that power is bragging rights: the church with the most toys wins. Another extreme is sheer momentum: we ran out of room, so of course we must keep building so we can keep growing, which will require more building. Discipleship is only marginally influenced in the context of a church's assets, if at all. But assets consume a lot of leadership's time and resources. (Some will want to say facilities are vital for discipleship, since youth groups and child care and attractive venues are necessary for discipling to flourish. Hold that thought for a couple of chapters.)

4. *Leading:* We saved the best for last. The duty of leaders is pursuing the mission. Too often, leaders think their primary job is in the three facets above. That's a fatal assumption. Mission is your number one job. Don't get distracted right now trying to define mission or untangle it from vision, purpose, values, and such as that. We'll clear that up soon enough. The point here is that leaders own this mission facet of their particular community exclusively. Discipleship thrives or dives here in the community mission, and it is the duty of leaders to motivate people to understand the community mission so that the individuals will clearly grasp their own personal call and duty. This leader-owned mission responsibility is true whether elder-, trustee-, or congregationally-led structures are in place. Every single leader is expected to be on deck declaring and driving mission.

Here's a situation where the disciple dilemma gains a lot of momentum: to really degrade discipleship, all you need to do is get leaders immersed in the insidious trappings of managing things, overseeing big operations and assets at the expense of the most important thing—the mission. Do not mistake the need for these other things to function well with the point about getting lost in them. The dilemma courses through gatherings, distractions in emotional political causes, in the institutional, and assets of the organization, but the real loss for discipleship is in mission loss. We'll think much further and deeper on this topic in chapter 14.

The common tendency in business and church is to use power and influence to get past problems and issues, thinking that surely the mission will only benefit from these trappings, which, outside of the mission, are simply power systems. It looks like strong action, big status, and tangible progress. But it usually doesn't last long.

Where do power problems frequently reside in the four organizational facets just described? Predominantly in the first three—gathering, operating, asset managing—because leaders tend to lean into the tangible and measurable issues. Why? Because most church success and performance metrics are centered on power and control. Think about the metrics revered in churches: attendance, giving, budgets, capital campaigns, baptisms, facilities, websites, blogs, staff size, and even the brand. We like to measure so we can compare. Against last year. Against the competition. For our own confirmation of progress. To show things are happening. Success becomes power management, not mission execution.

As mentioned earlier, power traditions, if not controlled by the mission, will co-opt it. In the corporate world, one observable indicator of power is the divergence between the written mission and how the organization actually operates. Take the mission statement of Enron for example, the energy trading giant that bankrupted in 2001: "The world's leading energy company—creating innovative and efficient energy solutions for growing economies and a better environment worldwide." In real life, Enron's leadership had cooked the accounting books and lied to their investors and regulators about sales, profits, debts, and toxic assets. As Enron's leaders lost their way, drunk with perceived power and promises of eye-watering bonuses, they engaged their exploitive influence to demand the silence and cooperation of their people. They trashed their values by living out a different mission in which the core value was this: Profit is god, so ethics are irrelevant. Said another way, when a mission is overtaken by power and influence, mission collapses. And that kind of power-and-influence tradition buries discipleship.

Power and influence are corrosive on the development of people, especially in discipleship. First, because power and its effects are enmeshed in the role and style of leaders. The TV series *Undercover Boss* used that power dynamic as its motif, disguising leaders as regular workers among employees to see the real world. Stunned and chagrined bosses experience firsthand the true corporation they're leading—exposing the symptoms and results of their power and ignorance of the regular folks, the customers, the product. Influence uncoupled from mission damages the standing and ethics of the organization, usually to the great surprise of oblivious upper management.

Common Symptoms

What's it like looking at power if you're sitting in the pews? It can be discouraging and frustrating, as you observe the firewalls between your life and the folks running things. If you're like me, you'd never think of yourself or your teams as guilty of anything like this. But here are some power symptoms commonly perceived by people in the pews:

- *Bureaucracy.* If you've ever had the privilege of spending time with the IRS, you know you're up against an impersonal behemoth. Bureaucracies are chock-full of mind-boggling policies, with multiple people who can say no, and very few people who can serve or actually say yes. There are complex committees and rules and forms. You may owe bureaucracies certain duties or obligations, but they're never obligated to reciprocate. Communication is political, specialized, and usually logjammed. In a bureaucracy, if the boss tells staff to do something they don't like, then nothing happens. Staff has other things to do, and the boss doesn't have the time or chops to follow up. Bureaucracy is a common power tool when regular folks try to bring up ideas or offer assistance in larger settings. In smaller organizations, bureaucracy power comes across as the-way-it's-always-been-done, and no one knows how to do anything differently. Change is hard in large and small bureaucratic power structures, a virtual firewall protecting the organization from effective relationships and from discipleship.

- *Branding.* Our brand is the perceived difference between this organization and others in our niche. Brand is king, and there are no exceptions, no messing with it. In branding, staff thinks it up, and the people follow. The brand is power, no walk-ons allowed, and we don't need help from the pews. The brand means no experiments or turning people loose to try new things. The brand dictates the play. And it's not happening if not invented inside. It can be very neat and tidy. But discipleship by its nature is not so neat. Discipleship needs maneuvering room outside the confines of branding.

- *Busyness and aloofness.* How is that power? Leaders and staff, maxed out with budgets, programs, and doing everything else important in running a church, have no time to connect with people. It isn't bureaucracy, but it looks a lot like it, at least to regular people. It's weird. A pastor says, "So good to see you!" But there's no time for relationship. That's what those groups are there for—connecting with you regulars. Disciples? We have groups for that. After all, you're not on staff or in leadership. Relationships? See your small group leader.

- *Assimilation.* Remember the Borg in *Star Trek*? Resistance is futile. People feel they can't raise concerns. If you were to speak up or to vote against something, well, that's a problem. There's a sense that maybe the ideas from the pews aren't simply unwelcome; they're indicative of rebellion and resistance. Tithe, attend, volunteer. Keep compliant, and carry on—or you may be banished to teach boys' fifth-grade Sunday school. It can even go so far as overt bullying. Sam Allberry writes of real time examples and damage done when leaders use bully or intimidation power to control and force conformity among disciples.[74]

- *Insignificance.* Perhaps you're sorted by age or education, or just by the fact that there are so many people. Church is a big gathering, and nobody knows my name. And almost nobody is trying to learn it.

- *Benchwarmers.* There are a lot of talented people in the pews itching for a chance to get on the playing field. But they have to be invited. The bulletin or website might list opportunities, constantly. But leaders must understand that individuals want to be invited in, given a sense that they're personally known and wanted. "Follow me!" They long for a calling to do something that matters. Put us in coach. Don't just preach to the team. Grab me, get to know me, call me, send me.

- *Spiritual concierge service.* You don't need to know how to fish. Come relax and be an audience. We'll spoon-feed you several times each week, and there's always the website. As society demands more time from people, and prosperity requires more disposable income, families have less time and far less effort to put into discipling. This full-service church approach actually reduces relationships rather than inspires them. Concierge Christianity can make for microwave versions of home-based Bible study and prayer, and of interaction too. We'll do the heavy lifting for you on Sunday. Just show up. So church organizations add programs and seminars and more staff to offload busy peoples' burdens, like discipleship. The result? More programs, where too few staff have too diffused a focus for individuals. Just groups. And the spiritual deflation at home keeps bleeding down.

- *Mutiny.* There's also a reverse polarity power scenario, where people can decide to mutiny against the leaders. Mutiny is power, disunity and disaster. We have a defined system (see Matthew 18 for example) to deal with heretical or abusive and bullying leaders. Aside from such abuse, disciples must submit and never become power pirates.

In the early fourth century, the church's endorsement by Emperor Constantine gave it power and influence over almost all of society. It was a bureaucracy. Power to punish errant sinners with the state's penal ire was theirs too. With the emperor at their back, the influence message was "Serve the church, or be afraid." It was a cold and ominous fellowship. Discipleship was lost to conformity. Relationships were converted by this influence to en masse groupings. Relationship? Talk to the confessional, the face isn't listening. The pros were busy, the congregants were an audience, and discipleship withered.

The same threats lurk among bodies of the believers today. Unless leaders are listening, asking, probing, and building sentinel relationships among their people, then honest communication and more crucially, a discipling atmosphere does not survive. How personal is your staff in among all the people of your church? Do you know when your people are missing or fading away?

Power and influence—whether perceived or real, and whatever the size of distraction—will co-opt relationships and leave an institution in place of disciples. I want to implore leaders to consider this: If a leadership team is too busy, too big, too small, or too detached to personally connect across all congregants and members—to understand them, to perceive what they perceive, to help them embrace the mission—then that fellowship isn't likely to support discipleship.

We rarely read Scripture from a leader's fiduciary perspective, meaning to understand how leadership's role and influence in an organization helps or hinders people in making and being disciples. But if you look for God's design in the Old and New Testaments, you can see how he charged leaders to organize so that his people could encounter the full orb of being his followers—as disciples. Jesus didn't do discipleship with campuses and gatherings, as many of us do today. But he did deal with the problem of power and influence in leaders damaging discipleship among believers, ignoring believers for organizational form or function or efficiency. Some of Jesus's teaching about power and influence may not be readily apparent glancing over his words. Yet much of what he taught is designed for leaders and organizations to address the way power short-circuits discipleship. His words were actually quite blunt for leadership. Consider these warnings from Jesus just in Matthew alone:

- Be on guard for burdensome and discouraging influences on disciples. (13:22)
- Be alert for the broad and sweeping power tactics that crush discipleship. (13:29)
- Beware the tradition traps in false teaching—about purity, tithes, vain worship practices. (15:6)
- Don't use your leadership influence to sow bad thinking among your people. (16:6)
- Don't allow your role and its power to make disciples stumble. (18:6)
- To restore lapsed Christians, use fair evidence and humble outreach instead of power. (18:15)
- Don't exploit believers through jealousy or cruelty. (20:25)
- Don't allow manipulation and abuse into your gatherings. (21:13)

On that last one, rooting out false teaching would be an obvious power abuse to highlight. But the stereotypical strawman isn't what we're after. Discipleship impaired through inappropriate influence and power can be much more subtle. As an example, let's consider one passage where Jesus focused on the power to induce people to stumble. I hope you'll consider how this single verse illustrates power's sway over discipleship:

If anyone causes one of these little ones—those who believe in me—to stumble, it would be better for them to have a large millstone hung around their neck and to be drowned in the depths of the sea. Woe to the world because of the things that cause people to stumble! Such things must come, but woe to the person through whom they come! (Matthew 18:6–7)

If we isolated that verse to adolescents, we'd miss the point. This applies not only to pastors promoting bad teaching. It applies to every one of us as believers in disciple-crushing abandonment, apathy, and arrogance of people looking to us for reason for the hope within us. Someone in power, whether pastor or pal, must never cause someone else to be tripped up or compromised in their fledgling (or even in a mature person's) discipling journey.

How many leaders, by design or default, convince people that accepting Jesus for salvation is all that matters? That's a millstone-worthy heresy. Underdiscipling by way of power abuse, neglect, bureaucracy or the bad traditions is a spiritual crime, because "salvation alone" isn't what Jesus taught. Allowing that kind of influence to soak into disciples is abdication of duty for leaders.

Discipleship Cultures

There's a formulaic influence trap in some Christian communities that defines Christianity something like this: Believe in Jesus + attend + give + think this way + pray some = all good. That kind of Christianity is an influence-driven stumbling block.

Organizations caught up in power and influence traditions will always struggle to make relational discipling even a small part of the fabric of the community. Most are, well, they're powerless to start the discipling journey. Think about how many discipling-capable people you have. Not just pastors, but experienced disciples in general—small group leaders perhaps, elders, deacons, teachers. Be generous and assume that all staff are capable too. Divide the number of experienced disciples into your total adult congregation. What does that ratio look like?

Jesus operated with 12 to 1, and in his daily, close-in, life-on-life discipling it was 3 to 1. Twelve as a number won't likely be as workable for us in today's world—it's too many. Our work silos, the pace of life, our families, travel, and community all wash out those intense disciple-building times that we read about in Scripture. And by the way, if you're a really relational church today, our research suggests your ratios for disciples to disciplers is *at best* between 25 and 50 to 1. That says nothing about actual discipling relationships, which may be far more diluted than 25 or 50 to 1. More than 100 to 1 as a ratio of leader to disciples was not uncommon in our findings, and in larger churches, running upwards of thousands to one. Moreover, these exercises make a questionable assumption that everyone counted as a leader is able and willing to disciple. How do we make disciples or live as disciples with such numbers?

Another counterintuitive statement on influence and power is the apostle Paul's ongoing discussion with the Corinthian believers about operating from weakness (see 1 Corinthians 1:18–31; 2:1–5; 2 Corinthians 11:16–33; 12:1–10). Which means leaders must humbly decline to exercise or lust for power and influence. We see Paul's embrace of so-called foolishness, not influence, and his choosing intentionally to refrain from using trappings of power and influence. He asserted that weakness and foolishness were Christianity's touchstones in society. Power is power by definition because it's society's strength and force of coercion in controlling people. Christ is about weakness and foolishness in management. Not a common go-to in the Harvard B-School playbook.

To see more power and influence examples, look through the Gospels, how the Pharisees and their friends use raw power to zealously attack Jesus's relationships with people. And in the chaos that finally ensued (in Matthew 27; Mark 15; Luke 23; John 18–19), see how Pontius Pilate scrambled to keep his own power intact.

Discipleship isn't about power and coercion. It's about closely aligned relationships lived out openly among people. It's leaders and emerging leaders leading regular lives, learning and then living out the mission Christ gave to individuals (as in Matthew 28:18–20). Power, much like the thorny ground in Jesus's seed parable (Matthew 13; Mark 4; Luke 8), will choke and marginalize discipleship as it parasitically takes hostage an organization and its mission.

This is not to imply that most churches run on raw power like Kmart and Garden Grove. The point is that when duty and mission are left behind in the thrill or press of responsibilities, another power trap, mission change will soon follow. Whether power seeps in disguised in amazing or in ominous circumstances, whether it thunders in through strong-willed people or crops up as organizational chaos, power will traditionally pull churches off their mission.

Leaders cannot be expected to make everybody happy. Nor to compromise doctrine nor orthopraxy to placate factions—many factions often being on their own kind of power kick or influence tantrum themselves. In John 13, the greatest leader ever known—Jesus Christ—is portrayed leading in humility and meekness. That's not a cringing servile set of traits. Humility and meekness can only be truly what they are if they have power under control within them. Not leading in power, not driving with social influence, but discipleship in humility and meekness. That's real power in Christ's discipling.

Practically every distressed company I've worked with over my career has suffered from power problems. Often it's detachment disease. Executives and leaders usually had no clue that they had no clue about their domineering reputations or their isolation from people and business. Everyone else noticed it, but not the executives. It crushed morale and development.

Discipleship is relational and engaged. Not managerial, not programmatic. We instinctively seek to follow traditions to make things bigger, better, more influential than we found them. We want to make more converts, or help bring justice or hope into a world of political or social chaos. In all of that, leaders often turn to power strategies, thinking "It's ok, just for this moment." But power invoked will not readily take its leave. Power reprioritizes itself ahead of mission, ahead of discipleship. The result trades the intimacy of church relationships for upwardness, or opportunities, or fixing chaos, or survival. And leaders become hostage to the dilemma. Either stick with the old ways, or take the risk in confronting the traditions.

Surely smaller churches are exempt from these power traps, right? Oddly, no. In smaller churches—running, say, fewer than a hundred worshipers—survival may be a power priority. Or perhaps just keeping things steady, just getting by week to week. In that case, the power trap is sustaining the status quo, or aversion to change, or the pressures of money problems, or just finding and keeping a pastor. None of that is discipleship favorable. These circumstances are not the mission. They're just circumstances. Yet leaders will often default to power as they try to fix them. Which arrests the mission, subverting disciples.

Power traps degrade the mission of any church. And keep in mind, small church congregant-to-leader ratios can be just as daunting as the bigger churches.

Lastly, the default mission often becomes growth, a power trap of its own, one that seems edgier, bolder, exciting. The mission statement on the website—probably more rote than reality—may speak of global missions, or ending poverty, promoting the gospel, social justice, or even making everyone a disciple. But the observable agenda tends to be echoes from Constantine's power era. Getting more oomph, more credibility, more influence on deck. Programs and preaching to attract the curious, to make converts, to pull in casual believers. All these will co-opt the mission. Then they take over the strategies—yet another subtle form of power encroachment.

* * *

To summarize our material thus far:
- Optional lordship degrades discipleship.
- A catch-and-release, converts-only focus dilutes discipleship.

- Influence and power, detached from the mission, disable discipleship.

We turn now to another tradition in the early church, one in which the leaders are clerically distanced from people. That trend would ensure the pacification of disciples. Only the few would have rights to deal with God and wow the watchers. And the laity would be only too happy to oblige.

No institution can possibly survive if it needs geniuses or supermen to manage it.
It must be organized in such a way as to be able to get along
under a leadership composed of average human beings.

Peter Drucker, *Concept of the Corporation*

5

Christian Tradition:
Clerical Distancing
(No Liturgies without a License)

Business Tradition:
If I Want Your Help, I'll Give It to You

Basil of Caesarea was ticked off. This eminent theologian of the fourth century—bishop of the church of Caesarea Mazaca in Cappadocia (part of modern Turkey)—was already busy opposing the heretical Arians, who were out there gossiping that there's no Trinity, no redemption. And now, there was payola among the church's rural clerics— backwoods bishops who let their presbyters and deacons sell off church titles and church standing to cronies.[75] Something had to be done.

Who were these people under Basil's wrath? They were the *chorepis-copi*, meaning "rural bishops"—the country pastors and lay ministers out in the hinterlands. Having them aboard had made sense enough in the beginning. There simply weren't enough trained metropolitan bishops (yes, actually referred to as "metros") to go around. The hills and farmlands were too remote, too scattered. The city boys didn't want to live out there. The locals would have to step up and be part of the solution.

The metros were more reliable of course. They were educated, trained under formal teaching and practice before taking their bishopric roles. But there were so many villages, so many farmlands, so many house churches that still needed leaders. So church leaders recruited another layer down for the country congregants. The rural bishops were rarely as qualified or experienced as the metros, but they filled a hole.

The metros weren't happy about these interlopers sharing their bishopric titles. The metros believed they were apostolically tethered to the twelve original disciples of Jesus (as they frequently reminded Basil). Basil could already hear the metro prima donnas ranting about the rural embarrassments. "Those religious rednecks are unworthy! These farm boys are hicks! Either you put them under our control so we can rein them in, or we're going to the pope!"

Clergy were fed up with irascible and incompetent laymen. If you want church done right, you'd better call a pro. Hand over the key duties and power to us. Then we can get on with being big. We can recruit better converts who'll sit serenely in their pews. Which, by the way, we can charge rent for. Don't sweat the small stuff about relationships, or about discipleship. It worked for Constantine, didn't it? "In all thy getting, get more people." Don't look for that strategy in Scripture. The Bible didn't get credit for inventing that one.

Motivating pep talks were developed to soothe ruffled feelings and delivered to the country folk. "Us metro guys get to do the really cool churchy-teachy things. Yes, we know many of you used to have pastoral roles. Get over it. Clergy will read Scripture; you will listen. Clergy will preach; you shalt sit there, because clergy understand (or pretend to understand) Latin, Greek, Hebrew—and you don't. Clergy will baptize; you get wet. Clergy will administer communion; take it and move on. Clergy can excommunicate and bury you. Get the hint?"

This kind of professional arrogance came to be known as clericalism. What does clericalism mean exactly? Get your hands off the altar; just show up and pay up. And don't call us, we'll call you.

It was a power consolidation play by the bishops. Lots of people would be affected as the metros snatched authority and responsibility from the rural bishops. Basil would feel for his country brethren being usurped: they needed churches out in the sticks. "But the metros will agitate this mess all the way up to the pope if they don't get their way. And God help us if word of this gets to the emperor. Somebody will have to take a fall over it, and he's already looking for an excuse to exile me over the troubles I've caused him with the Arians." And after all, the country bishops were troublemakers in their sloppy theology, not to mention letting nepotism and graft infest their churches. Truth is, they never were discipled by anyone, really. Just laymen with a title, thrown in to fend for themselves as best they could. And the people under them? Those country presbyters and deacons were another rung down the food chain altogether. So—time to slip a tighter noose on the neck of the farmers and herders. We have to snatch away their authority to do practically anything ministerial. Maybe they can still mop the floors. Looks like we'll be increasing the travel budget for the metros.

Taking responsibility away from the common people would upgrade the quality of the church's organizational game, and eventually quash the whining among the jealous metros. But it wouldn't solve the problem of bizarre discipling. Beginning in Basil's time, and running through the tenth century, the metro bishops would curry to the community chieftains. Kings, emperors, regional lords, and landowners were the target audience. Which also meant more church and state confederations in the making. To lower a bit the daunting ratios of clergy to everybody else, the gentry, the educated, and the social noblesse became the focus of clergy. In classic top-down organizational brilliance, the metros came up with a plan where the elites got religion, then they would assemble their commoners and pass on the faith. People would listen to the landed, and not rail so much, right? They were the elites, after all. They owned the land. Want to work? Straighten up. Listen to us. Fly right.

It was perfect. The gentry would get valet treatment from clergy. Preaching, teaching, double communion helpings, frequent friars, discount funerals. The whole nine yards. The enlightened elites would of course run right out and bestow their couth and Christian wisdom to all the common folk around them. That strategy would reach the world. It would change the game with the heathens.

Except it didn't. What resulted was a well-informed but very apathetic aristocracy. Another unintended consequence was that the clergy began to really like their less frantic pace. They now had smaller territories and wealthy, interesting clientele. The privileged and less needy folk were so much more fun. And the clergy got to rub elbows with power, money, and persons of desired peerage. All that was pretty nice. Soon the wealthy families—some noble, but many having violent and cruel reputations not unlike the Borgias—would even be supplying the church with its bishops. That the bishops could enjoy both clerical power and monetized largesse in all this was—well, it was just a peripheral blessing.[76]

How *do* you run a disciple-making ministry, when instead of twelve disciples with Jesus, you're solo, facing the fifty, five hundred, or five thousand with no fishes or loaves? What to do when weird and cultic practices are being taught by some bozo in Belfast? The chorbishops were an embarrassment to the elite bishops, to their papal boss, and to the pope's governmental big brother, the emperor. The answer to the problem was just like in *The Apprentice*: "We have two strategies for that." One: Blame somebody. Two: Fire them.

Some church traditions and behaviors seem to have been the basis of a script written for modern-day broadcasting. Remember the aforementioned TV show *The Apprentice*? As the program's host for most of its fifteen seasons (beginning in 2004), Donald Trump was the big boss. Teams would compete, running some kind of wacky venture. Someone would screw up on results. Big boss wanted answers. Who was to blame for the mess? The team leaders, faced with the threat of personal oblivion, had to act fast. The solution? Somebody (else) takes the fall. Shame and blame are the hot potato. After a few elites gathered in a smoke-filled room, some poor schmuck got fingered by his teammates. The scapegoat was picked, plucked, and pushed out for sacrificial reckoning.

And then there's that oh-so-familiar line from the big boss. "You're fired!" The shocked contestant was escorted out of the building, loaded into a New York cab, banished to the dustbin of digitally syndicated history. The temporarily vindicated, having scapegoated somebody else, bought time to play another day.

Does that have anything to do with the disciple dilemma? It may be more applicable than you'd first guess, looking back at the early church.

No Rube Goldberg distortion of biblical discipleship would be complete without putting the gears in neutral for discipleship—the gears of relationships and development for regular people. The modern management term for this is *centralization*. Pull up the ladder of responsibility so the folks downstairs can't screw up whatever it was we never taught them to do in the first place. The folks upstairs get to do all the cool stuff, burnishing the image of being higher, better, special.

One encounter between Jesus and a centralized committee of priests is found in Luke 20.

> One day as Jesus was teaching the people in the temple courts and proclaiming the good news, the chief priests and the teachers of the law, together with the elders, came up to him. "Tell us by what authority you are doing these things," they said. "Who gave you this authority?" He replied, "I will also ask you a question. Tell me: John's baptism—was it from heaven, or of human origin?" They discussed it among themselves and said, "If we say, 'From heaven,' he will ask, 'Why didn't you believe him?' But if we say, 'Of human origin,' all the people will stone us, because they are persuaded that John was a prophet." So they answered, "We don't know where it was from." Jesus

said, "Neither will I tell you by what authority I am doing these things." (Luke 20:1-8)

Jewish central committees don't particularly like to share ministry roles, and they especially don't like outsiders getting any limelight or making waves. In the story about Basil and the country bishops, it's the laity who are the losers and the metro clerics who are threatened. The metro bishops were the regional leaders, the Chorbishops the local leaders, and the emperor was the Bishop's big boss—a religious/government hybrid that would make Iran's ayatollahs jealous. To avoid losing face from the local antics the clergy scapegoated and sidelined laity, who deserved some of the blame, but not all of it. And in preserving their own status, the clergy would start another tradition: Only the pros can do things really well, professionally, actually. The laymen can't handle it. The pros are better, greater, separated. They're on a higher plane with God than the rest of you.

Clericalism's Messages

This scenario is known as clericalism. Clerical social distancing if you will. Clericalism is a niche form of power and influence that sends a message to regular disciples: that they're unworthy of doing things that the professional Christians do. So don't even try. Even though Scripture eliminates all such status and privilege after Christ's atonement, the tradition lives on. The *ism* in clericalism is an unhealthy tradition, with clergy holding back roles for all disciples in spheres of worship, ministry, and certainly discipleship itself.

The other big issue in clericalism is cultural. That big issue is reprogramming people in the pews to actually believe they're the lesser, the lame, the theological lepers, and that it's clergy's job to handle the big stuff—teaching, communion, baptism, giving reason for the hope. And laity would upload that programming and fall right in line. The result? A tradition of laity no longer being the hands and feet of the churches, relegated largely to being benchwarmers. They would do their menial jobs well (if there were any), and revere or reject roles now monopolized by clergy.

Why is Old World clericalism a threat to modern-day discipleship? Because what was a fourth-century countermeasure to crowd control and amateurish behavior is today normative Christian culture. Concierge Christianity. Show up, be served, and be dazzled by the pros. You couldn't possibly pull this off as a layman, you see. Step aside and stay seated.

We commonly train and reinforce leaders to think of themselves as the responsible people, the only legitimate leaders, just as we program laymen to stand down. Sometimes it's the paradigm that only highly educated specialists can do good work for God onstage. Or sometimes it's the reverse problem—people in the pews looking down their noses and saying, "That's what *those* people do up there. They care for the kids, give talks, visit sick people, talk to heathens." In either case, it's clericalism: control, professionalize, specialize, elevate, isolate, passivate.

The result? It domesticates (breaks) disciples. Those with "Pastor" or "Reverend" or "Elder" next to their names are by this tradition bestowed a false veneer or a mistaken identity as better-qualified-than-thou. The tradition goes further, reinforcing the myth that people should view leaders as the anointed Christians, with special knowledge and secret access to God. Plus other traits and tax exemptions that regular mortals don't possess. And there's a weird inverse to that thinking—usually unspoken, but no less alive among modern disciples: There's no need for those of us in the pews to sully our hands doing this or that, since that's what plumbers, proctologists, and priests are here for. The help will take care of it. They watch the kids for us on Wednesday nights, preach something, make people feel guilty, bury the in-laws. That kind of stuff. That's what we hire those people to do.

The star power and inaccessibility of a pope is a classic example of clericalism—that relational distance and separation from regular Roman Catholics worldwide. But the same problem also emerges in a small church pastor, so busy doing everything that there's no access to him, or connection with people. Small church example: I visited with Chris, in Nevada, a pastor of about fifty people. "What do you do to develop disciples there?" I asked. The surprising answer: "I don't. I don't have time. Too much to do, and everyone telling me that discipleship isn't their thing. So I take care of it all."

It's not necessary that every member of a church have a deep and close relationship with every leader. But leaders must eliminate perceptions and trappings of clericalism in their organizations. That means leaders must retool typical Christian expectations for discipling. Retool so responsive and engaged disciples emerge. You can delegate that kind of discipling responsibility, but you must not presume delegation solved it. That's how you foul up execution—by presuming simple delegation equals performance and follow-through. You have to disciple the disciplers.

In the business world, delegation only means you told someone what you expected them to do. Until you come alongside them to coach and practice it, delegation isn't worth much. Few leaders realize how little their words of delegation mean, and how little comes of it. Instead, you have to practice it out with your own people until they get it, so they can start practicing it with their people. This means sharing and giving up some of the plum jobs, or ensuring and verifying that the not-so-plum jobs will be covered so the leaders can lead, and the disciples can go be disciples. Leaders must instill involvement and responsibility by disciples where full-service professionalism can never do so. You cannot staff discipleship's development any more than you can hire real relationships.

Leaders must break clericalism's grip on their people, lest another generation of marginalized and passivated disciples emerge. This is not to suggest a down-with-clergy agenda. Christianity needs specially trained scholars and pastors to help us with the technical and fulsome truths found in the history of Scripture, to help disciples learn to deal with life issues they encounter, and to combat crafty pseudo-intellectual mud hurled against the faith in order to unsettle disciples. We need those kinds of well-equipped people. Yet leaders must recognize that the historical tradition of clericalism erodes and dissipates leaders as much as it passivates those in the pews.

Distancing in churches between leadership and laity is a major road-block in discipleship. This is not implying leaders are the means to make individual disciples. Leaders are called to a specific role to organize the mission and culture for further discipling. And just like the rest of us, leaders are equal in the sight of God with everyone else. Although a leader's charge is significant to the organization, it's not an impossibly lofty role—as Peter Drucker notes in the header quotation for this chapter. Unfortunately, tradition has driven a false wedge of elitism between clergy and disciples. And that wedge is perceived as normal and right in Western Christianity. It becomes the formal and informal segregation of clergy while the rest of us rest. Spectators in the pews watch the pros. And as laity became accustomed to such a caste system, they came to like it. Clericalism would dilute Jesus's standards for disciples, and it would isolate and paralyze disciples.

It might surprise some people to learn that prior to Constantine, the duties performed by laity and clergy were nearly indistinguishable. The case is strong that there was little or no difference between laity and clergy responsibilities until around the thirteenth century.[77] Even so, with Constantine's arrival in the fourth century, political and societal changes would begin eroding the role of disciples in churches, from small, intimate, persecuted gatherings to overnight fame, power, and social influence in the big cathedrals. And as bureaucracies are wont to do, the clergy became rife with nepotism and cronyism. Catholic historian and author Sean O'Conaill describes the situation this way:

> This relationship between church and state always severely distorted the church's message and limited its evangelical impact—giving rise to the very scandals that led to the secularist reaction in the modern era. When the church aligned itself with emperors and kings who had acquired their power by violent competition, its bishops were soon mostly recruited from these very same military-aristocratic elites, and the Gospel message of social

humility, peace, and welcome for the stranger was necessarily compromised. The pattern of seeking to "convert" social elites in the expectation that their underclasses would then conform made clergy generally content with mere conformism, not at all the same thing as deep Christian conversion.[78]

Note the profound implications of O'Conaill's discipleship prophecies: "scandals [back then] that led to the secularist reaction in the modern era," and "clergy generally content with mere conformism, not at all the same thing as deep Christian conversion." Here's another testament to debilitating traditions from long ago running strong in our present day. And O'Conaill suggests that those old events induced the secularist reaction we're experiencing today—prospective disciples—hurt, angry, and deserting. Starting with ancient clerical power plays, the implications flow into our own world. When leaders allow scale, power, and influence to eclipse Christ's model of life-upon-life, it can impair generations of would-be disciples. This clericalism tradition would make for very thin soil in which to sow discipleship's seeds, much like the New Testament metaphor in Matthew 13:1–9; Mark 4:10–20 and Luke 8:4–15.

Church leadership was not prepared for the fourth century's membership boon. Three problems flooded the churches, inducing many bad reactionary decisions. First, it was a time of overwhelming numbers arriving at church doors—commoners coming out as their landowners, chiefs, and lords turned to Christ, or as they at least virtue-signaled the social status and benefits of church association. Second, there simply weren't enough experienced laity nor clergy to go around—to live out discipleship at a personal level with the masses. Third, the growth, coupled with the overwhelming rural social needs, resulted in just about anyone with a pulse getting the nod to lead in church gatherings and ministry. Some did quite well as newly appointed deacons, presbyters, and bishops. Yet many were immature in their faith, and sometimes their beliefs were downright weird—bizarre mixtures of pagan and Christian rites, tribal bias, and corruption. It was mass production of theological chaos. And it was precisely what Paul warned Titus about (in Titus 1:5–16).

Two Models

In researching church discipling, two models predominantly rise up. One is the incubator model, the other a lean model.

Incubator models discover and employ the gifted talents of people in the pews toward discipling. This model excels in probing gifts and exploring motivators among people, to help them be disciples and make disciples, and connecting all that energy and talent to the mission. These kinds of incubator leaders want to know who's in the room, and to relate to these people—to foster real discipling relationships among the people there. These are leaders who aren't confined to their Sunday staff roles. They're opportunists—finding capability, enlisting it, driving relationships forward. Helping people learn how to make relationships that make disciples who make generations of disciples.

The other model is the lean model. You need sophisticates to run a lean operation. Without getting too bogged down in business systems, this model aims relentlessly at being in control, getting professional results, minimizing waste and defects. There's an intended production objective. There must be no distractions or problems or waste associated with the production outcomes. Just conform to the process.

The story of Dawson Trotman (founder of the Navigators) illustrates this notion of lean. Dawson made a commitment to God to share the gospel of Christ with someone every single day. No waste, no exceptions. He sometimes picked up hitchhikers along the Pacific Coast Highway to meet that goal, explaining the gospel to them, then dropping them off. He remembered one guy as particularly unpleasant and foul-mouthed. But this guy heard him. He accepted the gospel. Dawson dropped him off and headed home—mission accomplished. No waste, no worries. It's about production, you see.

A year later Dawson picked up an unpleasant, foul-mouthed hitchhiker who appeared to know nothing of the faith. Dawson started sharing the gospel with him—and discovered it was the same guy from the prior year! There'd been no impact on his lifestyle, no evidence of conversion. Right then and there, Dawson realized that the lean model is not discipleship.[79]

There can be a lot of time-burn and chaos in building relationships with people. Yet people are precisely the reason for discipleship. Funny, how relationships like that, with all those not-like-me people are key to successful business ventures and discipleship. Yet people in organizations often reverse what's important. They control the periphery—things like budgets and programs—while the core people languish.

You might be familiar with churches that are lean—no waste, no surprises in the organization itself. There's a program for everything. Budgets are nailed or else rapid cuts follow, just like a Wall Street playbook. The services are scripted to the minute, and staff are the big draw, everybody sitting in their designated places at their designated times waiting to hear from the big names. It's hard to get to know the leaders—but boy, do we have programs! Relationships? Yep, they meet in that room over there. Discipleship? There's a seminar on that coming up next month, be here at 8 a.m. sharp. If you want to feel included, fill out the website guest form and we'll get back to you shortly, or at least before you move away. Please sign up for a small group so we can feel assured you're being discipled, and staff can go back to working on the budgets.

Businesses frequently think (mistakenly) that their technology or their intellectual property or their budget is their most important asset. In reality, it's the people. Just as Christian organizations can mistake programming and staffing in place of the real mission of disciples.

There are real-world business examples of organizations that lost their way, people who thought that a program could supplant relationships. A major home improvement chain launched a lean management initiative when they hired a Fortune 50 manufacturing executive to take over as its leader. A production oriented lean makeover did not go well for the employees or the customers of a folksy do-it-yourself (DIY) business. DIY quickly became known as "Dumped In a Year" as the home improvement giant tried to claw its way out of its lean crisis and move back to a people-centric service model. Similarly, the way church leaders organize has to serve the mission, and not the other way around. Otherwise, as we've seen, the mission will collapse under the tyranny of the urgent.

Which model is right for a church or business? Well, it depends. Thermo Electron's mission was the incubator model—diversifying their businesses with motivated employees who had gifts and talent to lead new ventures. It worked well for them. On the other hand, lean has its place too. For example, I really like the fact that commercial airlines operate under lean principles, with tightly controlled procedures that result in the same safe flight every day, instead of harebrained experiments in aviation like, "Hey! Let's see if this thing can land sideways."

But for disciples, relationships (much like incubators) will drive better KPIs (key performance indicators, which are the things that are crucial in an organization's pursuit of mission) than any perfectly starched process could ever hope to offer. This is not to imply we throw out Paul's call for order in church in 1 Corinthians 14:40. Order is crucial. But considering Jesus's true nature, as God incarnate, is it possible to design a better discipling process than Christ's? How do you do discipleship other than Christ's personal, intimate, relational life on life way?

When we were drafting this book, Brent, a theologian in Chicago pointed out how the occurrence of mass conversions are implied in Acts 2:41: "Those who accepted his message were baptized, and about three thousand were added to their number that day." The takeaway is evangelistic gifting at work and many coming to faith. What we don't know is the rest of the story. Were they discipled, or dismissed, or derelict? We honestly don't know. But what we can know is that Jesus, Paul, and the apostles repeatedly gave us the example of life on life is the rule, not the exception. The evangelical events were indeed for mass appeal, in the way of drawing people toward encounters with Christ, and relational life with his disciples.

Basil's dilemma in the fourth century was dealing with the arduous work of making disciples rather than simply pleasing his bishops. Basil's dilemma showed us that a church cannot delegate discipleship to staff and expect things to go well, nor can it dumb down robust engagement for untrained disciples and expect disciples to follow well. There must be balance. Discipleship will not succeed with the pros alone. There aren't enough of them, ever. A single pro mentor will only bog down, eventually, in a morass of underdiscipled believers all dependent on that one person.

Disciples are to be developed well, then multiply new disciples, who then make disciples who make disciples. Otherwise, in the pro-only model, the process is mere addition. One person relating to many people in cycles or waves of proselytizing. Not many for many. One for all the many. Which cannot be all that many.

Groups and events may well draw a person in to start a disciple's journey, but groups and events, church or otherwise, are not discipleship. Sermons equip, but they do not make disciples. Programs do not make disciples. People, empowered and coached personally by their disciplers, make disciples who make disciples. The Christian community depends upon the empowerment and employment of the laity. One person over many as a mass discipler is simply not enough relationship.

Jesus and the apostles across the New Testament made it plain that the body of Christ is built by disciples, not by staff, and not by insulating or distancing people from one another.

When Jesus demanded that the organization's handlers (his own disciples) allow him to personally relate to the "little ones" (Matthew 19:13–15), is it possible that Jesus meant only people under the chronological age of eighteen? Without close and personal relationships, whether infants or new believers, disciples cannot fulfill Jesus's commission on discipleship. Leaders own the job of building that community, where disciples build and enable real relationships.

Making leaders something higher or bigger than laity is a dead end for discipleship, because it reinforces the false notion that the "lesser beings" have a lesser calling, which is a lie. Building a church strategy on growth or some famous name or social or political agenda is a classic power diversion, and a biblical dead end.

Leaders must know their people. Do you know the names, stories, talents, and lives of your people? Be worried if the first response from your staff is "We're too big for that." Or its alter-ego: "That's what the small groups are here for."[80]

* * *

We now have four dysfunctional traditions on the table, traditions still alive and well that have degraded Jesus's teachings for discipleship:

- Optional lordship degrades discipleship.
- A catch-and-release, converts-only focus dilutes discipleship.
- Influence and power, detached from the mission, disable discipleship.
- Clericalism—distancing people into concierge Christianity—passivates disciples.

Now we're ready to see how size fits into these traditions. Is it curtains for discipleship in big churches? Are the small churches diminished in discipleship? The next chapter will size it all up.

The radicalism of Christ's way must challenge us.
He does not want to win numbers but dedicated hearts.

J. Heinrich Arnold, *Discipleship: Living for Christ in the Daily Grind*

6

Christian Tradition:
Herd Community Causes Disciples

Business Tradition:
Too Big to Fail

Pope Gregory the Great was a visionary man, and a most capable leader of the church at the end of the sixth century. Almost a thousand years after his death he would be lauded as "the last good pope" by the famous reformer John Calvin.

Gregory's father was a wealthy Roman senator, while his mother would later be venerated as a patron saint to women. Gregory grew up very blessed, and apparently quite humble. He was an academic wonderkid in law, the sciences, and literature. And though Gregory eschewed attention and the limelight, they would have their way with him nonetheless.

He would hold public office by age thirty-three. Upon his father's death, Gregory converted the family's substantial Sicilian estate into a monastery. During this time Gregory would view all that he'd grown up with—the estates, the money, the power—as *contemptus mundi*. He felt disdain for this life's trappings. He wanted a smaller life, to live in close relationships with the people around his monastery. He was always among the people, giving away food, comforting the sick, talking to and relating to the community. Gregory had chosen to serve Christ by living out his life in close relationships among the locals.

Or so he thought. Known at home and abroad for his ability to relate with people and draw them in to the teaching of the church, his talents gained the eye of Pope Pelagius II, who ordained him a deacon. The pope would soon send Gregory to Constantinople. Emperor Maurice was there, and the pope sought troops and aid from his head of state in order to defend Rome against the invading Lombards. Gregory, with hesitance, went. He moved freely among the very worldly elite and powerful in the Byzantine capital, and he did so without compromising his own standards. Yet military support from the emperor would never materialize. Realizing that the emperor wasn't going to help in Rome's plight, Gregory returned home.

When Pelagius II died of the plague in the year 590, the hands-down choice as the new pope was Gregory, the reluctant hermit. He would in vain try to continue living a monastic life as a pontiff. It would prove impossible to command a global church while living off the grid. Reluctantly he was extracted from his monastic closet. And so, he acted. He would see and move on the need for great scholarship and reasoning to challenge the church, to upgrade missions work and outreach, and to be his people's leading servant. And he would heed the call to serve the poor when citizens of Constantinople turned away from their own people's gut-wrenching needs. What Gregory did in his time as pope would be worthy of a Harvard Business School case study in entrepreneurial genius, leadership, truly compassionate capitalism, and an attempt to reignite discipleship in a very large Christian institution.

Gregory would organize his own logistics systems, a revolutionary accomplishment for that time. He would devise supply chains, accounting practices, and equity-incentivized farm operations with delivery nodes to ensure food supplies arrived for the needy, diverting what would have been church revenue into supplies for starving street people. Gregory the ever-serving deacon would even develop his own version of Meals on Wheels, where people who were incapacitated from ravages of plague and poverty could be assured that food would arrive in the hands of stewards. Stewards who were compensated only upon discharging their duty. Gregory knew how to extract performance from stodgy staffers. And his keen sense of strategy would launch successful mission endeavors to the Anglo-Saxons, the Netherlands, and Germany.

In Gregory's life we can begin to comprehend the challenges of personal discipling in the small church environment as well as seeing him lead disciples in an institution of massive scale and size. Gregory truly understood serving people, reaching them at a personal level, leading them to serve other people in need.

But our interest in Gregory goes further than his administrative and managerial savvy. As leaders, we need to consider a big question that gets little attention: Is there a "right size" in bodies of believers, an optimum scale and mass for discipleship? Gregory succeeded in ministering personally; he succeeded in managing ministers, whether in his own small hometown environment, or as a global pontiff. His work, words, and scholarship as a pope were significant. Yet the question of organizing the first Giga-church (10,000-plus members) toward effective discipleship is before us. How did Gregory do in that regard? He was, after all, snatched from a local deacon's life, one of relating and walking and living among his peers, to become the administrator of the most massive church with a massive staff, massive social problems, and massive numbers of congregants awaiting what's next.

Until Gregory's arrival on the scene, it would be fair to say the Roman church had chosen to set aside discipleship for market-share. And in that growth rollup, a culture of "too big to be concerned with discipling" had arrived. Leave that to the executives, the cardinals, the pope. The church was too big to fail, discipling too failed to be big.

"The radicalism of Christ's way must challenge us. He does not want to win numbers but dedicated hearts."[81] Too-big-to-fail numbers thinking wrecks businesses too. In 2008, Bear Stearns, one of America's oldest and most prestigious investment houses, was sold to JP Morgan for less than ten cents on the dollar of its value twenty-four months earlier. Bear Stearns had been worth $66 billion USD back in 2006, going big with more than $300 billion under management only months before the crash. Books aplenty have dissected the company's downfall,[82] many pointing to its concentration in subprime derivatives, questionable assets, and collateralized debt obligations, all stretching them well beyond their capacity to operate when the financial crisis of 2006 arrived. In other words, they were in debt way over their heads and loaded with bad collateral. Others point to a perfect financial storm in the housing market, or simply to Wall Street greed. These are all subcomponents of a much larger issue that caused Bear Stearns' demise—and that same issue torments churches today as much as it does Wall Street: When numbers displace the mission, the numbers rule. When numbers rule, the rule of law is not a mission, it's numbers. Said another way, what really matters—the mission, or the numbers? Only one can have top billing. A lot of business people will say the mission of any business is to maximize returns to its investors—the numbers mantra again. But that's a dilemma in itself. The prize of a business is the returns it garners in money and market share. But the mission is something else altogether. In sports we focus on the game, not the trophy. We want the trophy. We like the accolades that go with the trophy. But we play the game our way, using our talent, our mission. If we succeed, the trophy comes with the winning performance. Numbers may indicate things like market share and monetized success, but numbers are not the mission.

As an organization grows, it must either have faithful followers committed to the mission, or the organization becomes its own mission—which is to say mission failure begins. Bigger always justifies more staff, more policies, more facilities, more numbers, and more layers in order to build up more size and planning for rinse-and-repeat like that all over again. Don't assume this means an organization cannot become big and still hold to mission. But leaders must realize that size has to be subservient to the mission, it cannot be a goal in itself, and not a casual add-on feature independent of mission. As size demands more attention at the cost of mission, mission becomes cut flowers, which is to say nice looking, but no longer functional, no longer rooted in a mission. Numbers, success metrics, and influence—subsets of a growth-based approach, loosed from a mission will become…the mission.

The tradition of growth (or avoiding growth) is an old but very common mission distraction that can crush discipling just as clericalism and lordship-lite production thinking can. In fact, these three dysfunctions can often be found emerging together in the rush and crush to deal with growth. These were the kinds of things that Gregory inherited. But is that a fair assessment? Think about Gregory's dilemma: Coupled with the twin crises of plagues and wars, how could anyone criticize priorities of ministry over something less immediate? It would be natural for a leader in that situation to focus on that moment and all its chaos rather than the mission. "We need tourniquets, not teaching!" So, we have an opportunity to learn something about leadership that is much harder to grasp in the fog of the issues and conflicts Gregory faced in his time. Gregory led by example throughout his life, ministering directly to people. To rephrase it, he gave away a lot of fish, yet he was not much into teaching fishing. Great compassion. Making disciples? That's a trickier read. Why? He may well have been pouring his life into others to make disciples pursuing Christ. But we cannot point to that, so we cannot be sure. A beautiful ministerial and managerial life. A discipling legacy is less obvious. And here we see a vital point. Gregory's papal life offers much in terms of personal doing, but little in his impact as a maker of discipleship culture. By all accounts, Gregory proved he understood what it meant to be an individual follower of Christ serving distressed people. He proved also that he was a master of organizational management and strategic planning. But so few around him understood and rightly valued discipleship. So rather than nit-pick this marvelous man of God, let's learn from him. What must it have been like to take the reins of leadership in the midst of that huge organization, at such a time of disease and death?

What should leaders take away from Gregory's great works? Not simply how to compassionately serve people, and how to set up savvy systems to leverage the bigness of a church for God's work. Gregory showed us outstanding vocational aptitude as a disciple of Christ. He showed us excellent ministry leadership, finding ways to motivate people to serve and perform. What he demonstrated is that some of us will attain or inherit roles of leadership, influence, and power. And when that happens, if we're not prepared for it ahead of time, our personal discipling and discipleship will fall to the tyranny of the urgent, the tyranny of administration, the tyranny of growth, fame, and power. Mission cannot succeed if we don't allow it to change a culture centered on works, causes, and tribes into a culture that sticks to the mission of enabling disciples of Christ. The point? You'll get all the beautiful things of justice, unity, real and effective agape love only when you pursue the real mission—making disciples.

There's wisdom to be found in looking at what Gregory did, and wisdom in hearing Jesus telling us (in Matthew 26:11; Mark 14:7) that yes, the urgency of the poor is always there, but focus (the mission) on him, then let that focus drive ministry, drive results.

For leadership, following Jesus's strategy to develop (or rebuild) a community of discipleship lets disciples multiply disciples, which is precisely what leaders should desire for their people. And in that journey, that strategic process to help enable people to minister greatly, and enable people to pursue causes passionately. Then disciples go into work life, home life, civic life, and ministry roles, and out across the globe. A mission of making constant followers of Christ, as disciples, is the true means of multiplying service and ministry, rather than plugging temporary holes where there are ministry gaps or chronic troubles. Leaders must organize in that way. Plug the mission, not the holes. Then the disciples will plug the holes. Holy hole-fillers thrive because leaders are wholly committed to discipleship's holy call.

A Man with a Big Plan

What does all this tell us about the size tradition? Is size constructive or destructive for discipleship? And a natural follow-up: How am I, as a leader, supposed to deal with size and its impact on discipleship? Glad you asked.

A preeminent name in corporate growth strategy is Peter Drucker, one of the most highly regarded business thinkers of the twentieth century. Ask anyone with an MBA about Drucker, and be ready to sit back and listen. Born in Austria in 1909, he fled Nazism for America as a professor in the late 1930s, where he wrote thoughtfully on politics through the 1940s—especially the evils of totalitarianism—before turning his brilliant mind to business in the 1950s. Drucker's career spanned tenures at both New York University and the Claremont Graduate School in California. His monographs in *Harvard Business Review,* and his more than thirty published works, along with a plethora of fascinating speeches, are widely embraced today in boardrooms and the most elite business schools.

He's the name behind modern management strategy. Corporate titans such as General Electric, General Motors, and AT&T credited Drucker with their massive strategic and financial gains in the 1970s and 1980s. In other words, this guy had credibility with big business. And the odds are likely that half of those reading this book in America are worshiping under Western church traditions introduced by Drucker's personal influence—influence that altered the course of Western Christian churches. And with it, he altered the course of Western discipleship.

Peter Drucker—born Lutheran, and later in life an Episcopalian—stated, "I'm not a born-again Christian."[83] Drucker's passion was sociology, especially the welfare of society. He wanted better for humanity than what he fled from under the Nazis. As one of the original social justice warriors, he saw things in corrupt political power that reviled him. His aim was to find a better way to address human evils, *acedia* (spiritual sloth and apathy), and social failure, and he frequently railed against totalitarianism, greed, and poverty. Drucker wanted to enable real change in a culture, change that would alter society from the bottom up, outflanking the powerful. Drucker surmised that change would best be brought by the regular folks, and thereby force the topside people—government leaders, business titans, nonprofits, and elites in society—to come around to a better way.

In the 1940s and early 1950s, Drucker thought and wrote about political enlightenment. But after recognizing politicians' addiction to power, he gave up on politics as a way of culture change. Corporate strategy became his go-to path forward through the 1960s, when many of his bestselling business works were produced. But by the 1970s, Drucker had come to realize the same power addiction trap lurked in businesses. He was coming to think that while the aim of changing Western society was feasible, it wouldn't be by either political or commercial means. Those ships had sailed, many of those leaders using Drucker's ideas to grow, but without taking aboard the ethical freight Drucker felt was necessary for society. And those political and commercial ships would not willingly relinquish the power and wealth journeys they were on.

Drucker saw that a new path was needed. It required lots of people. It required conviction and enthusiasm that wasn't lured away by opportunistic power, wealth, or fame. This new way would need to be made up of two special assets. First, a highly empowered social machine that could rally millions of regular folks to a just and moral cause. Second, leaders immune to power traps in order to successfully pilot that new cultural machine.

In the 1970s, Drucker could already see the machine in its prototypical phase. Scattered around some of the big cities were these peculiarly big churches. You might recognize names like Brooklyn Tabernacle, Liberty Baptist, National Presbyterian, Coral Ridge. These were mega-sized gatherings where thousands attended each week. They were faithful people who sought a moral order, who weren't in it for monetary or political gain, and who wanted things to be different, to be better in the world. Where these churches stood theologically didn't matter at all to Drucker. He was after the social leverage, not the soteriology. He called his idea "the phenomenon outside my window." One of those big churches that was right outside Drucker's window was Robert Schuller's drive-in Garden Grove

Community Church. It was a mere twenty-six miles from his Claremont office, where thousands of these nice church people gathered every week.

Along with his new approach, Drucker needed fresh leadership to implement his idea. He needed leaders without guile or aspirations of grandeur who would spend significant time with him, learn from him, and emulate his thinking in societal change—in a word, Drucker would need disciples. They would be "playmakers," borrowing a football term, winsome leaders who could attract many alongside them to scale up the work, scale up the size of the voice, and thence scale up the social agenda Drucker sought to influence through the Western church.

He found his disciples in three men. Perhaps these names are familiar to you. The three Drucker disciples were Rick Warren, the pastor of Saddleback Church outside Los Angeles; Bill Hybels, former pastor of Willow Creek Community Church outside Chicago; and the late Bob Buford, a cable-tv mogul and founder of the Christian Leadership Network. A casual tour around the web will reveal personal stories from each of these three very influential men telling the world that Drucker mentored them and architected their organizational game plans.

The notion of these three Drucker disciples was to integrate the gospel with people's passions and wants. This so-called "attractional" model would scale to mega-size, pulling in members who wanted to sync up their personal agendas with a moral or Christian kind of venue. And he thought, these people would want to see their participation become an influential platform. It would be leverage to broadcast the gospel even further, do ministry bigger, and change society by means of power, by means of influence. It was a new approach. Unless you want to look back to the fourth century and Constantine. The Drucker plan wasn't intended to make disciples, even though that may have been on the minds of his protégés. The Drucker approach would attract people into churches. Gathered up mostly from other smaller churches, it would turn out, with many of those people attracted to the megas actually sticking around and becoming wonderful followers of Christ. But the concept itself was classic business school: a marketing campaign aimed precisely at gathering power in market share.

The secret ingredient for the early megas was a seeker-sensitive venue. This seeker approach was detailed in Donald McGavran's 1965 book *The Bridges of God*. Seeker-sensitive meant that you figure out what people are looking for in their wants and wishes in a church experience, then you give it to them. You market Christ to personally felt needs. It would put church growth on steroids.

Willow Creek and Saddleback prove that strategy out convincingly. Both churches grew to more than twenty thousand members each within a few years of their founding. With growth like that, all the benefits and baggage of big could not be far behind. Size and influence were Drucker's objectives. Bigger meant more. More influence, more attraction, and more shots-on-goal to change a culture, with the crowds hearing and then taking goodness into society, just like the landowners didn't in the fourth century. Some traditions never die, they just keep coming around and around.

Some would argue that the Drucker approach was so novel that even Jesus hadn't thought of it. But Drucker had one very prescient thought we do need to learn from: Get a community of believers focused on something motivating, like discipling, and you generate people who'll go out into the world and influence the world as humble followers of Christ, not as power brokers. That's a key point for Christian leaders, no matter what size organization you lead.

This idea of size and influence in the 1970s and 1980s was already in motion with Christian organizations outside the churches. And politically conservative thought leaders figured out how they could catch a ride on it—two familiar examples being the Moral Majority, led by the Reverend Jerry Falwell in the political space, and a conservative resurgence among Southern Baptists to power-wash religious liberalism's influences away from their membership.

So now the megachurches were on the rise too—intentionally designed as Bigs for Jesus, to give glory to God by virtue of size and influence. At their core, these megachurches relied on size as the brand for their continued propulsion. This kind of approach was not, I would argue, a discipleship-oriented mission, but it does create buzz and enthusiasm.

Bill Hybels began Willow Creek Community Church in 1975, and Saddleback started under Rick Warren in 1980. Both were focused on reaching people and serving God through Drucker's mentoring model. Hybels made an art of surveying community needs, then asking people to come experience what they wanted, in a church-lite setting. Saddleback would lean more into a discover-what-God-wants-in-you approach that would eventually produce a blockbuster book, *The Purpose Driven Life* (twelve million copies sold). Both churches had a common logic: You matter a lot, come hear how God's way aligns with you. We can do big things for God together.

This Big model became a template put to a program by Bob Buford's business, the Christian Leadership Network, which became a megachurch consulting system. Buford's protégés would train thousands of pastors worldwide on how to do mega.

So how did Drucker's game plan perform? In 1983 in the US, there were less than a hundred so-called megachurches (with two thousand or more attendees), which all in were hosting about 250,000 people on a Sunday.[84] Today there are about a thousand such churches, with a combined total attendance of more than five million. (Those numbers are understated, because most Baptist and Presbyterian churches—many of them megachurches—don't usually participate in surveys by the Hartford Institute for Religion Research, the leading observer of the megachurch movement.) The known list shows at least a tenfold growth in the number of these churches since 1983, and a twelvefold increase in the headcount.[85] One other interesting point: Most of the growth into megachurches is by attrition of members from smaller churches. Attracting big, pulling big— from smaller churches.

Today, about 10 percent of US churches host over 26 million people. That means 30,000 churches out of 300,000 average 900 people or more. In other words, over half of US church attendance on a Sunday is concentrated in a big (or mega/giga) church, some headcount live, some virtual. Think about that. Ten percent of the churches in the US account for more than half the attendance. The other 25 million attending worship are spread out across 270,000 churches, those smaller churches averaging about ninety-five people per church.

Size Dynamics

This new normal is an old tradition: size is good. For some churches, that means big is where it's at. Big preaching, big music, big facilities, big names—the venue is in going big.

For others, small is holy. In the small churches, it can be intimate, it can be exclusionary, the purposes being to keep things personal, intimate. Or it might be church polity—small is a doctrinal emphasis for the Quakers, for example. Or maybe small is just circumstantial—a church too remote to draw large crowds.

But in either tradition, small or big, size can overtake mission, all supposedly for success and glory for Jesus and the gospel. In both cases, big and small, the centuries-old tradition is in full force: Size matters; headcount done our way is what matters. Our discipleship? I think you meant membership, didn't you?

Popularity tends to attract wanna-be's to mimic, and the mega model did just that. Some people just enjoy the buzz of the big event. Others go there to hawk health, welfare, prosperity, fame, and books—all in order to glorify God, we're told. Oh, and often creating vast wealth for celebrities, validating William Cowper's lines: "A business with income at its heels furnishes always oil for its own wheels."[86]

With churches hewing to the tradition of size as the mission, the mission to make disciples was being lost. The laity—Christ's true agency for disciple-making—would be told to tithe and show up to hear the anointed. Size was kingdom power. Focus on size. Whichever size "fits" you.

Don't get lost in the debate over whether small or large churches are biblical models. Ask what the mission really is supposed to be—not the mission statement words, but the actions that demonstrate what the mission *actually* is. There's the true soul of a Christian community. Watch how that community functions as a body. Track what's important to them in action, not words.

If you watch the actions, you can see that discipleship is irrelevant in so many churches because size and popularity and capital campaigns are what actually matter. Elevation Church, Life Church, Willow Creek, Garden Grove are examples of size-centric missions. While the virtue signal (a message of dubious sincerity meant to market a message of "go with us, we're with your values and issues") might be "To draw people to Christ" or "To make him known," it all looks to be a path ending at conversion or membership. Many of the big missions that are seeking seekers will use intersectionality to attract headcount: this theology + this political stance + this view = folks like us. Drucker knew how to establish a culture that would scale up. I'm not a fan of Drucker's model for megachurch social engineering, but I really appreciate his insight into culture being a leader's responsibility. One of Drucker's famous lines makes the priority crystal clear: "Culture eats strategy for breakfast."

For some large churches—such as Francis Chan's Cornerstone Community Church—bigness was a surprise, not a brand. There were a few people meeting in a house church, then it morphed into thousands in a big church over a short time. Lots of people came for the truth being served up straight, without seeker-sensitive pandering. Churches like Cornerstone in Simi Valley and Redeemer in New York grew because they were already located in major population centers, and preaching winsomely without specifically aiming to boost headcount. Their bigness happened as a consequence of mission delivery, not as a branding strategy.

The thinking by Cornerstone and Redeemer's leaders is beautiful. They faced the implications of size head-on. They knew what was necessary for relational Christianity to emerge. Big was not going to deliver on relationships. Tough choices were confronted. Redeemer broke out into six venues versus one. For Cornerstone, Francis Chan deployed house church and small church ministry to reestablish relationship and discipling traction among gathered believers.

In both intentional size and unintentional size—whether big or small—we can recognize one very important thing: Leaders (meaning not only pastors but also trustees, elders, committees, and small groups) will encounter a size challenge, whether by design or default. Leaders are responsible for the thinking, the decisions, and the organizing to achieve discipleship whether serving in Big or in Small. To fail to do this is leadership dereliction.

Even before the Covid-19 virus became an issue, it was clear some larger churches were grappling with the risks and complications in being big. Some—like Seacoast in Charleston, South Carolina, and Church of the Highlands in Birmingham, Alabama—use satellite churches to offset growth constraints, allowing the popular senior pastor or church to remain front-and-center by streaming a common digital sermon to all campuses, even while shrinking the size of any single campus. Some churches, seeking to fuel stalled growth, have launched autonomous daughter churches. Others launch members into a new area with seed capital, an autonomous pastor, and a separate governance body, just as New Testament churches often did.

The point to be grasped here is that a mission of Big is often textbook MBA—and a significant discipleship challenge. Go edgy and grow. Brand it. Diversify and deconcentrate risk. Push capital and facility liabilities off the home church balance sheet. Franchise music, books, celebrity names, and really comfortable pop-theology. Are these strategies and motives biblical? I don't know how to answer that for any single community. But size absolutely impacts the complexity and quality of a disciple's development.

For leaders thinking about discipling, a common assumption about discipling is….prepare for a bad pun…."herd community". Herd community is the idea that given enough people sloshing around together in gatherings, discipleship will evolve. That kind of strategy defies organizational reason, unless you happen to hold to the Darwinian recipe that enough time plus enough stuff plus enough chance will cause coherent life to splash up. In herd community, the bet is that enough people, time, and fellowship will surely generate disciples.

Size is not the mission for effective discipling, big or little. Gatherings and programs are not the mission for effective discipling. Yet most churches have the same basic playbook, which is group gatherings like sermons, Sunday school, mission trips, and small groups. None of that is bad. Much of it is very good. But it fails in assuming that discipleship is occurring for the regulars in all that.

Why Be Concerned with Size?

Why should leaders even consider the organization's size when it comes to disciples? Why not just let God do what God will do in our church? Well, there's a biblical reason for that, and organizational behavior validates that biblical reason. Let's step through a few of those passages.

Acts 6 describes problems in the church arising from conflict between Hellenists and Hebrews, problems emerging from sheer headcount growth. There was intentional redesign to put relational leaders back out among the people. The purpose? To drive ministry and discipleship forward:

> In those days when the number of disciples was increasing, the Hellenistic Jews among them complained against the Hebraic Jews because their widows were being overlooked in the daily distribution of food. So the Twelve gathered all the disciples together and said, "It would not be right for us to neglect the ministry of the word of God in order to wait on tables. Brothers and sisters, choose seven men from among you who are known to be full of the Spirit and wisdom. We will turn this responsibility over to them and will give our attention to prayer and the ministry of the word." (vv. 1–4)

Factionalism came from growth. That growth, in underdisciped people, was causing chaos, which bred more chaos, as Paul would later describe to the Corinthian church:

In the first place, I hear that when you come together as a church, there are divisions among you, and to some extent I believe it. No doubt there have to be differences among you to show which of you have God's approval. So then, when you come together, it is not the Lord's Supper you eat, for when you are eating, some of you go ahead with your own private suppers. As a result, one person remains hungry and another gets drunk. Don't you have homes to eat and drink in? Or do you despise the church of God by humiliating those who have nothing? What shall I say to you? Shall I praise you? Certainly not in this matter! (1 Corinthians 11:18–22)

Growth with thin discipleship allowed paganism and generally bad thinking to multiply in churches:

Now about the gifts of the Spirit, brothers and sisters, I do not want you to be uninformed. You know that when you were pagans, somehow or other you were influenced and led astray to mute idols. Therefore I want you to know that no one who is speaking by the Spirit of God says, "Jesus be cursed," and no one can say, "Jesus is Lord," except by the Holy Spirit. (1 Corinthians 12:1–3)

Impoverished discipleship allowed heresy to fester around the most foundational and obvious truth—the resurrection of Jesus:

But if it is preached that Christ has been raised from the dead, how can some of you say that there is no resurrection of the dead? If there is no resurrection of the dead, then not even Christ has been raised. And if Christ has not been raised, our preaching is useless and so is your faith. More than that, we are then found to be false witnesses about God, for we have testified about God that he raised Christ from the dead. But he did not raise him if in fact the dead are not raised. For if the dead are not raised, then Christ has not been raised either. And if Christ has not been raised, your faith is futile; you are still in your sins. Then those also who have fallen asleep in Christ are lost. If only for this life we have hope in Christ, we are of all people most to be pitied. (1 Corinthians 15:12–19)

The business of well-designed organization matters greatly to discipleship, and in organizing well, a mission must be surrounded by an intentional culture just as a home must have walls to surround floors and ceilings. Culture must be designed and deployed around the true mission Christ gave us—of disciple-making. Surrounded by a supporting culture, the mission can execute crisply. Organized traditionally, where culture is separate from the intent of the mission, the mission will likely hollow out and collapse. Any organization focusing on growth or nongrowth, or just letting "whatever" happen about discipleship in larger gatherings (more than three) is at great risk of being controlled by a symptom, which is size. Size displacing the real mission of the church. Just as insidiously, any organization that allows size to be a free radical (a "whatever happens" approach) will be enslaved by the overhead, administration, and distraction of that uncontrolled circumstance's demands over time, often unaware until it's too late.

Growth is cancer for organizations that don't prioritize mission over size. And even more commonly, letting underdiscipled growth simply happen, like an untended grapevine, will mean the choking out of the mission. If discipleship is to succeed, growth must be a symptom of a strategy, not the strategy itself, and not an unintended happening. To say this in context of Scripture, Jesus directed disciples to go and make disciples who would drive discipleship, not membership.

In the fourth century, people were coming to churches and seeking assistance, education, guidance, mentorship, direction. The few parishioners capable of developing disciples were swamped, as was local clergy. To fill the leadership void, less experienced people were thrown in. Problems emerged—bad teaching, hurt feelings, feuds. Clergy became concerned that the lay people weren't educated enough, or committed enough, or trustworthy enough to do the job. Clergy began to absorb the authority. Crucially, they sidelined the duties of believers and also usurped the mission of the individual believer—the mission to make disciples. The church unprepared to pursue Christ's mission ballooned Big, absorbing the masses. And the size tradition trap was set. Discipleship's critical roles were yanked away from regular people, which spawned clericalism and spectator passivity. Leadership vacuums meant fewer leaders available as disciplers, and it meant more people leading who weren't ready to lead, thus straying and wrecking discipleship. Congregants had little exposure to any discipleship development. Then, too few clergy leading too many congregants choked off relationships further.

The laity, now sidelined, took their new benchwarmer roles seriously and became spectators of the Big. An audience. Or the opposite problem emerged: People left the Big and went out on their own. Heresies and exclusionary thinking often filled that gap. Where big meant a professional and productionized church that marketed to the curious, small opened up gates for unprepared people even if they couldn't handle leadership or discipleship. Size meant focusing on the urgencies of distractions instead of relational discipling.

Because no organization nor program can actually make disciples, the results of such mass production efforts are clones. There are risks in biological cloning: early morbidity and dysfunctions. Disciples who've been mass-produced show similar high risks of abnormal learning, spiritual muteness, or rejecting and leaving fellowship altogether (see 1 Corinthians 3:2; Hebrews 5:12).

* * *

Where are we in the traditions journey? We've looked at five subtle but negative church traditions leaders must deal with to grasp the disciple dilemma:

- Optional lordship degrades discipleship.
- A catch-and-release, converts-only focus dilutes discipleship.
- Influence and power, detached from the mission, disable discipleship.
- Clericalism—distancing people into concierge Christianity—passivates disciples.
- Size, large or small, is a disciple-stifling mission challenge.

The last tradition to consider is when leaders make the *not* main thing their main thing in doing their thing. Let's take a look at that thing.

The duty of the fighter pilot is to patrol his area of the sky,
and shoot down any enemy fighters in that area.
Anything else is rubbish.
Manfred von Richthofen, the Red Baron

My head is in a bad place
But I'm having such a good time
Dr. John, "Right Place, Wrong Time"[87]

7

Christian Tradition:
The *Not* Main Things

Business Tradition:
Mission Drift

Cyprian, as new bishop for the third-century church at Carthage, faced a dilemma. Hooligans were demanding their restoration, back into the church's fellowship. They were a sorry lot of apostates, adulterers, idolaters, recanters, drunkards, and the like. Cyprian's staff wanted immediate excommunication for the ne'er-do-wells. Others across the church were pleading for gracious restoration of the purgatory-bound revelers. Anger from every direction. Something had to be done to appease a deeply divided church—some way to right the rogues, pacify the passionate, and indulge the indignant.

Wait! That's it! Let's indulge them! Indulgences. It has a warm ring to it, don't you think? A price paid to reduce time in purgatory. A barter. In exchange for works of merit or donations to the church, the church could then be motivated to assist the paid-up penitent.

Purgatory was a kind of pay as you play penalty box for the naughty-but-not-eternally-damned, a sort of time-out awaiting entrance to heaven. It was an ingenious plan. Right out of the temple moneychangers' playbook. A kind of covenantal commerce. We, the clergy, will assume pardoning powers from God to dispense credits—credits from heaven's treasury against less egregious sins. Don't bother looking it up in your concordance, because we had to, more or less, traditionalize it. Everybody knows there's a treasury, probably, maybe like that, yes? Work with us here. This treasury simply must be composed, mostly, of Christ's merit, but also merits from the good works of martyrs and the saints. Monetized merit. Bartered blessings. All we need to do now is set up an exchange rate. We can broker holy credits against the debits of the penitent purgatorians. They petition us to indulge their hot mess. Or maybe it was a relative's mess they're paying for. Anyway, quid pro quo. You do this for us, we do that for you. To get these indulgence credits we have several convenient payment options to choose from. You could, say, do extended prayer time with the rosary. Or we have the Hail Mary plan, or adorations, or even pilgrimages, if you're more inclined to stay up off your knees.

You want forgiveness, and we want publicity, cash and people in the pews. You have debits, and we offer credits. It's commerce. And the church can be flexible on terms. Cash, if you're so inclined, to help with construction (or wars). We can even broker petitionary letters of credit from worthy people who God really likes, transferring their good deeds to people the church really likes. That is, if the letters have legit bar codes—as in prison bars of the persecuted and the martyrs, which are worthy credits indeed, to redeem the errant. The saints in persecution can offer somebody else a break if they sign over their persecution credits. The saint doesn't need them, the church gets paid, the penitent gets a break.[88] Someday the Wall Street folks will congratulate us for inventing arbitrage. Brilliant!

Indulgences took on bizarre forms and uses. One wealthy congregant made a novel inquiry to the pope's chief indulgence officer, a priest named Tetzel. "Could indulgences be purchased in advance for a future sin?" Upon assurance that indulgences could indeed buy future forgiveness, cash was exchanged, and a certificate of future pardon issued. The member then proceeded to beat the indulgence-issuing priest senseless, apparently electing to exercise his option immediately on the short market.[89] How about that? A futures market in forgiveness! Are indulgences great or what? In other news, Pope Pius X launched the first quantitative easing program around 1903, granting two hundred days of purgatory discounts as indulgence authority for his cardinals' discretionary use, one hundred days' authority for archbishops, and fifty days for bishops.

Like most social engineering programs, indulgences would become a bureaucratic nightmare of graft and corruption that churches would struggle with for centuries. Indulgences would also become a doctrinal, administrative, and political morass, with codified rulebooks large enough to make an IRS regulator envious.

More to our point, indulgences were a distraction and drag on the mission of the church. Mission must be the basis for dealing with circumstances like rebellious followers, lest the circumstances and their trappings hijack the mission, then become the mission.

This illustrates a principle known as keeping the main thing the main thing. Making the *not* main thing the main thing is a common foible for believers and businesses alike. And a very common ambush to mission.

GE—the General Electric Corporation—is the recordholder as the longest-standing member of the Dow Jones Industrials—over a hundred years. The market value of GE in 2000 was an eye-watering $524 billion,[90] a number larger than the gross domestic product of all but the top forty nations in the world.[91] From its start in 1892, GE was manufacturing. Beginning with lighting, GE expanded rapidly, producing power grids, jet engines, consumer electronics, and home and medical appliances.

By the mid-eighties, GE's growth had slowed. When you're one of the largest corporations in the world, it takes a lot of growth to move the results needle to satisfy Wall Street. Diversification yielding better profits became the new path forward. The appliance credit division, around for years to help people buy GE washing machines and refrigerators, was upgraded to Version 2.0, becoming an industrial bank, an insurance company, as well as a consumer credit powerhouse. Meanwhile, back at headquarters, GE bought into entertainment, acquiring RCA and NBC, Vivendi, and Universal Pictures. GE would declare in 1990 that it was pursuing a whole new strategy known as "the boundaryless company."[92] Think about the term boundaryless as you read this old quip: "Whenever we attempt to remove a fence we should always pause long enough to find out why it was put there in the first place."[93] Boundaryless can get to be a pretty confining strategy.

By 2000, GE's stock price peaked at $60 a share along with its afore-mentioned balance sheet showing a net worth of $524 billion. As the complexities and distractions from "boundaryless" weighed on the Fortune 100 darling, a slide began, tilting its valuation downward.

As of press time for this book GE's stock price trades regularly in single digits, down more than 50 percent in value since 2018 alone, when its legacy seat in the Dow Jones Industrials was lost from its demise. As of 2020, the company's net worth is around $54 billion, just 11 percent of the 2000 peak.

What happened? The business consensus is that GE's leaders made the *not* main thing the main thing.[94]

Distraction Dangers

How does this story about a corporation's slide from glory have any-thing to do with discipleship? Indulge me if you will.

Like GE's acquisitions, and like papal indulgences, distractions from mission as the main thing burn leadership's time, resources, and commit-ment to the mission. They bleed organizations out from that main thing they're supposed to do. Distractions that pop up may look like decent things—such as new land to build on or new causes to pursue. Or they may be emotional and political crises demanding immediate attention, like the things driving indulgences. It can all seem right and noble—just solving the problem, taking advantage of opportunities. But these issues must find their place within the mission, not by distracting from it. As an example, no effort in discipling the revelers in Carthage was apparent in the stories of indulgences. Just papering over things with an eye toward revenue and social influence.

Outside the mission, such things become multiple twists and turns away from the real reason the organization exists. They may be wrapped in causes, but causes require loyalty, and that loyalty will negate any other issue that encroaches on or challenges its supreme cause, including the mission. What this means is that leaders must know and understand the main thing, focusing the design and operation on the main thing of the organization—whether a church, parachurch or business, which is the mission. That is leadership's perpetual duty. Said another way: When the main thing isn't driving all the other things, the other things drive the main thing. Not a good thing.

There's a joke about a driver on a bus route in London, and his bus was constantly late. As for how he might improve performance, he declared, "We could run on time if we get rid of the customers!" In other words, eliminate the main thing so as to fix a symptom. Does the distraction get the driver's seat, or does mission drive the encounter with the distractions?

Distractions come in many forms, all seeking to hijack mission. There are out-of-nowhere distractions, like Covid. There are also smoking-volcano distractions, always smoldering, waiting to blow up. Recurring allegations about a prominent person, for example. It smokes until it explodes, the consequences erupting large and in plain view. Or leaders can face deferral distractions—the proverbial can kicked down the road—such as not dealing with a prickly staff problem. The bill will eventually come due, in full, with interest. Often, church leaders end up entangled in business fads as a playbook instead of looking to the greatest management book ever written. It's a book that presciently informs Christian leaders about man as man, about rituals and traditionalism, and of course, about pursuing the right stuff in structuring organizations and people. Which means the root cause of the disciple dilemma—and the path out of that dilemma—is found in sixty-six management texts that you probably carry (in print or digital form) into church every Sunday. The Bible is a fantastic leadership playbook. My career is a proof-text that even mediocrity can be made effective by relying on Scripture. (btw, references are available about that mediocrity.)

Other examples of the *not* main things are the tendencies that Bill Hull describes in *The Complete Book of Discipleship* as he contrasts "the Jesus way" with "the consumer way": competence beats prayer, individualism instead of community, impatience rather than endurance, and celebrity over humility.[95] But boy do we look good!

And there's fear and despair, which often manifests as anger and outrage about the way things are, or ought to be. Despair is contagious mission distraction too, especially as despair contaminates leaders fighting tough circumstances and problems.

There are also "firefighting" distractions, a very addictive straying from the main things, where leaders forget mission as they're caught up in the thrill of momentary crises and quick fixes.

Lastly, and becoming a more common threat today, is distortion distraction—heresy sold as virtue in currying to modern man's favor. An example of a that could be today's obsession with sexual identity over Christian identity—as some churches fall all over themselves to accommodate the views of everyone other than the authors of Scripture. The distortion is not in being kind, gracious, and welcoming. The distortion comes in altering plain biblical views about a subject simply to pacify someone's demands about what they personally view as fair, good, or right.

All these distractions—the good things and the bad—are corrosive when mission doesn't hold sway over them. Take another look at Baron Richthofen's quote at the head of this chapter. Shooting down the enemy is indeed the fighter pilot's mission, just as a leader's duty is to avoid the trap of distraction reaction—to keep everyone on their duty, their mission. "Everything else," as the Red Baron said, "is rubbish."

Consequential issues will always erupt in life, and those issues will be distracting. That's precisely where mission must be intentional and influential in leadership thinking. Rather than reactionary moves against distractions, leaders must know ahead of time how all this works, and be capable of looking through the mission for thoughtful engagement with any circumstance. Without such depth perception, distractions prevail and mission languishes.

One example of a distraction from mission is likely found in your organizational chart (if there is one). An organizational chart gives you a view of how the people structure supports the mission. For example, if we were to diagram Jesus's organization, it would look like this. Jesus had direct reports. He was discipling men and women in daily life and service. He also majored intently on three men. Then when disciples were ready, he sent them out to make more disciples. The takeaway from this chart is that Jesus intentionally structured his "organization" for the mission of making disciples:

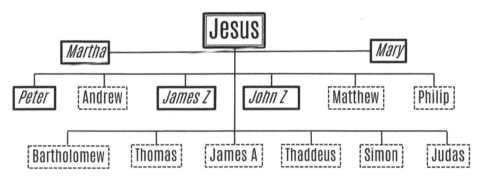

Most larger churches have an organizational chart that probably looks something like this next one. You can see the staff, and maybe small groups or Sunday school. All good so far. But the distraction is in the failed design. Notice what's missing. Once past a defined staff level, all the people—the very core of the church—are a blob called "everybody in the congregation" (if they're even represented at all).

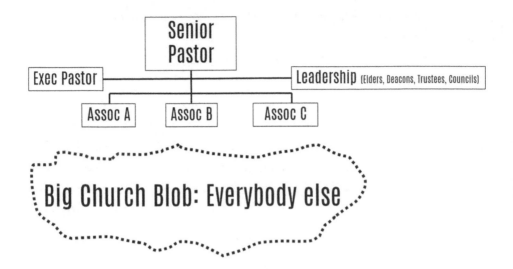

If discipling is the mission, then the people in the blob are the critical part of the design. But all those people are just the blob in most church designs. And according to Barna, we can see that the blob is languishing. Eighty percent of Christians in the blob are on their own, with no constructive discipling relationships to coach them. They aren't even visible as people.[96]

Imagine a pharmaceuticals manufacturing company operating like that, a company making drugs that you depend on. The human resources VP says to the CEO, "The structure of our company's people is shown on this org chart. We have very well-defined roles for the top people, as you can see. The rest of the employees hang out in what we call the blob. By our estimate, eighty percent of our employees are in the blob. We don't know how many are really there, or who they are, because—well, because they're in the blob. But they come in every day, sitting around in the factory. We don't really know anything about them or what they do. They'll head home at five after their workday, after whatever it is they do out there. Next day, they'll be back—getting paid to be part of the blob."

If you pitch a presentation like that to a CEO in a commercial enterprise, you should expect to receive sincere congratulations for your honesty. Then you'll experience a lively eye-watering lecture and get an assignment. The lecture may vary in its emotive ambiance, tone, euphemisms, and such. Your hair may even be wafted a bit off after the chat. But the assignment you'd get will go along these lines: "Fix this. Everybody has a mission. Everybody has a place. Everybody reports to somebody. Fix this really fast, or *you* won't be reporting to anybody."

Now why would it be that Jesus had visibility and direct reports for all the disciples he lived life with? Why do corporations have specific name-by-name report structures all the way from bottom to top? Because they design their organizations, then place all their people in roles to pursue a mission.

Why, then, do so many Christian communities just go with the blob? If clericalism—keeping the pros in power—was the mission, we could be okay with a blob. Blobs aren't supposed to do anything anyway, the clerics do stuff. But blobs are not blobs. They're Imago Dei. They're disciples. Disciples are individual people with individual needs and skills. If disciples are what Christ told us to focus on—and he did—then we need to design the organization to serve that mission. We need specific visibility and relationship with the people who are the mission, the mission of discipleship—connecting people in ways where an intimate few can relate to one another as disciples developing disciples, and going through life with them. No blobs left behind.

The same challenge exists for smaller churches.

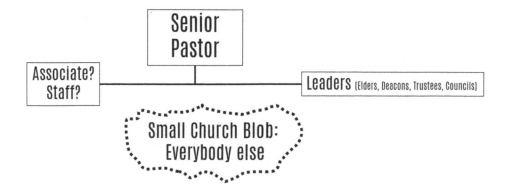

Although a small church has fewer congregants, there are also fewer pastoral and lay leaders to connect with. The same blob effect. Maybe a smaller blob, but a blob.

It's really hard to make a convincing case for discipleship in blobs of 15, 150, 1,500, and so on. Yet most Christian organizations are designed to support administrative management, not the mission. There's the distraction—doing the *not* main things so much that the main thing is lost. Distractions aren't supposed to be the main thing. If you plot out your organization this way, you may come to realize that it's not organized, staffed, or purposed for discipling. It's designed to run a business and to hope that small groups, programs, ministries, and Sunday schools are gathering enough people around to have discipleship hit here and there in the herd community.

Enable and Empower

Imagine an aircraft factory where the CEO and his staff design in depth and in detail the roles of the executives. They work to get all the senior management roles perfectly defined, deeply coached up, intensely developed. Meanwhile, out on the factory floor, 98 percent of the folks there get little or no attention. They're all out there, happily bolting together the airplane you're about to board for your next big trip. The factory folks have a colorful pamphlet from upper management showing them exactly how the senior team is organized. They had a town hall meeting to get pumped up about the new factory building being built. They saw a PowerPoint presentation on the strategic plan and thirty-six core values for the business (which nobody memorized). The factory folks received no personal development about building airplanes, but they understand the executive layout. Now, I don't know about you, but I want the guy bolting the wings on that plane getting a *lot* of attention and training as a wing disciple trained by seasoned leaders before he goes out to do his job.

Most church people—again, around 80 percent according to Barna, have no engagement at even the most rudimentary level as disciples.[97] And if they did want to be discipled, a church staff alone, including all its lay leaders, is never going to be large enough to disciple in the way Jesus discipled people. The leaders are outnumbered. Even if all the leaders—ministers and lay leaders combined—were fully involved in discipleship with a few, there would still not be enough disciplers to provide one-on-one (or one-on-few) discipling alongside everyone as Christ did, as Paul did.

Eighty percent of the people in the modern evangelical church have no study, no mentor, no younger disciples coming up behind them. It's a stunning number. Eighty percent with nothing other than a Sunday worship event, if even that, as discipleship. This kind of traditional practice may be unintentional, but it's very effective in producing passive Christians, individual spiritual isolation, confused thinking, and timid answers about hope in Christ. And in too many cases today, it prompts significant desertion as individuals seek saltiness elsewhere.

The distractions we've discussed are subtle ways to ensure the main thing is *not* the main thing. Just as indulgences consumed an inordinate amount of energy, time, and goodwill, so handling distractions outside of mission undercuts mission.

Defrauding the atonement of Christ with indulgences eroded discipleship because the main thing wasn't the main thing anymore. As GE discovered, doing the not main thing is not a good thing.

It isn't impossible, but it's a long shot to expect groups or congregational activities to produce wholehearted disciples. That's the job of disciples relating directly to other disciples. It's your primary role then, as a leader, to establish and sustain your community mission, such that your community enables and empowers people to disciple. To do otherwise is to subvert the main thing to other things.

In Luke 14:28–33 Jesus tells us that whether you're in construction, warfare, or discipleship, understanding the implications and costs of what you're about to do is necessary:

> "Suppose one of you wants to build a tower. Won't you first sit down and estimate the cost to see if you have enough money to complete it? For if you lay the foun-

dation and are not able to finish it, everyone who sees it will ridicule you, saying, 'This person began to build and wasn't able to finish.' "Or suppose a king is about to go to war against another king. Won't he first sit down and consider whether he is able with ten thousand men to oppose the one coming against him with twenty thousand? If he is not able, he will send a delegation while the other is still a long way off and will ask for terms of peace. In the same way, those of you who do not give up everything you have cannot be my disciples.

While there may be times when counting costs may not be possible in the moment, Christ makes plain here that issues of great import deserve thoughtful consideration.

Now, some Christians say forget assessing costs, that stepping out instinctively demonstrates faith, and that mulling over costs is a ruse, seeking a way out of being obedient. In other words, just jump, and expect God to handle it. But lunging has no basis in the thinking Jesus points to in Luke 14.

This warning from Christ is specifically given to people so they'll understand what they're in for before they commit to being his disciples. In discipleship and disciple-making, there are costs in dollars, reputation, risk, and time, as well as in the effects it will have on your people. It might even cost you your job. It will almost certainly stir up dissent, discussion, and probably some yawns, as the normal and the traditional stuff comes under scrutiny, and some people will wonder what this fuss is all about.

A few years ago, I took over as the CEO in a company that was doing well. Doing well except for a few things: multimillion dollar financial losses, failures in safety, quality, and delivery, major customer desertion, loss of confidence by the board, and collapse of employee morale. In other words, there were big problems everywhere. The business was within a few weeks of shutdown. I told the investors that if they really wanted things to get straightened out, they had to be prepared to put in tens of millions of dollars, and to let us work on the culture for two years or more.

The board was stunned. That much money? That much time? Things couldn't be that bad, could they? Surely within, say, six months or so, all could be made better—couldn't they? But in counting the cost in money and time, they came to see the challenges as massive, and they committed to fund and go ahead.

That experience reminds me of the disciple dilemma. The old ways aren't working, but they're familiar. Surely a couple of sermons and a new program can fix this, right? The likely answer is no. The changes will be hard, costly, and long-term. But changes are needed in Western discipleship, lest the trends and symptoms we've described keep reproducing, driving disciples further off course from Christ's call. Such a reformation will change how churches look. How they grow, behave, and serve. These costs are worthy of consideration before plowing ahead.

Christian leaders can get fidgety when ministry is compared to so-called business thinking. But what I hope emerges from this book is the realization that the business aspects of Christianity—which are ultimately about people—are key to mission and culture change. These "business" aspects are identical for biblical as well as commercial leadership: mission, culture, strategy, execution. These are not sacrilege. Just as God's laws of gravity apply to sinner and saint alike, so also do God's organizational principles and wisdom apply to people in commerce and Christianity.

The disciple dilemma emerged because the Christian community defaulted to methods that have consistently proven not to work in developing people. And they perform no better in Christian community than they do in business. Why not rely on the proven and published wisdom of God when it comes to people and communities? The knowns being:

- Uncommitted Christians, just like uncommitted employees, do not stick around.
- Power isn't powerful in the long run. Rather, it's debilitating to people, and to purpose.

- Brand obsession, social causes, and growth fixation will divert the mission.
- The notion that groups and lectures equate to discipleship is a myth.
- Converting or recruiting people without developing (discipling) them is a tragedy.

All people in a Christian community are discipling resources. God has always organized his people purposefully, from the ark to the exodus to New Testament churches. Organizational structure, policies, and roles (yes, job descriptions) were all alive and well with God's blessings under Saul, David, Solomon, and so on, and forward into the New Testament. Even financial systems existed and functioned, just like the financial system the Lord and his twelve disciples maintained (which included a crooked CFO named Judas). There were logistics and supply chain systems serving the Jews as they moved around the deserts to support their journey and warfare. And of course, God was making very plain—repeatedly—his specific direction for the Hebrews, which was their mission. People were operating by departments and specializations (the tribes and crafts), dealing with disciplinary issues (the laws), and staying on track (the schema). Organization mattered back then for God's followers just as much as it matters now. We serve an organizing God, and he demands that we organize for discipling people—*all* the people, as disciples. For example, read Genesis 2:19 to see the organizing God discipling man to set up the taxonomies and categories of created things for our good.

> Now the Lord God had formed out of the ground all the wild animals and all the birds in the sky. He brought them to the man to see what he would name them; and whatever the man called each living creature, that was its name. So the man gave names to all the livestock, the birds in the sky and all the wild animals.

Likewise, we serve a strategic God who directs us to count costs and think through things before we act. And then to act strategically, within a community that serves God's mission laid out for people. The leaders of the Jews, of Jet Blue, and of your Christian community own the responsibility to ensure not only that clear direction is known and understood by people but that the mission gets executed.

Christian leaders, just like business leaders, don't always get things right. Sometimes the mission is aimed at the wrong things, as it was for the Judaizers in Acts 15, or the numerous misses by Pharisees and Sadducees in New Testament times. In other ways, the right mission gets lost in the hustle and bustle of life, of stuff, and of things. It can be a slow drift, like the Galatian churches confronted by Paul in his letter to them. We were on track, then we weren't on track. Or mission loss can come in a moment; we just put it in the ditch, like the bad practices among the churches in Corinth. In each of these situations, leadership must own responsibility, get things back on the track, encourage people to stay the course. It's what leaders do.

We spoke earlier of the main thing. That main thing is precisely what leaders must make plain for the organization, the culture, and their supporting strategies and systems to drive toward. The main thing is the mission. For Christian community, it's fundamentally a mission about making and sustaining disciples. Anything else that's given control of the mission—whether worship, theology, global ministry, size, or status—will degrade the true mission, which will hinder disciples from flourishing as Christ intended. As mentioned earlier, one recurring example is making gatherings and groups the mission, rather than personal, relational discipling. Programs and crowd size are not proportionate to discipling.

Imagine an art school where students are encouraged to create beautiful art through lectures about techniques and method in compelling artwork. Yet if no one comes alongside them personally to show them brushstrokes, colors, or technique, what kind of artists will emerge? Or imagine learning to fly by being given books and videos and simulators, but no instructor goes with you on your first real flight. Think of a car manufacturing plant with no skills training—you get a talk, a uniform, and well wishes as you step out on the manufacturing floor to assemble cars. It simply does not work that way. Leadership has to set the pace, the culture, the mission.

In discipleship, just as in each of those scenarios—art, flying, and manufacturing—people must be mentored, accompanied, coached, developed. Only then can they learn and practice what they're there to do. Otherwise, the talent is squandered, the mission lost. In the business world, people whose talent is squandered will tend toward poor workmanship and they will not stick around long. There are better places to go, better relationships, greater fulfillment toward a destiny. It's no different in discipleship.

* * *

We've looked at six consequential church traditions leaders must recognize to confront the disciple dilemma:

- Optional lordship degrades discipleship.
- A catch-and-release, converts-only focus dilutes discipleship.
- Influence and power, detached from the mission, disable discipleship.
- Clericalism—distancing people into concierge Christianity—passivates disciples.
- Size, large or small, is a disciple-stifling mission challenge.
- Getting distracted off-mission makes the *not* main things the mission.

It's time to move beyond the traditions that cause the disciple dilemma, and to follow a path forward. Time to start putting the pieces together. Let's go from "What's happening?" to "What do we do about it?" What then, exactly, does a disciple look like, act like, live like? What are the attributes leaders must design into the institution and community to encourage, to motivate, and to drive expectations in discipling? The next chapter will lay out key traits for disciples, then illustrate how leadership must promote that kind of discipling.

Part Two

The Dilemma's Effects

Things that cause people to stumble are bound to come,
but woe to anyone through whom they come. It would be better for them
to be thrown into the sea with a millstone tied around their neck
than to cause one of these little ones to stumble.
So watch yourselves.

Jesus, in Luke 17:1–3

The waking God may draw us out
to whence we can never return.

Annie Dillard, "An Expedition to the Pole"

8

The Dilemma and the Disciple

In the original *Men in Black* movie there's a scene involving Tommy Lee Jones and Will Smith as they encounter a crowd of little creatures, whose entire world is the inside of a locker. These tiny creatures see the large humans peering in on them and start shouting, "All hail Jay!" (Will Smith's character). The critters thought that their little locker was the universe, and that these men were gods. So, while the rest of the galaxy is spinning out of control, the locker creatures were oblivious to it all, just hanging out in their idyllic world.

The scene may have been intended to be a dig at religion, about how silly and mistaken people can be in their myopic and mythical beliefs. The scene got something right though. We can be lured into thinking our slice of life is the way it's supposed to be. The traditional way, so to speak.

Inside the Locker

Let's reflect again on the background for the traditions and how they came upon Christian community. The traditions we're describing came about because an unprepared and burgeoning church was forced to react to massive changes, and they had to act immediately to avoid a crisis. These arguably knee-jerk-reactions-turned-traditions are at the root of the symptoms impacting discipleship, symptoms of a stunted discipleship that have taken over in much of Western Christianity.

What were the massive changes? The church had been declared a cohort of a ruthless Roman government. People were suddenly piling into the churches to be counted among the emperor's new religion and hence escape being left out of favor, or worse, being labeled a rebel. The onslaught of new arrivals was too much for the nascent church to handle, especially since the changes came without warning and certainly without any planning by its leaders. Relational discipling, which had been prevalent in the house churches of fives and tens, became nearly impossible in the massive gatherings of hundreds and thousands. Congregants in this gold rush of church growth were folded into a partial gospel, one that left out lordship and a real disciple's life. Christianity was traditionalizing the idea that getting saved, plus becoming and staying a good member of the Church, was the *summum bonum* of Christianity. Yet conversion and membership left out Christ's lordship and the better implications of discipleship, or at least professionalized most of it under the job description of a seminarian.

So, pack them in, catechize them, get their confession, and collect tithes became tradition. Oh, and have them exit speedily, please, so the next shift can enter the pews. Meanwhile, in smaller towns and villages, whatever laity could be deputized to help in churches came with little or no experience in the faith. Theology in outlying areas often became mixtures of old pagan stuff mixed in with the reality of our risen Christ. Eerily, it was just like the passage in 2 Kings 17:41: "Even while these people were worshiping the LORD, they were serving their idols. To this day their children and grandchildren continue to do as their ancestors did."

Corruption and power-mongering were rampant among clergy and lay leaders alike. Clergy, seeking to clean up fuzzy, corrupt, and heretical wackiness among lay ministers, had snatched away church duties that were meant for relationship building, personal development, and spiritual growth for all followers of Christ. It was a hostile takeover. And as in most hostile takeovers, the pros spirited away a majority of the voting stock rights. There's an old saying about professional-only control: "A layman built the ark—it took professionals to build the Titanic."

A strength of this period of time—the formal education of pastors—was squandered in staff takeovers and control, which curiously, caused loss of control. Lacking heads but desiring quality, or power, or both, staff could not effectively relate to the massively expanded parishioner base. Such control and so few heads would stifle discipling. Congregants need not apply to the church's new standards of a formally credentialed team.

Professional standards became such a tradition that today we can see that most people tend to sit back and be the audience—a concierge community—while the pros do their thing up front. Pros and pew folk alike think this way, traditionally speaking.

There are many knots entangling discipleship: Pastors and their people alike are conditioned to think the roles of disciples and pastors are separate and unequal. Professionalizing the ministrations of the church would be a crippling blow to disciple development. It would promote a tradition of professional church, bureaucratic systems, spectators, frail disciples.

In this professionalizing and spectatorship, the church began to orphan believers, because by combining worship and discipling in mass (literally), any hope for deep relational growth was lost to bigger and more efficient gatherings. Life-on-life discipling was unauthorized trespassing on pro turf. *Traditional* now meant that simply having people in church and participating in activities would be discipleship, reimagined. This underdiscipled laity, increasingly unable or unwilling to talk about their hope in Jesus with outsiders, would now look toward the clergy to carry the heavy freight of gospel conversation. Discipleship atrophied.

Then came the recanters, the people leaving the faith. Frustrated with the impersonal, the isolation, the hypocrisy, and the elitism they were seeing in an underdiscipled church, many began to walk off, seeing nothing different in Christianity than one might find in any other mystical or governmental experience. It was mystical whereby only the enlightened could speak, and where the adherents were unqualified. That status led to congregants as mutes, or simply oblivious to the hope that was in them.

Old traditions efficiently replicate an anemic faith. The traditions may get a little cosmetic work here and there to stay culturally in vogue, but they're disciple-smothering nonetheless. With salt and light ebbing from voices and lives of disciples, the result was that markets, schools, the arts, the sciences, and civic life heard less and saw less, as these Christians replicated more weak and dysfunctional Christians, and in fewer numbers as well. This situation fares little better today.

Aside from a few awakenings and revivals along the years, the traditions have accomplished all that might be imagined for them. The trends tell us that disciples have peaked out in Western Christianity, as the millennial and Z generations depart the faith faster than they come in, while the greatest and boomer generations gray out and give out. So people looking to Christianity for answers and meaning by coming into Christian community are becoming rarities, and disciples offering the hope of Christ are even rarer. All the while the tradition beat goes steady on, with consequences morbid to discipleship.

With slightly different, secular labels, these same types of symptoms and traditions have proven corrosive to business as well. Both channels—spiritual and commercial—demonstrate the same dysfunctions toward people from life lived among bad traditions.

Slowly Learning

Leadership cannot be half-hearted, which is to say timid or uncommitted in helping an organization. A daunting struggle for me in troubled businesses has been changing deeply embedded bad traditions held by leaders who wanted to do right, but were fearful to go all in on big issues. In one company in the deep South, I encountered a factory with no air-conditioning and temperatures that would soar well above 100 degrees in the Summer. The tradition? Noble motive (trying to save money), wrong choices: Employees, trying to keep things running would take off safety gear in the heat, which meant cuts, strains and sprains would skyrocket on the factory floor without safety gear. Factory leaders were half-hearted, at best, about safety and adamant against spending money on cooling.

Unless change leaders were present for months on end reinforcing, almost daily, what needed to change, the old ways would snap back, the symptoms coming back in full bloom, the trends sliding back down. It took years to change the culture, to get rid of the bad traditions.

In the Old Testament, Israel's and Judah's kings had similar problems. Some kings are described as acting with their "whole heart" to right things, but faced an entrenched bad culture. Others did a few things well, but let a lot of the traditions stay. In other words, they were half-hearted about their dilemmas. In both cases, allowing the bad traditions to stay wrecked Israel and Judah over time. Examples:

- Although he did not remove the high places, Asa's heart was fully committed to the LORD all his life. (1 Kings 15:14)
- In everything he [Jehoshaphat] followed the ways of his father Asa and did not stray from them; he did what was right in the eyes of the LORD. The high places, however, were not removed. (1 Kings 22:43)
- He [Joram] got rid of the sacred stone of Baal that his father had made. Nevertheless he clung to the sins of Jeroboam son of Nebat, which he had caused Israel to commit; he did not turn away from them. (2 Kings 3:2–3)
- Jehu destroyed Baal worship in Israel. However, he did not turn away from the sins of Jeroboam son of Nebat, which he had caused Israel to commit—the worship of the golden calves. (2 Kings 10:28–29)
- Joash did what was right in the eyes of the LORD.... The high places, however, were not removed. (2 Kings 12:2–3)
- Then Jehoahaz sought the LORD's favor.... But they did not turn away from the sins of the house of Jeroboam. (2 Kings 13:4, 6)
- He [Amaziah] did what was right in the eyes of the LORD, but not as his father David had done. In everything he followed the example of his father Joash. The high places, however, were not removed. (2 Kings 14:3)

- He did what was right in the eyes of the Lord, just as his father Amaziah had done. The high places, however, were not removed. (2 Kings 15:3–4)

Can you see in these texts that even with a whole-hearted King, it is a challenging ride to change a culture? Over the years I've wasted millions of dollars half-heartedly poking at symptoms, only to realize that the roots of the traditions were left untouched and would return to haunt me. Because of me—a leader, not acting with a whole heart and following through to uproot bad traditions, the problems ebbed, but then they flowed right back. It's a traditional approach.

As a leader, you've probably been handled, complimented, condemned, heralded, and hated, and heaven knows you're very, very busy. Being handled (kept away from truth so as to keep the boss from blowing up or taking action) can be very distracting—it can even become a tradition itself. Examples of leadership being handled are visible even between Jesus and his own team. The disciples wanted to formalize the haves and have-nots in the new organization:

> They came to Capernaum. When he was in the house, he asked them, "What were you arguing about on the road?" But they kept quiet because on the way they had argued about who was the greatest. (Mark 9:33–34)

This was clericalism against Christ.

Another example of clericalism is elitism, where jealousy guards the flanks to ensure no personal advantage is allowed others. Near the end of John's Gospel, Peter was coveting John's situation, as he coyly probed Jesus:

> Peter turned and saw that the disciple whom Jesus loved was following them…. When Peter saw him, he asked, "Lord, what about him?" Jesus answered, "If I want

him to remain alive until I return, what is that to you? You
must follow me." (John 21:20–22)

The quest to get and consolidate power is a tradition that presses constantly onward. It feeds on specialization and differentiation in organizations. The bigger the staff, the greater the threat of spin and bureaucracy,
further isolating individuals, further leaning into groups as a mass produc-
tion/low relational answer to discipleship. Highly specialized training is a
wonderful and necessary thing in our complex world's many industries,
technologies, and administrations. But it's not the key to developing disciples. God intends disciples to be individual priests, and to serve min-
isterially in their individual walk of life. A disciple is fully forgiven, able
to walk into the holy of holies, which before Christ was possible only for
the anointed high priest. Disciples now commune directly with God. So
discipleship must not be subcontracted to staff and elites. This is true first
of all because we're already in God's presence, and he deserves our fullest
and best. Second, subcontracting simply doesn't work for discipleship. It
must be personal, lest discipling fade away into program plays, and the
passivated spectators stay on mute.

Seeing things from a CEO's chair, or a pastor's chair, or the chair of
an elder or deacon or other leader, is to be almost fog-bound in trying to
see clearly, in getting at unvarnished truth, perceiving consequences, and
especially discerning old-but-not-good traditions, the true roots that are
diverting individuals from their discipleship. Being underdiscipled is so
normal in Western Christianity that it's hiding in plain sight. Being discipled in Christ's way can be so rare that most people have no idea what the
concept really even means.

This isn't a new problem. A few consequences of underdiscipling
examples are readily found in the Bible:

- unrealistic expectations about life in a fallen world (John 9:38;
  Titus 1:10);
- pressure from causes, generational shifts, or tribe, and caving to
  their message (John 12:42);

- captivation by bizarre philosophies (Galatians 3);
- living enslaved through undue fear of mortal death or difficult circumstances (Hebrews 2:14);
- distorted interpretations and applications of Scripture (Colossians 2);
- cultic influences that eclipse the gospel (Galatians 1:6; 2:11);
- being "tossed about" (James 1) in fear, doubt, and ambivalence;
- giving up and walking away (John 6:66).

More consequences of the traditions: Many disciples today have little idea of what death to self, or taking up one's cross, or counting the cost, or surrender are all about. Yet this expectation of Jesus's followers— "Unless you do this...you are not my disciple"—is plain in his words:

> Whoever wants to be my disciple must deny themselves and take up their cross and follow me. For whoever wants to save their life will lose it, but whoever loses their life for me will find it. (Matthew 16:24–25)

> Why do you call me, "Lord, Lord," and do not do what I say? (Luke 6:46)

> If anyone comes to me and does not hate father and mother, wife and children, brothers and sisters—yes, even their own life—such a person cannot be my disciple. And whoever does not carry their cross and follow me cannot be my disciple. (Luke 14:26–27)

> Anyone who loves their life will lose it, while anyone who hates their life in this world will keep it for eternal life. Whoever serves me must follow me; and where I am, my servant also will be. My Father will honor the one who serves me. (John 12:25–26)

The tradition of lowering the bar to sell converts is a cheapened grace, and to morph discipleship into membership was a shrewd organizational move. It was power consolidation, and it put disciples into a tradition of serving a church instead of following the Christ. Christ changed the rules. We're all priests in Christ's service now (1 Peter 2:5–9). And since Christ has done away with temple blood sacrifice and professional and tribal priest-doms, clericalism is an anachronism—it's outdated. Again, we must not mistake having wonderful and highly competent professional ministers with clericalism any more than the false notion that we don't need great professional coaches for a sports team. Nevertheless, the overt and covert messages from the tradition of (dysfunctional) clericalism are short-circuiting discipleship:

- This is a professional event. Sit back. Be amazed.
- The professionals do the important stuff—ministerial things, intellectual things, speaking-about-Jesus-to-nonbeliever things.
- We professionals are busy the rest of the time working on budgets and capital development and professional presentations, so don't expect to have a relationship with us.
- A few select members like elders, deacons, and small group leaders may assist in the upfront roles from time to time. The rest of you sit quietly.
- Drop your kids off in our children's programs so they don't distract from the professional presentation.
- Volunteerism is encouraged. You really should help in the nursery, and with Vacation Bible School too, and you can occasionally pass the offering plate.
- We have programs and an app for your spiritual development.
- Find your purpose in a small group or Sunday school. Remember, however, that if you get real and bring out personal stuff, you may cause others to be uncomfortable. This would require professional involvement, which we really don't have time for.

Underdiscipled believers will always be at risk of cultural conformity, silence, faith collapse, spiritual abandonment, exploitation, and gullible fables. Having looked at the dilemma through the lens of the individual, let's take a look at the broader impact of the dilemma in the Christian community.

It is difficult to imagine how the religiously mature,
socially respectable, and psychologically adjusted church member in our situation
can come to terms with the naked horror of Calvary or the blazing glory of Easter morning.
Both his religion and his culture compel him to sentimentalize, neutralize, assimilate
these Christian images. If he did not do so, they would challenge his religiosity
and his respectability and might even threaten his so-called mental health.

Peter L. Berger, *The Noise of Solemn Assemblies*

9

The Dilemma and the Christian Community

"It is difficult to imagine how the religiously mature, socially respectable, and psychologically adjusted church member in our situation can come to terms with the naked horror of Calvary or the blazing glory of Easter morning. Both his religion and his culture compel him to sentimentalize, neutralize, assimilate these Christian images. If he did not do so, they would challenge his religiosity and his respectability and might even threaten his so-called mental health."[98] In the beginning of the book we asked, "Is something amiss?" We looked at symptoms impairing discipleship, and we identified six ancient traditions, prime contributors to those symptoms. These six aren't the only things responsible for negative consequences affecting Christian institutions today. But they're very good at being very bad for discipleship.

All six traditions might be present in your particular Christian community, or only some of them, or perhaps none at all. But even if your leadership team were exempt from those bad traditions, your children, your friends, and the broader Christian community are being reprogrammed under their influence.

As we've seen, the trends stifling discipleship in the West are myriad. Even if we discount the disturbing trends that are reported, the symptoms we personally encounter linger around us, persuading us that a dilemma is lurking out there.

A recap of the big questions is in order here: Why is the Christian voice fading today from the marketplace, from government, the sciences, the media, and the arts? Why so much disdain and disunity among followers of Christ across denominations, races, ages, nationalities, and political stripes? Why the significant exodus by Christ followers today? If there's a root cause to all this, what is it, and what should we do about it?

These are strategic organizational questions. Strategic discipleship questions. And strategic questions such as that are about culture.

Culture is a powerful game changer. Old Testament leaders like David and Asa changed a culture of idol worship, high places, and cults into God-seeking communities. Wilberforce and Abraham Lincoln forced change to begin in national cultures rife with division and oppression, moving toward nations transitioning away from slavery. The common links in these success stories are leadership, mission, and culture.

Leaders in every Christian community are charged with an agenda that's no less game-changing: set the mission, pursue the mission in the outworkings of an intentional culture, and ensure that those ancient, harmful traditions don't creep back in to alter the course. And when leaders realize the mission has been compromised, correct course, correct culture.

This stuff of mission and culture is vitally important, because the people who pass through a culture's orbit and influence will be discipled in that environment—programmed by it, so to speak. The ominous consequences of the six traditions lie in their capabilities to divert the mission, hijack culture, and produce people who think anemic discipleship is just fine the way it is.

The disciple dilemma requires leaders willing to take the risks to reestablish mission and rebuild culture so their people can be restored to the full implications in discipling as Christ intended.

The six traditions affect the institution as well as people individually. For the community of believers, those tradition-bound challenges show up as:

- wrong mission—some as social causes, or politics, or power, or simply busyness
- leaders awash in distractions
- culture that tracks to circumstances instead of mission
- bureaucracy in programs and policies, arising from the assumption that these things make for credible discipleship
- staff as the originator of all things legitimate
- members more inclined to be observers than disciples
- contentment with the traditions, just as they are

Let's unpack this list in terms of a Christian community. Wrong mission can come in two forms. One is brandishing mission statements to resonate with a target market—to attract the kinds of believers drawn to populism instead of a mission about Christ's purpose for believers. We'll pursue that specific issue later in depth. The other failed mission form is when words say one thing, but actions point another way. Mission cannot be written and shelved. Mission must become and remain the core of community, decisions made, resolve held.

Culture tends to conform to circumstances instead of mission because circumstances are very distracting and demanding. A discipleship culture succeeds only when leaders are intentional about mission leading the culture, not the other way around. All else is subservient to the mission. Culture is easily compromised by leaders not establishing clear mission-to-culture ties and expectations. Examples of such fuzzy boundaries include things like nice mission statements without any tie to the culture, or leaders letting society take the reins of influence (and the community wanders off), or letting the distractions become the mission and allowing culture to follow suit.

As for bureaucracy: administration and policy are key tools to employ, but such things cannot take priority over developing individuals in the way Christ demonstrated discipleship. Leaders must stay on mission.

Likewise with staff. It's one thing to have coaching and support by a staff in a community, but using staff as the engine for discipling (a symptom of the clericalism tradition) will make staff overload or power or bureaucracy a real threat to mission. Meanwhile the regular folks continue to be just spectators or adjunct workers. With clericalism comes passivity and disenfranchisement, weakened minds among believers, and a concierge mentality that creeps even into biblical home life compromises, impacting children and adults alike.

All these issues create a diluted discipling rhythm, reinforcing a sense of complacency that replicates the traditions. These mission failures induce a sense of normal, and lines are drawn, expectations set.

Another result is syncretism. Steve Turner's tongue-in-cheek poem "Creed" has some lines that I find especially interesting: "If death is not the end, if the dead have lied, then it's compulsory heaven for all. Excepting perhaps Hitler, Stalin, and Genghis Kahn."[99] If someone in your church told you they were a disciple of Jesus Christ, and then also said they're convinced that other faiths and beliefs provide the same opportunity for people to get to heaven, you might be tempted to think they're a one-off mistaken believer. But if half your folks felt that way, could it be there's a cultural problem? Something that's replicating that thinking among people?

The Westernization and pluralism of Christianity has weakened disciples. Underdiscipled believers thirsting for development have sought out the sages of web browsers, social media, movies, surveys, politics, causes, and scientism for answers, because they rarely have discipling teammates helping them navigate real life. Like salt water, the spiritual brews drawn from the wells of modernity and wokeness cause people to thirst even more. In their thirst, they become less capable of thinking critically in and about their faith. And without basic discipling development, people take up mythologies that have no basis and no hope. Those mythologies resonate in minds that have nothing better to anchor on.

Let's return to the cultural symptoms facing discipleship today that were listed in Chapter 1:

- Eternal life is not exclusive to Christianity, according to six out of ten Christians.
- Absolute truth does not exist for 40 percent of Christians.
- Talking about faith is considered "not my job" by 35 percent of Christians.
- 92 percent of Christians do not believe sharing faith is very important
- 65 percent of Christians say living out faith is better than talking about it
- 65 percent of the US population identify as Christian, which suggests there are around 200 million believers. Less than a quarter of those Christians—about 50 million—attend a church.
- In Great Britain, 60 percent of the 60 million people (about 38 million) claim Christianity. Of those Christians, 8 percent—about three and a half million—actually attend a church somewhere.
- 82 percent of US Christians surveyed say they have no Bible study, no faith community, no mentor.
- 80 percent of Christians say they lack the skills or relationships to talk about their faith.
- The average US tithe today is 2.5 percent of "income" and declining. As a comparison, it was 3.3 percent during the Great Depression.
- 41 percent of believers say spiritual growth is an entirely private matter.
- 33 percent of believers say going it alone in spiritual growth is right for them.
- 52 percent of Protestant church leaders say small groups are key to discipleship.
- 74 percent of Christians say that they're satisfied, or almost where they want to be, spiritually.

- 65 percent of congregants think discipling at their church is good; but only 1 percent of pastors believe that same statement. Who's got it more right?
- 59 percent of millennials dropped out of church and the kids did not bring them back.
- From 1990 to 2016, "Nones" (no religious affiliation) quadrupled from 4 percent to 17 percent.
- "Nones" are 17 percent of the boomer generation, but for millennials the rate more than doubles to 36 percent.
- US church membership is down 17 percent from 1999 to 2016. Protestant headcount trends are down 8 percent from 2007 to 2019, and accelerating downward. And for the Roman Catholic Church, for every person who comes in, six leave.

We asked this question early on: *If discipling is doing well, what gives with these numbers?* On the other hand, if we're programming people to stay on the sidelines, underdiscipled, all these trends make sense. Unconvinced of the truth claims of Christ, feeling marginalized in their pews, encountering example after example of leaders who are wrecking their credibility across the headlines, and lastly, Christians lacking any real discipling development or incentives to do so as individuals—why would anyone stick around? In that kind of context, would Christian muteness, confusion, despair, and departure be at all surprising?

Jesus taught that love between disciples is the primary attraction for the world. Yet common fracture lines emerge between and within churches, suggesting anything but love. There's always some give and take over serving the poor, widows, orphans, immigrants, and the infirm. But there are gigawatt fights among Christians over big social issues: LGBTQ, abortion rights, and racism, with schisms and charged rhetoric getting front-page news attention. How should leaders deal with advocacy and issues like these? Does discipleship prepare people for maturity in Christ, and for unity and polity around Scripture? Or is Christian community becoming just another social media rage tribe? Social media, much like sewers, are useful things. But immersing ourselves in either is not a particularly healthy thing. I think you see where I'm going with this… What looms on the Christian community's horizon in the days ahead if we run silent, scared, dumbfounded and angry?

Pollsters suggest that the driving issues in the next decade among Western Christians will include these:

- schisms (like those among Methodists, Southern Baptists and Episcopalian/Anglican denominations)
- "SOGIE"— sexual orientation, gender identity equality
- abortion rights and fights
- complementarian and egalitarian ministry conflicts
- racism litmus tests and victimism
- social justice
- climate change
- politics as morality standards
- age, income, and nationality silos

In the years ahead, will leaders focus on Christ's mission of discipling—or find something else to zero in on? Unfortunately, leaders seeking social significance, power and acceptance rather than following Christ abound. An example? Consider these words from a 2017 address by Bishop Stephen Cottrell of the Church of England, about sexual rights versus a biblical worldview:

> "It would be particularly foolish for us to ignore the missiological damage that is done when that which is held to be morally normative and desirable by much of society and by what seems to be a significant number of Anglican Christian people in this country, is deemed morally unacceptable by the Church."[100]

To get along better with society, Cottrell offers an interesting proposal: stop looking to Scripture and go with popular opinion, whatever that happens to be this week. In other words, let's start a new tradition. If you grew up as a millennial in his church, wouldn't this kind of influence shape (distort) your discipleship?

Here an incoming British archbishop is saying in effect, "What I teach you is far more palatable to society than Scripture, so get in line." This is a leadership failure worthy of Baal's best leaders in Jeremiah 7:9–10:

> Will you steal, murder, commit adultery, swear falsely, make offerings to Baal, and go after other gods that you have not known, and then come and stand before me in this house, which is called by my name, and say, "We are delivered!"—only to go on doing all these abominations?

Cottrell's thesis is a manifestation of clericalism at its finest, derailing biblically sound disciples as the objective.

Leadership failure like Cottrell's is not uncommon among an under-discipled and disunited church. And the liberation from inconvenient biblical texts points back to leaders letting someone in power sell a truly false religious pablum. The traditions exploit both ends of the leadership problem, from heretical teaching down to simple individual apathy. In one form it is leaders just letting traditions rumble on so as not to cause problems. In others, it's heresy packaged as the new way under the power and clerical authority of renegade theologians.

Leaders allowing these errant traditions to continue means big trouble for disciples. It means replicating the problems at ever higher rates among believers. It means many will fall silent. It means underdiscipled people who are puzzled by Christianity's lack of salt and light will stop thinking. Or it means angry Nones and Dones will walk away at increasing rates.

None of this is new. All this has plagued the church from sixteen hundred years ago (and longer) until now. But the production rates of bad discipleship are accelerating, the recovery rates diminishing. The traditions are the catalysts for all that, because we lashed community to the traditions—and because we lost our grip on the mission, traditions are all we have left.

If the goal is really evangelism—to save as many people as possible—discipleship is the only rational approach. Why?

The traditions in conversion Christianity are hub and spoke, meaning one person as the hub evangelizing many, as in a speaker speaking to many in the room. That means each leader or speaker or pastor makes converts in a series—1+1+1+1…. Essentially, this is brute-force marketing.

Think of a professor having two hundred students, and every one of them knows nothing at all about the subject being taught, and most have no interest in it either. The individual relationships required by such a professor to those many students is unworkable at any significant level outside the classroom. A similar problem is faced by leaders in pulpits, or on YouTube—or even in small groups of ten or twenty—trying to disciple many people. Real depth in relationships isn't possible in numbers that large, and development occurs only meagerly in class or worship.

Jesus demonstrated a max discipling ratio of one to a dozen, with a deep emphasis on one to three. How many leaders will we need in order to disciple every twelve people, if it's the leaders that have to execute on the task? A lot. Factor in a 69 percent washout rate among believers today, and you can reach only one conclusion: There aren't enough pastors, speakers, evangelists, elders, deacons, trustees and small group leaders in Christianity to disciple the converts. We're back to the third-century problem. Either disciples do discipling, or attrition math gets us to zero over time.

Jesus has a different formula: one to one, and each one to another. This results in multiplication—two become four, who become eight, who become sixteen… The former ratio (one to many) assumes that most people leave the converts to the pros, while the rest of us stay quiet. That conversion technique will only add, not multiply. Each cycle adds one more direct report to the pastor's list, either swamping the leader or maybe yielding one new convert.

Again, Jesus's model (one to one, one to a few) is a multiplier. As Jesus set it up, every disciple gets trained, then goes out and makes other disciples. And each cycle doubles the aggregate of the earlier round.

If you think about the pandemic and variants we face as this book goes to press, there were one or two people who contracted the Coronavirus in late Summer or Fall of 2019. Two became four and so on. By Spring 2020 the replication had spread worldwide. Replication multiplies fast! To illustrate this more in numbers, run thirty discipling cycles (each cycle runs a year or two) in the addition method, where one pro disciples two people who, unless they're pros too, are not replicators, but move along as believers. Our noble pro keeps on going, discipling another two, and his life work yields about thirty or forty disciples over a career. Be generous and say that a few of those do some discipling too, also through the addition process, and then maybe the number isn't just 30 or 40, but even as many as 300 or even 3,000 after those thirty cycles, which together take about thirty years. Impressive, right? Top that off by assuming, amazingly, that none of those people walk off on their faith.

Yet with disciples making other disciples, doing multiplication discipling, starting with just one person, thirty cycles in thirty years will equal 568,870,912 disciples—roughly equivalent to the present population of the entire continent of North and Central America. Assume the current rate of 69% drop out and we drop down to a paltry 280,000,000 new disciples who are out making more disciples. The cycles themselves aren't linear in true discipleship, because more and more people are entering the cycle, so time is not a fixed interval; it's compressing.

There's another important issue here. Conversionism (the goal of making converts instead of disciples) remains shaky at best, because when you get converted, you're on your own, if we're really honest about it. This one person simply cannot keep deeply discipling every one they've added. Overload sets in if you have dozens of disciples connected with you. Popular college professors and preachers can vouch for that. But if we use Jesus's method, which is life-on-life discipleship, each round of disciples ensures that the next round is equipped to make more mature disciples, and the network it creates means huge numbers of disciples are not dependent on one person.

Mission and culture change is the only way to escape addition conversion—the only way to address the traditions and consequences that run wide and deep in Western Christianity. History is full of examples about traditions and symptoms destructive to serving our God, much as we read of the Asherah poles, high places, cults, and god-worshipers in the Old Testament—just as we see the totalitarian traditions and intolerance movements afoot today, reprogramming many in the faith of Christ. Disciples today live with the baggage and practices of long-embraced but dysfunctional traditions. These traditions are silencing, intimidating, and isolating disciples across the Christian landscape, taking the voices and lives out of the visible world.

The situation is complex, deeply embedded, and poking around the traditions means all this will be emotionally charged. So now we have met the dilemma. What to do?

Part Three

Moving Forward—a Better Path

Costly grace is the gospel which must be sought again and again.
It is costly because it costs a man his life,
and it is grace because it gives a man the only true life.
Dietrich Bonhoeffer, *The Cost of Discipleship*

10

A Disciple of Christ

There are so many good books written on being a disciple and on making disciples. For example, a great read is Dann Spader's *4 Chair Discipling: What Jesus Calls Us to Do*, published in 2019 by Moody Press. It's a clear and cogent read, progressing from "Come and See" to "Follow Me" to "Fishers of People" to "Go and Make."

The aim of *The Disciple Dilemma* is to serve leaders. To make a case that the entrenched obstacles and symptoms Christian community faces in discipleship can only be addressed by leadership. Which brings us back to Os Guinness's statement "Contrast is the mother of clarity." This chapter is a contrast—about what a disciple "is" to modernity versus the "ought" of Scripture.

What is a disciple? How do you explain the notion to people? The modern often suggests a disciple is a higher order being, someone saved and then upgraded, to the highest Christian order, like a frequent flyer ranking program: there's the regular believers, then pastors, then missionaries, saints perhaps next, and then the ultimate martyrs of holiness—the fifth-grade boys' Sunday school teachers. Yet there's scant biblical evidence that we should think of disciples that way.

Discipleship is usually ranked by people as a standing above regular believers, even so far as going to the very top of the heap—limited to the twelve guys with Jesus in the New Testament. Such assumptions can imply that true lordship, reserved only for the rigors of a disciple must not apply to me, or worse, that since I'm not one of the original twelve, being a disciple is not even an option. "No thanks, I'm good" becomes a perfectly rational response in that line of thinking. But caste Christianity isn't real. And discipleship is *not* optional for believers. Every believer is a disciple, a priest, an adopted child, and a slave. No believer can opt out of any of that. And every disciple owns the job of making more disciples.

The New Testament word for "disciple" (Greek *mathetes*: "learner/student, follower") applies to three distinctly different kinds of disciples in the Bible. Two are believers in development. One is a non-believer. A look at all three of these can help us understand the fuller context of a disciple.

Our first kind to discuss is a discipler of disciples. Jesus was that. But we can see that a discipler is not isolated to just stories about Jesus and his twelve. For instance, we read of Paul and Peter and Priscilla and Aquila living that life as a discipler in the New Testament too. These were disciples who lived with, as in deep connection with, not simply near other believers. I had someone like that growing up.

Mickey was our youth pastor in high school. He knew us—I mean he *really* knew us. He wasn't just a guy leading the small group then fading away to be with the adults. He was among us, inside our heads and our hearts, and we knew he loved us. He was a change agent for a lot of young casual Christians. I'll never forget a chat with him one evening. A nice, fun, easy chat. Lots of laughs. Mickey was like that—fun. But when the time was exactly right, the scales perfectly balanced in the silence of the moment, he leaned in on me and he said, "Listen you turkey, it's time you made a choice. You're a lukewarm believer. Get off your butt about Christ. Choose! Are you fully in, or dropping out?" Mickey, that faithful disciple was a game changer for me. And forty-seven years later, that disciple's impact on me refuels my convictions to run the race of a disciple. Those specific words aren't the perfect pitch for everyone by a discipling mentor.

But that approach illustrates a mentoring disciple building a relationship, then putting that relationship to work getting another (casual) disciple going on a better journey. You can see this same dynamic in Acts 18:26 when Priscilla and Aquila worked closely with Apollos—to teach him a better way as a follower of Christ.

> Meanwhile a Jew named Apollos, a native of Alexandria, came to Ephesus. He was a learned man, with a thorough knowledge of the Scriptures. He had been instructed in the way of the Lord, and he spoke with great fervor and taught about Jesus accurately, though he knew only the baptism of John. He began to speak boldly in the synagogue. When Priscilla and Aquila heard him, they invited him to their home and explained to him the way of God more adequately.

The second kind of a disciple may be the most well-known concept: A student, learning from and serving Christ. And living out life with other disciples. The traditions teach us that if we get saved, and if we have a little continuing education and participation along the way, all is well as a believer. But in the Bible we see disciples studying, gaining practical experience, in a Christian community, but intensely living and developing alongside a very few (ideally, three or less). Now, we can all gain from being part of Christian community, from the friends, the sermons, the lectures, the mission events and the small and large groups. But life with a very few is the way Christ discipled Peter, James, John, Martha, and Mary. And it's the way the Apostle Paul did it. These disciples worship Jesus as God himself. They realize who Jesus truly is, God himself. They're dedicated to him, sold out, surrendered and serving him. John 21 describes the twelve as having now come to this realization. These are the disciples we read about in Acts 11:26, with a new name intended to mean the same thing as disciple: Christians. "The disciples were called Christians first at Antioch". These are not members. These people are disciples, Christians, lives fully in, wholehearted, with their own life given away. These are wor-shipers and students and followers of the Most-High God, the Lord Jesus Christ.

But one more kind of disciple is found in Scripture: *unbelievers* who are disciples. Does that surprise you? A lot of people think you cannot be a disciple unless you're a believer first. Give me an opportunity to make a case. It matters as we think about the life of a disciple.

I'm going to employ a set of phrases to describe a disciple, then unpack them so we can illustrate what the dilemma has done to dilute discipleship. The attributes of a disciple I want to walk through with you are based on Jesus's words and are in the middle column. To keep the traditions in view, we'll map also the traditional functions often used *in place of* discipleship in contemporary Christianity in the right column:

Christ's words:	Traits of a disciple:	Christian traditions:
"Come follow me"	being invited	seeker venues / proselytizing
"Who do you say I am?"	evaluating, realizing	"just accept Jesus"
"Take up your cross"	surrendering, growing	optional lordship, optional discipleship
"Unless a man take up his cross and follow me…"	Bondservant, "death to self"	be baptized, small group, mission trips
"I send you out"; "baptizing…teaching…"	teaming up, being sanctified	solo endeavor, works, virtuousness
"Go therefore and make disciples…"	inviting others: fishers of men	conversionism, moralism
"He indeed bears fruit and yields… a hundredfold"	lifelong development, inviting others	membership

Let's step through these traits to get a fuller grasp of the disciple's life. Here's a progression of the process lifted from the New Testament descriptions of the disciples:

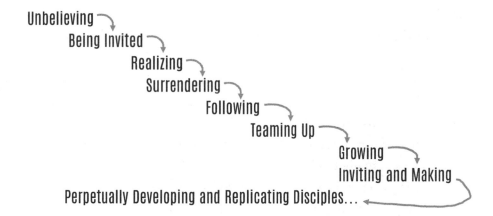

In the case of Jesus's relationship with Peter, for example, we see Peter morphing from a curious and unbelieving fisherman to a faithful apostle and martyr:

- Peter the unbeliever, invited to come and follow and evaluate Christ (Matthew 4:18; Luke 5:1).
- Peter who still did not understand who Jesus really was (Luke 18:34; John 16:17).
- Peter now truly believing in Christ as Lord and God (Luke 24:31-32).
- Peter learning under others—being matured and equipped (John 21:22; Galatians 2:14).
- Peter going forth into life, work, and communities (which may have included foreign soil) (Acts 10:24; 11:1).
- Peter's lifelong development while teamed with other disciples (Matthew 10:5; Mark 6:7).
- Peter making more disciples, discipling other disciples (John 21:15–23).
- Peter repeating his ministry and disciple-making throughout life (before being martyred in Rome around AD 66 while serving as bishop for the new churches there).

Unbelieving

Could this be right? Unbelieving disciples? Well, you have to start somewhere.

Jude verse 22 reminds us: "And have mercy on those who doubt" (ESV). Disciples in their opening moments don't believe Jesus is who he is. For example, his original twelve and their friends—who were all known as his disciples from the start—did not collectively believe or even suspect that Jesus was actually God.

Notice these examples of the disciples' shortcomings in understanding and faith: "The disciples *did not understand* any of this. Its meaning was hidden from them, and *they did not know what he was talking about*" (Luke 18:34, emphasis added). And a similar example: "When they came back from the tomb, they told all these things to the Eleven and to all the others. It was Mary Magdalene, Joanna, Mary the mother of James, and the others with them who told this to the apostles. But *they did not believe* the women, because their words seemed to them like nonsense" (Luke 24:9–11, emphasis added).

As leaders, does this set of passages about Jesus's disciples matter in modern discipling? Yes, it does, and here's why: a disciple may or may not be a believer yet. For me, this recognition that a nonbeliever can be a disciple is a profound thing. Our duty as an individual follower of Christ is not to make Christians, or to make converts, or to make church members. We're to make disciples, to invite *unbelievers* to start a *discipling* journey.

Here the Christian community has to teach disciples that their duty is not about conversion of people, but to be disciples making disciples. This thing of inviting people to come and see is not a sales call, though we must always be prepared to give reason for the hope within us when asked (1 Peter 3:15). We aren't sales people. We're billboards. Not selling, but rather pointing and inviting, while living among people. This discipling thing is about the idea of "come and see," much like the Samaritan woman declared after meeting Jesus at the well.

Christian communities often operate with two faulty assumptions. One is that everyone's an evangelist, which is untrue biblically (Ephesians

4:11). The second faulty assumption is that unbelieving people usually find God in churches or in ministries. That isn't the way things worked for God's disciples in Scripture, and it hasn't changed in our Western society today. Yes, some people do walk into churches and surrender to God. But statistically there's very little walk-in trade in the Bible or in the present day. From the beginning, discipleship was mostly believers going out in the world and meeting and relating to people, who then became curious.

We need to retool our disciples to seek out unbelievers and live among them as disciples, so they'll ask about hope, rather than hoping we can sell them a deal, or that they'll come looking for us.

Unbelieving disciples might range in their traits from skeptical curiosity, like Nicodemus, to condemnations and assault, like Saul (which, when you think about it, may not seem like we're describing a disciple at all). Others may have some exposure to really solid Christians, yet these exposed folks are still unbelievers, just trying to figure out who or what to follow—like the puzzled disciples of John the Baptist.

Not everyone is going to sign on, of course. Judas was named as one of the original twelve disciples, but never believed Jesus was the Christ (Matthew 26:23). Others will say encouraging words like "Christ is Lord," yet they never actually own it, never believe in him, and they eventually trail off (Luke 6:46). But some nascent disciples begin to realize that this is no ordinary religion. The Christians were different, weird actually, in some alluring way. These (emerging) disciples listen, they come to think the evidence is perhaps reasonable and deserves a deeper look. They may be your children. They may be close friends or family, coworkers or mentors, recreational friends or neighbors. But disciples begin as unbelievers.

Discipleship starts with *not* believing—not yet. And as a follower of Christ, by being with these discipling unbelievers, you'll be hanging with a lot of people who aren't at all like you, maybe not ethnically, perhaps not politically or philosophically; they may not even be in the same age bracket or have the same sexual identity as you. That's who disciples are to be out among.

Leadership's role in Christian community begins here, helping believers who are disciplers, to feel confident and willing to be among unbelievers of most any stripe and style. Leaders owe their disciplers a culture that reinforces and makes normal a seeking out of relationships with people in their work, their surroundings. Of course personalities play in here too. Some are extroverts, easily able to connect and converse, while others may be introverts, wanting to crawl under a rock and be left alone. Disciplers are both types and more, and they deserve development in their own individual ways and styles. Disciples need a culture that tamps down huddling indoors, away from the unbelievers. How? There are lots of other books to read about day-to-day discipleship. This book is meant to be different. This book is about the ways that leaders must shape the strategic choices of an organization, so that those day-to-day results will become long-term outcomes.

This is not to suggest that leaders are doing all the discipling. It's about leaders establishing an environment so disciplers will take up true biblical community, which includes living, mostly out there, among unbelievers.

Being Invited

Inviting is how Jesus won disciples. Not selling, not shaming, not slick messaging. People were invited to come and learn about him for themselves.

Likewise, disciples are to invite others to explore who Christ is, who God is, who man is. In a word, it's an invitation to relationships. Not making people projects or objectives, but inviting and hosting people. Not saving them and ditching them, or converting them and plugging them into a membership program or small group, but inviting and going along with them—questions, ridicule, reasoning, and all—whatever it is they uniquely require in order to see Christ.

Yes, we can read of Jesus acting as an evangelist to large crowds. But he and Paul would go on to say that not all will be evangelists. Yet Christ demands that all be disciples.

Leaders must enable a community to escape from simplistic conversion quotas and formulas, and to be released from shame-based messaging or expectations that intimidate many believers into silence, or distort who they are in Christ by pretenses of evangelical conformity.

Leaders must help believers learn that invitation is a unique person-by-person talent, using their personality and nature as God intended them as individuals. Unique individuals. Leaders help believers learn what to expect from being an inviter. Sometimes invited people will push back and walk off. Or sometimes it will become a relationship, as unbelievers walk with you, watch you, question you.

Larry Alex Taunton's book *The Faith of Christopher Hitchens* is a true story about a prominent atheist, Christopher Hitchens, who travels the country with Taunton, a believer. Taunton invited this famous atheist on driving journeys to go to their debates, but in time the two became true friends—able to relate, able to see each other's world. A similar example of relating and inviting people into your life is found in the book *The Doubter's Club*, written by Preston Ulmer. That's how this all begins. They meet you, they watch you. They watch your Christian community in action. That's how Jesus made disciples—he invited people. Those invited might be enthused intellectuals like Nicodemus, or impulsive fishermen like Peter. And not all of them followed, even though they came face-to-face with Christ (Luke 18:18). Some will bail on you. Others will stick around and ask questions. They'll probe, and go on to realize who Jesus Christ is, and keep going.

The point here is that we're to be believers who invite people to come and see. Invite people to check out the reason for the hope we have within us. Jesus in the New Testament is predominantly an inviter (consider passages like Matthew 4:19; 8:22; 9:9; 19:21; John 1:43; 10:27; 21:19; 21:22).

Leaders owe their people a community that motivates and equips disciples to invite others to come and see, to investigate Christ. Inviting is what results in some unbelieving people coming to Christ and belonging to him forever. A lot of church people (82 percent by some studies) will tell you they don't want to have anything to do with inviting people to come and see. That's fine. Move on. A few will want to know more about being an inviter, and how that can be genuinely and sincerely lived out in their workplace, their schools, their communities. Start there, with those people. They will be your early disciplers. And if I'm reading Scripture right, the invitation isn't a fake interest so you can get people saved. It's an invitation to teach a disciple of Christ how to love by truly understanding someone else's story. To really get to know them. Really relate to them, listen, care, connect. To have an honest relationship because you were gifted an unbelievable love, called to live alongside unbelieving people. Eventually, they just may ask you what your story is. Be ready to talk about your reason for your hope within you.

Realizing

For the disciple, a revelation arrives. For some, it arrives slowly. For others, suddenly. It's the revelation of who Jesus Christ is, who they are, and what God has done—and what all this means, ultimately and personally (Matthew 27:54; Mark 15:39; Luke 23:47).

Then at some point, as they're deeply influenced by the recognition of the majesty and reality before them, the scales tip. It may be easy and fast, like Thomas facing the resurrected Jesus. It may be long and arduous, like the faith journey of C. S. Lewis, tormented, pushing back, finally processing and getting it—who Christ is as Lord and Savior—while Lewis was riding in a motorcycle sidecar, arriving at a zoo.[101]

Surrendering

"Costly grace is the gospel which must be sought again and again.... It is costly because it costs a man his life, and it is grace because it gives a man the only true life."[102] With that awesome realization comes a handing over of the keys, as it were, to the lordship of Christ as God incarnate.

In modern parlance, surrender often means deference, a willingness to go along, a little give, in exchange for expected benefits. "I surrendered to my wife's demand to wear a blue shirt instead of a red one." Surrender as Christ meant it is a misunderstood concept to people in Western civilization these days. The lordship part of Christianity is often thought of as more like negotiations in a real estate deal, rather than true surrender: "I'll do this, you do that, we'll meet halfway on those other things. You want me to do what? Well, that's a bit much, really. Let's not have some policy thing like Jesus as Lord clog up a freebie eternal life offer, ok?"

But surrender is nothing like that. It's a removal of liberties, rights, and entitlements. All now belongs to the Conqueror. No idolatry—personal or religious—allowed. In other words, your life is no longer your own. And disciples are actually joyful about that.

The stories of surrender in Scripture, and of surrender for Christians in the years since, are fascinating. Christ's lordship begins to soak through a disciple's thinking, through their psyche, through their lifestyle.

Christ nixed any idea that one could be a disciple without full and unconditional surrender (Matthew 16:24; Mark 8:34; Luke 9:23; 14:26; John 8:31). A disciple begins to absorb and soak in the ways and words of Christ in their life. In experiencing life in a broken world with Christ alongside them, it's an apprenticeship. And it will not be a perfect journey. But Christ's discipleship is fault-tolerant. It does not imply life without failure. Lapses, sin, and even denial of Christ are all typical life stories for disciples (Luke 22:54).

To contrast surrender with modern deference, discipleship means enslavement to the Most-High God. No rights, no options aside from the Lord's bidding. I don't know about you, but *surrender* and *slavery* aren't my first word choices in a motivational speech to potential new employees. "Hey, we're really glad you're considering joining us here at XYZ Corporation! Exciting things happening, can't wait to tell you about the pay, the benefits, and the growth opportunities. But first, a couple of other things. You'll be required sign a paper whereby you willingly give over your entire life to us. No holdouts. Keys, kids, 401(k)s, dreams, hopes, and all your rights. You may even be selected to die for XYZ. You're our servants now. Whatever we tell you to do, you do. So drop your cell phones and car keys in the baskets coming by, and put on the chains! Now about that great dental plan…" No company could possibly get away with that speech, right? But Jesus did, a lot. Examples:

> And whoever does not take his cross and follow me is not worthy of me. (Matthew 10:38 ESV)

> If anyone would come after me, let him deny himself and take up his cross and follow me. (Matthew 16:24; Mark 8:34 ESV)

> If anyone serves me, he must follow me; and where I am, there will my servant be also. If anyone serves me, the Father will honor him. (John 12:26 ESV)

Cultures can be rotted out by false distractions like power and finances and disunity, all displacing reality. Leaders have to rid cultures of the popular myths that are false, or risk losing the culture over time. Example: We offered free flu shots to employees every year. Two guys, no matter what anyone said to them, refused to get vaccinated. They both seemed to get the flu nearly every year, missing days of work; they were contagions, and doing their own health no favors. I asked them why they wouldn't take the shot. Their ominous reply: "The people giving the injection will put these little microphones into you. Then the government can listen in on everything you say!" That myth was false, but it spun off from conspiracy theories and bad thinking about risks, and it generally led to fewer people getting flu shots, which was a culture of mythology-displacing truth. We brought in the instigators and showed them the evidence to prove their fears and stories were not true. One of them took the shots after that. The other refused, and kept up the microphone antics. We dismissed him.

To focus this back on our lordship issue: Leaders have to root out damaging myths, such as the falsity that a Christian can actually be a Christian without yielding to Christ's lordship—that lordship is some works-based add-on. Enter leaders—they design and influence the community to point people to true things, and to motivate people to pursue those true things. They graciously and firmly root out the heretical things. This is not to say we must run people off from our community, but we must turn people away from promoting heresy. Not little technical disagreements like how much water does it take to baptize someone, but big ugly lies that promote something like optional lordship.

Whether it's employees or Christians, people have to be shown the better way by their leaders. If people won't cooperate on the consequential stuff, they have to be dealt with in grace and in honest confrontation. People need to know both the what and the consequence of these false traditions and practices. If they can't accept that, they have a decision to make. Does that sound cruel to you? If people in consequential matters like discipleship will not go all in, they need to be put into more basic discipling. "Though by this time you ought to be teachers, you need someone to teach you the elementary truths of God's word all over again. You need milk, not solid food!" (Hebrews 5:12). For those who refuse reformation in the consequential stuff like lordship, Matthew 18:17 applies: "If they refuse to listen even to the church, treat them as you would a pagan or a tax collector." As does 1 Corinthians 5:11: "I am writing to you that you must not associate with anyone who claims to be a brother or sister but is sexually immoral or greedy, an idolater or slanderer, a drunkard or swindler. Do not even eat with such people."

Leaders have to come to grips with what's consequential and what isn't, to point disciples to the main things. Those main things come down to this: a real disciple will begin to deprogram from a "me" agenda and begin to live a life underwritten by serving Christ, dying to self and following Christ, alongside a few other disciples. For a person to seek him with all a disciple's heart and mind and strength is God's formula for encountering him (Jeremiah 29:13). Such a true encounter with our living Christ has a way of clearing a person's mind of the trivial. There are plenty of mythologies to combat in a Christian culture. Yet leaders absolutely must kill off the damnable tradition that Jesus is Savior but not necessarily Lord, and that lordship is just another word for membership in an institution. Jesus

Christ owns us, body and soul. Lordship is to be a centerpiece of each person in a Christian community. Teaching, sermons, and study series equip and outfit disciples. But those are tools. The transmission of lordship is one person in a relational walk with another, living out life together as surrendered servants of the Lord God, practically, real life alongside real life.

That's the environment, the relationships, and the culture leaders must foster and replicate.

Following

Disciples follow. They volitionally choose to pursue Christ. To unwind the me-centric virus we all have raging within us, a disciple must uproot their agenda and go where Another tells them to go (Luke 14:33).

The term *follower* suffers from much the same language trap as the word *surrender* does. Today, "following Jesus" is often code for a groupie or a fan. Such as "I like Jesus better than I like Foo Fighters or Widespread Panic". But the sentiment of "I like Jesus" is still as a fan or a groupie. It can be like a Facebook follower: stealthy, shadowy, stalking Jesus from my easy chair or small group, but not up and obvious in broad daylight. Jesus said disciples must really, truly go after him with their whole life, or they're not disciples (Luke 14:27). It meant day-on-day walking with and talking with Christ, not sporadic drive-bys at the temple. It meant following him into tough terrain, harsh environments, really dangerous circumstances, and maybe an occasional party or wedding.

In our following, Christ tells us to take up our cross and follow him. What could Jesus possibly mean?

It's similar to the phrase used today: "whatever it takes." It suggests someone is willing to do many things that most others would not do in order to prove loyalty, or to get your business, or to gain your favor. In other words, I'm fully committed to you.

Here we see something that the Bible associates with several metaphors. One is standing firm (1 Corinthians 16:13), which is to say that nothing can shake me loose from serving God, "whatever it takes." Nothing, not even life-threatening terrors, can move me from my convictions about God.

Another way of saying it is found in the phrase about doing things for God "with all your heart and with all your soul and with all your mind" (Matthew 22:37), or its twin, to follow God with your whole heart (1 Chronicles 28:9). Which in contemporary terms means no half-hearted or conflicted conformists. Again, whatever it takes. Today, and practically, that means shedding any personal pre-disciple bucket list to execute on the new disciple's marching orders. This doesn't necessarily mean a new disciple must give up medical school in mid-stream, but it might mean that. Or it may impact where the med student goes after graduating, or who they go with. These will be personal and individual assignments, journeys of time, prayer, counsel with discipling friends, whatever it takes, with full enthusiasm (heart), intellect (mind), and energy (strength).

A wholehearted disciple pursues God with the passion of the thirsty deer desperate for water (Psalm 42:1); any substitute, or any partial or half-hearted pursuit, would now be unfulfilling. Day by day, moment by moment, for the rest of life, disciples follow.

There's no negotiating whether or not a disciple must actually and fully follow Christ (Matthew 16:24; Mark 8:34; Luke 9:23, 14:33). Which is daunting, and completely impossible without grace and forgiveness. This is the biblical concept of following God with a whole heart. The same concept of the committed heart ties back to Christ's command as disciples to take up our own cross. No room remains for anything to displace the wholeness of a disciple's surrender, crucifixion of self (1 Samuel 7:3; Matthew 16:24; Mark 7:6; Luke 14:26).

I think here of Paul's sentiments: "I consider my life worth nothing to me; my only aim is to finish the race and complete the task the Lord Jesus has given me—the task of testifying to the good news of God's grace" (Acts 20:24).

What does this wholehearted follow-and-pursue concept mean for leaders? Leaders recognize the pull and push of the times, how they affect their people. Leaders build, tweak, and sustain an environment that encourages people to be freed from the idolatries, fads, and rages of the times. That environment frees disciples from traditions and symptoms that distract individual disciples from their individual, personal, and unique pursuits of God.

Leaders as leadership are not the disciplers to everyone in a Christian community. Either the leadership builds the culture in fostering person-on-person tailored pursuit, or else leaders are back in the disciple dilemma's trap of doing it all themselves, or hoping numbers and groups and programs will make up for discipleship.

Ponder these examples of God's expectations for the wholehearted follower:

> Jesus said to him, "Follow me, and leave the dead to bury their own dead." (Matthew 8:22 ESV)

> To another he said, "Follow me." But he [the man] said, "Lord, let me first go and bury my father." (Luke 9:59 ESV)

> Jesus told his disciples, "If anyone would come after me, let him deny himself and take up his cross and follow me." (Matthew 16:24 ESV)

> Calling the crowd to him with his disciples, he said to them, "If anyone would come after me, let him deny himself and take up his cross and follow me." (Mark 8:34 ESV)

> He said to all, "If anyone would come after me, let him deny himself and take up his cross daily and follow me." (Luke 9:23 ESV)

> Jesus said to him, "If you would be perfect, go, sell what you possess and give to the poor, and you will have

treasure in heaven; and come, follow me." (Matthew 19:21 ESV)

And Jesus, looking at him, loved him, and said to him, "You lack one thing: go, sell all that you have and give to the poor, and you will have treasure in heaven; and come, follow me." (Mark 10:21 ESV)

When Jesus heard this, he said to him, "One thing you still lack. Sell all that you have and distribute to the poor, and you will have treasure in heaven; and come, follow me." (Luke 18:22 ESV)

Jesus said to them, "Truly, I say to you, in the new world, when the Son of Man will sit on his glorious throne, you who have followed me will also sit on twelve thrones, judging the twelve tribes of Israel." (Matthew 19:28 ESV)

Again Jesus spoke to them, saying, "I am the light of the world. Whoever follows me will not walk in darkness, but will have the light of life." (John 8:12 ESV)

My sheep hear my voice, and I know them, and they follow me. (John 10:27 ESV)

If anyone serves me, he must follow me; and where I am, there will my servant be also. If anyone serves me, the Father will honor him. (John 12:26 ESV)

Jesus said to him, "If it is my will that he remain until I come, what is that to you? You follow me!" (John 21:22 ESV)

Teaming Up

Hopefully this chapter is reinforcing the word *relationships* in discipling. For leaders, here's another challenge in the disciple dilemma: How does leadership establish and sustain a community that does relational discipling? Ideally we can dispel a notion that throwing together ten or twenty or five hundred people in gatherings will reliably slosh discipling to life.

I'd like to try and explain the concept of teaming—working closely together—using a fighter pilot illustration. Weird? Let's see if it flies.

To be a fighter pilot, you have to give up everything else that competes for your time and attention. Nobody gets the job without surrender, sacrifice, and sweat. You have to be all in. *Really* all in. Like, you may get killed doing this. You must learn how to operate in teams to be effective. You'd better have your mission, your weapons, your limits down cold, making your flying skills and knowledge into reflexive thinking, instead of something you need to look up on the web.

You start out as a "wingie" flying with an instructor. You learn to be a good fighter pilot living around excellent teachers. Practicing. Screwing up. Nearly killing yourself at times. Multiple "deaths" in the simulator. But you get better being part of this fellowship. You listen a lot, you learn, you try things out. And if you go all in, you might just become a fighter jock.

I chose to use Air Force F-15s, nicknamed the "Eagle", for the fighter pilot illustration. (I could have used other fighters here, like F-16s or F-18s or F-22s or F-35s, but you deserve much better than that.) The mission of an F-15 fighter is to drive out or destroy enemy aircraft (see the Red Baron's quote at chapter 7's heading). If you have bad guys looking for a fight in an air war, the F-15 Eagle is the jet you want for the fight. It was designed with the power and the weaponry to take on multiple enemy jets at once, win, and come back to fight again. It is an amazing weapon.

Now, don't think our job as disciples is to attack other people. The "bad guys" in a disciple's fight are

1. our own sin nature;
2. satanic attacks; and
3. the evil in societies attacking us over the centuries.

Not to get too dramatic, but the people we're called to interact with as disciples are the enslaved and oppressed of the enemy—they are not the enemy themselves, even if some act like it. We can certainly agree that the evil of a Hitler or Pol Pot or Mao or Stalin, and social ills such as abortion and racism and oppression and such, must be actively advocated against, fought against. But in a disciple's context, the fight is against the three enemies above.

The disciple has amazing weapons for the fight: "The weapons we fight with are not the weapons of the world. On the contrary, they have divine power to demolish strongholds" (2 Corinthians 10:4). As a Christian, you're strapped in to operate an amazing weapons system that you could never humanly match. If you're willing to use the weapons granted to disciples in the way they're designed, you'll be in position to enter the fight and win.

In the illustration here notice how the jets are teamed up—in formation. They fly together for several reasons. Flying alongside each other means the bad guys have a tough time trying to sneak up on either one of them, and by flying together, when troubles come, they can support each other, coach and encourage each other.

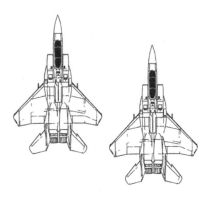

This echoes a similar concept for disciples: "Though one may be overpowered, two can defend themselves. A cord of three strands is not quickly broken" (Ecclesiastes 4:12). "Two are better than one, because they have a good return for their labor: If either of them falls down, one can help the other up" (Ecclesiastes 4:9–10).

Disciples, like fighter pilots, rely on each other and have confidence in their wingman. You understand each other's strengths and weaknesses. You get to know some wingmen (wingies) so well, you even know what they're thinking without anything being said. You know your wingie is there for you, that they will have your back. Training and living out life together, to make each other better, support each other day after day.

Fighters can operate alone, if they must. But they do their best work in teams. There's a flight lead, and there's a wingman. The lead is usually the coach, the Jedi knight for a younger or less experienced wingman. So, for a while, you'll learn as a student. A wingman.

There's submission in this formation. What a strange word to stick in a fighter pilot illustration—or a discipleship illustration, for that matter. A wingman, in submission, can be in complete control of the formation.

The idea of a wingman's power is found in the Greek word for submission (*hupotasso*). Submission gets a bad rap in Western thinking. In the Greek, it doesn't mean being a doormat or a weakling follower, as some think of it today. The Greek word for submission—as literally a sub-mission to the mission—means "to place in good military order; to accomplish the mission." Think of it as either person being able—and also obligated—to be in control when it benefits the mission. Ponder that concept next time you attend a wedding with the word *submission* in the vows.

Submission is how fighter pilots work offensively and defensively together. The lead may be a general officer, the wingman a second lieutenant. But in true submission, the wingie can take the lead from the general using that fluid (submission) leadership concept.

One objection I often hear in talking about discipling relationships is "We can't relate like Jesus and the disciples did in that time, that agrarian world, that slower world." That's factual, but not pertinent. Discipleship does not have to be rigid and minute-by-minute, face-to-face. Discipling can span the gamut from intense daily education to daily life with intermittent contact. It may be one-to-one, it may be multiple people discipling one. It can be a portfolio of mentors/disciples across work, play, family, civics and missional settings. But it should be intentional, consistent and ongoing.

Back to our aviation example. Over time as a fighter pilot, you fly with lots of wingmen. Some will outrank you and you're the student so to speak. Many will be peers, people you can count on to be there for you.

Others will be new to the game, looking to you to lead while they act as a student. You get better working with every one of them. And when your own lead, your coach, says you're ready, you'll become a flight lead. You take what you learned, and you'll begin to teach new wannabe fighter pilots the ropes. And this is key: you never stop learning yourself.

For the rest of your life as a fighter pilot, and even beyond those days of flying, you keep networking, learning, broadening yourself to be better, and to be pushed to be better in being around others. And for the rest of your life, you associate, you mentor, you learn, you raise up new wingmen, new students and operate in the real world with these people.

Disciples, like good fighter pilots, are the product of the culture you are immersed in. The concept for leaders to think about here is a community that builds micro relationships—twos or threes among a community of tens, hundreds, or perhaps thousands. Disciples are to be benefactors of those they're tightly grouped around.

Growing

Fighter pilots like to hang together, but they know the real development and learning happens in one-on-one development, usually up in the air where their real fight is underway.

As we've mentioned before, the popular Christian tradition is to hope the small groups and ministries are causing the discipling. Like the odds of the Mariners getting to the World Series, real group discipleship might happen, but it's a low probability event. Growing in Christ—much like growing in any professional domain—demands self-driven ambition. In Christian speak, it's sanctification. You don't get sanctification going to class. Sanctification comes from the choice to put self to death and grow into what Christ wants, not what I want.

Peer pressure is often thought of as an effective solution to drive personal surrender to Christ. Usually though, once the peers have left and their pressure is off, so is the surrender. A community selling seminars and classroom-and-group-based sanctification is missing the meaning of growth in Christ. Like vitamins, they're helpful, but not sufficient.

Inviting and Making

Let's think about how disciples relate to the broader world, in day-to-day life, so to speak. This is the "going into all nations" concept.

Consider a term coined by the famous Dutch theologian and statesman Abraham Kuyper—*spheres*—vocational spheres, civic spheres, and missional spheres.

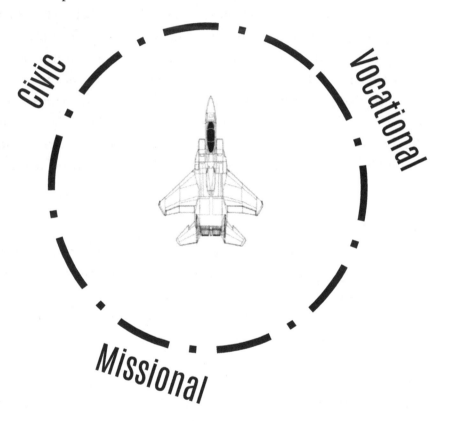

What does he mean by spheres? Territory may be helpful to explain this. Each sphere, like the civics sphere has its own turf that encompasses many things—life as a local citizen, a national citizen, serving in civic events and activities, such as a volunteer in a polling station or volunteer fire department as examples. The spheres, as Kuyper explained, each have their own unique purpose. In some ways they may overlap—such as a police officer who has policing as vocation, but in that policing role her vocation also intersects with her civic role in caring for people in her community.

Our lives as disciples exist, in all these spheres. There are other spheres too—like recreation or church life. But for the sake of brevity, we'll use three broad spheres of mission, vocation, and civics to discuss discipleship.

Vocation is about acting on a summons or call. The Latin root word *vocatio* is also the basis for "vocal"—calling or directing someone to do something. Vocation implies a personal and specific use of life talents to add value to God's kingdom and creation. We're all specialists of some sort in a highly specialized world, doing whatever we do. "You do you" has validity in the individual call, using unique talents from God, for God.

Whether we think about a disciple's vocative work like the task God gave to Adam in Genesis—to name and categorize creation—or as specific taskings as seen in Ephesians 2:10, directing best practice and best effort in all we do vocationally, we aren't actually "working for the man". We're working directly for our Father, our King, the Most High God, our Lord.

Surely if, as a disciple, I understand what God did for me, and what has been given me, and that my work is God's expectations, purpose, and call for me, I should want to be at my best—doing it with all my mind, strength, and enthusiasm, to borrow from Deuteronomy 30:10. Doing my best—whether that's brain surgery, baling hay, buying lumber, or babysitting.

Vocation places us in a fascinating position, a place where people, watching this crazy work ethic, will eventually want to ask us for the reason for the hope within us. Which becomes a chance to invite them to come and check out what we've found, what we've been offered. Vocation offers us the chance to invite people to meet the Son of Man.

A few will make civic duties part of their vocational life, like a career in politics, or working for government, the military, or their community. But for most of us, civic interactions will be much more voluntary and secondary to vocation and family. Civic involvement connects disciples to other people—to organizations and societies and governments in our local, regional, state, and national communities. We're to "contaminate" our culture with the beauty of disciples living and walking among people. Disciples are to live among others, serving them and building relationships, even in sometimes adverse settings:

> This is what the LORD Almighty, the God of Israel, says to all those I carried into exile from Jerusalem to Babylon: "Build houses and settle down; plant gardens and eat what they produce. Marry and have sons and daughters; find wives for your sons and give your daughters in marriage, so that they too may have sons and daughters. Increase in number there; do not decrease. Also, seek the peace and prosperity of the city to which I have carried you into exile." (Jeremiah 29:4–7)

Today, this kind of civic involvement may look like volunteering at a school, a library, or a hospital, or helping at a polling station, or working in societies and philanthropies. None of these purposes have an explicit mission to promote the person and work of Christ, but each of them represents arenas where people meet disciples in action, where they can ask why you are the way you are, why you believe what you believe.

For a disciple, civic activity is not a virtue signal, or doing what people will applaud, or something we do in seeking protection from social criticism. As disciples around the world, we owe our governments—republics, democracies, monarchies, and even dictatorships—the benefit of Christ's excellence in his disciples serving the civic sphere we live in.

This civic sphere can be a hard pill to swallow for many Christians. The civic space can incite feelings of contempt, frustration, and anger, as causes or groups we may disagree with crowd the headlines and places we live. People are just not like us. And yet, what better place to be asked about our weirdness, if not among the ones who don't understand us?

Disciples owe their civic community their relationships. This is prime space to demonstrate civility, unity, compassion, and diplomacy—all in rather short supply these days, it seems. Being a disciple—associating and engaging in the vast world outside the church—is where the action is. It's where somebody weird like you can make for compelling curiosity to all the normal people. It's where you can really flip over the basket and take that light outdoors (Matthew 5:14–16; Mark 4:21; Luke 8:16).

Missional work is explicitly that—a mission. It's discipleship, serving outside our workplace, perhaps inside or outside our community, maybe inside or outside a church with other disciples. Missional discipleship may be local, international, familial.

For pastors and professional missionaries, a domestic or global missional calling would certainly be a vocational as well a general call. But for most disciples, mission is serving God part-time, outside their vocative and civic life.

Do you think of your family as a mission? Family is grouped under missional life here because family is a primary obligation for a disciple—primary in serving God. Family can certainly represent personal gratification too, but that's secondary. This primary and secondary ranking has profound implications on discipleship in terms of why we have families. Family is first a calling, not a gratification. It's serving a spouse, raising up children, caring for parents. It is secondarily—which is not to say unimportantly—for our own pleasure and gratification.

And people watch disciples—watching why a disciple does not conform to typical social constructs in dealing with or running from problems.

My bride, Karen, was abused as a child physically and mentally by her troubled mother. But when her mother was a widow and facing cancer, Karen was there when no one else was—in the hospital, caring for her mother for hours at her bedside. Karen was there for the incontinence, the anger, the hours of waiting on someone who had not been kind to Karen as a child. That's crazy love!

So as a disciple, the way you interact in family, foreign posts, or food shelters all become visibly strange behavior around people who just won't understand you. And they'll want to understand. Get ready for the questions.

In going, disciples are operating with tentmaker strategies. Tentmaking is a term borrowed from the vocational life of Paul, who was both a highly trained theologian and a master tentmaker. Some people have written scholarly articles on Paul's missional role actually being funded by his substantial business holdings in the mobile home market.[103] But a tentmaking approach is a rarity in Western Christian community, more often because we want to separate from our discipleship at work, and be religious in our Christian community. A disciple is a disciple through tentmaking as well as Christian ministry. Some of us are missionaries on foreign soil, and our mission is itself the tentmaking. But all of us are to have some calling and skills we bring to the discipleship journey. Nobody is exempt from their calling to be a disciple as they make tents, whatever that tentmaking may really look like.

Missional work may or may not involve things God has equipped and called a disciple to do in professional life. No other religious system generates missional servants like that. Any religious worldview can support vocational work. Almost all belief systems can support forms of civic work. But only a disciple can be called by God to go and do missional work as a form of worship and gratitude.

Disciples do what they're told to do not because they're seeking credit with God, but rather from obedience and surrender and love toward God. The rest of the world's so-called virtuous works are actions about earning merit, paying off guilt, avoiding reprisals, or just karma. Cults like Mormonism that plagiarize the term *mission* serve only out of transactional benefit: You do those things, you may get these benefits.[104] The same can be said for Buddhists, Hindus, and Muslims—all these groups have many beautiful and gracious people doing works, but not as a mission of gratefulness and obedience. It's for merit. For example, in Islam, Allah's demands do not drive volitional and joyful action, but rather in seeking favor, and acting in fear. Only the disciple of Jesus Christ can operate in grateful obedience.

Secularists, while denying the notion of gods, may also borrow terms like *mission* or *calling*, and do nice moral things. Yet without a transcendent, the secular missionary is limited to virtuous hedonism—in other words, doing what feels good to them or looks good to others—because no higher purpose other than self-gratification can exist without a God-defining purpose. It may be wonderful work, except that *wonderful* as a word is now merely a relativist's opinion. Otherwise known as gratifying meaninglessness. None of that meaninglessness and fear and self-serving poverty is the life of a disciple.

This is the disciple's life: to do justice, love mercy, walk humbly with God (Micah 6:8). It's the disciple, who has no personal merit, who was a beggar, now inviting others—like the infirm, impoverished, alien, orphan, and widow—to experience the cool water that quenches life's thirsts forever (Isaiah 55:1).

How are disciples to operate in these spheres? The short answer is "in formation." This goes back to being teamed up. Disciples are not to live life solo. Jesus designed his discipleship as teams, not solo acts (Mark 6:7; Luke 10:1). Disciples grow in watching, following, and emulating, as well as in failing, forgiving, and getting back up again (Ephesians 4:29-5:4). A disciple without mentors and team-discipling relationships is criticized in Scripture, and the idea of going it alone is never suggested or demonstrated by Christ or the apostles (Ecclesiastes 4:12; Proverbs 27:17). It's a communal journey, with God and with other believers. Disciples will grow through relationships—or else starve spiritually, in solitude.

The aim is that a disciple will—in time, and with encouragement—go and make new disciples while inviting others, ministering to others, and being authentic and transparent for others. And then it's rinse and repeat for the rest of their lives as disciples.

Disciples are learners under other disciples, then becoming discipling mentors to others. In all cases, disciples are supposed to be networked with other disciples, and not out solo.

You may be plugged into all three areas—workaday life, civic duties, and missional commitments. This may mean you have one mentor and a couple of close wingmen. Maybe you're operating in one arena. Or you may be involved in all these spheres with multiple mentors, with several very close disciple friends who know you and are truly connected to your daily life. This is discipleship!

This illustration shows daily life for disciples (represented here as the two fighter jets in the center of the circles) with the three spheres we mentioned grouped together, shown as segments of life.

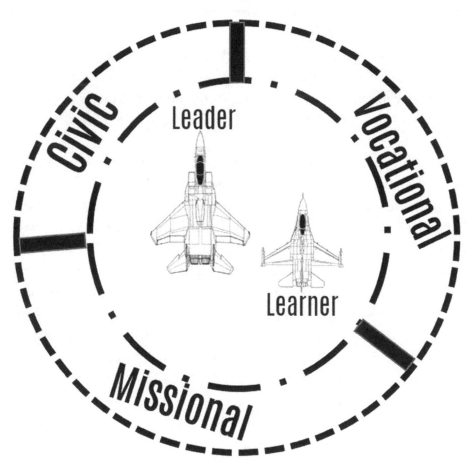

In other words, a disciple's life is made up of roles in vocational, missional and civic space.

Discipleship thrives by people connected with similar life interests and callings. Sometimes you're learning from others, sometimes coaching others, sometimes running alongside others. But the point is to operate with others. Intentionally solo discipleship is not discipleship. Solo is the concept from Judges 21:25— "Everyone did what was right in his own eyes" (ESV).

Teaming up can involve vocationally aligned people, like disciples who share a common profession of being doctors or bankers or builders. Or it may mean families teaming with other people with children of similar ages and in similar stages of family life. Or sports or hobbies may be the common denominator. The point is that disciples in the West need to reestablish and reboot with vocational, civic, missional, racial, and generational relationships in order to gain wisdom and depth as disciples, and to better relate to the rest of the world.

Examples of a disciple's life in the vocational, civic, and missional arenas are plentiful. A few of those examples, with a little more granularity are shown on the outer ring for each sphere of vocation, mission and civics.

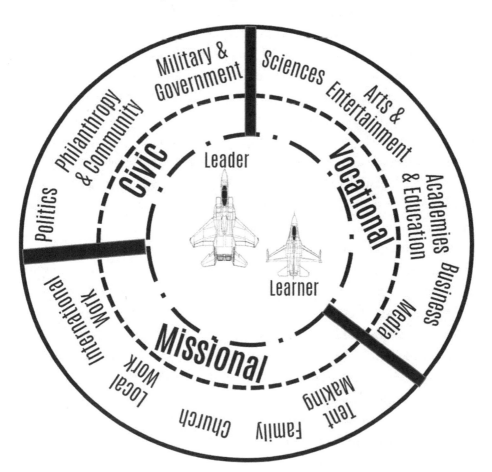

By operating "teamed up" with other believers, people will be watching closely, and trying to figure you out, perhaps even asking you about that weird alliance and life.

If we're to affect the trajectory of the disciple dilemma, we must re-capture these spheres. This is not to say there's no one doing this today. But the numbers are low, the voices hushed. Disciples must repopulate these spheres with credibility into business, military, and governmental prominence, and into the courts, the best of the academies, political offices, media channels, entertainment arenas, and of course the local communities and causes we live in and around. And certainly, there's discipleship in family life, shown here under the missional arena.

Finally, let's discuss the invite-and-making aspect of our discipling journey. This can be uncomfortable. Some of us are tangled up in guilt that originates in the false premise that all believers are to be evangelists. That's bad theology, unsupportable in Scripture. What we're called to be is inviters, rather than sales people. What does that look like? It looks like using your God-given placement in work, recreation, family, and social spaces to be seen, and to be inviting—sometimes verbally so—with the result that people come and check out who Christ is. Remember our concept from the last chapter—inviting often best begins by listening to the other person's story. Perhaps for months. But the time will come when they want to be invited to come and to see.

Some disciples are gifted evangelists and can jump on the soapbox and proclaim the call to come to Christ in any situation. Some are apologists who are designed to interact at some intellectual level with skeptics and scoffers. But all of us, as disciples, can say, "Come and evaluate Christ." In one way or the other, all of us are given that charge, and use gifts that apply to the people we resonate with and serve with. It may be a simple encounter where someone needs help, and you're there. It may be a two-year walk alongside a hardened scoffer who can't stand religious people. It might be your own kid, or your boss. Jesus makes plain that you'll be made ready when the time comes. Just don't duck out. Be a disciple—be the inviter, be the billboard.

Think of your life as a disciple like a portfolio manager. You have a variety of people in your life, some scoffers, others skeptics, and some true servants and followers of Christ. I have a relationship with a friend in Britain that started out in the first five minutes we knew each other with his declaration of "Oh God! You're one of THOSE people." (A long list of negatives followed.) I really enjoy him. Among many subjects and conversations, he still shudders at Christianity. But he says that the idea of real hope is his "*Kryptonite question*" because he has no hope at all for the future. He has accepted my invite to check hope out. He wants to understand the reason for my hope. What an invitation! Here's a post from him in the Fall, 2021:

"it seems unfair to ask me to engage in looking at a book that lacks historical authentication and is full of contradictions and downright nastiness and has been used to justify so much bloodshed, suffering and destruction."

My greatest challenge as a disciple here is getting past the apologetic triggers that distract staying focused on being his friend, and understanding his own worldview first.

Your duty as a disciple is to get ready, to learn and gain confidence, then invite and serve these varied and fascinating people, in inviting them into your life and perhaps, in meeting Christ. It can be as simple as "Come check out the evidence with me," or, "Come to church with me" (although you should develop into a disciple who can hold his own in basic thinking about Christ, rather than pawning people off on your church staff).

When people ask, or when people attack you, invite them. Find your voice and invite. Some of you will say "That's not my personality." Get over it. The Boss said that this is a common challenge for all of us as disciples. Get on board. Go. Invite. Learn how to befriend and relate so they might hang around and encounter Christ. The Holy Spirit takes it from there. The "it," by the way, may still be you as the fuller encounter, the voice, hands, and feet on that encounter. This is not exploiting people. If you really believe Jesus is the resurrected Christ, the Way, Truth and Life, and you are his follower, the kindest and noblest thing you can possibly do for people is to make that introduction.

Perpetually Committed and Ongoing

Larry Thompson retired in 2016 after twenty-two years as senior pastor of First Baptist Church in Fort Lauderdale, Florida. Except he didn't retire. Larry started Faith Foundry, a ministry to disciple discipling leaders.[105] Larry's program invites young pastors into a year-long discipling walk beside him and other leaders, with field trips, weekly interaction, and visits onsite with each pastor in their home setting. It can be a grueling pace. And the trauma, drama, and sure-don't-wanna that pastors dream of leaving behind did not go away for Larry. It multiplied! Now he's walking alongside multiple church situations, coaching, counseling, encouraging. Even pastors need mentors. In a word, it's discipling. You never retire in serving as a disciple of Christ.

When I was in my forties I dreamed of a time when I'd have made enough money to be able to quit work and do whatever I wanted to do. I have friends who retired at thirty-five, forty, forty-five as successful entrepreneurs, and who began playing, traveling, whatever they liked. Then I noticed something. Almost all those early retirees were unhappy. Their worlds often became small and tedious. They were bored. Restless. Some volunteered in the strangest places to escape their golden retirement years. Some died young. It seemed that living their American dream was becoming a nightmare. Listening to many of these friends, I realized something that recurred across their lives: they came to dread the loss of meaning that endless pleasure and leisure exacts in exchange for its presence.

Solomon's words in Ecclesiastes come to mind about who we are, what we're here for, and how work, pleasure, and purpose are gifts from God, but not ends in themselves.

A disciple must instinctively grasp the fact that purpose, meaning, and destiny are possible only in Christ. And that a disciple never retires from learning, going, teaming, and making disciples for all their days. Anything else that promises some kind of meaning is rubbish. "Grow or die," to use a business term, applies to development as a disciple. Discipleship is an ongoing growing and serving, not a once-filled stagnant pond.

My physics friends tell me that photons have energy and velocity, but no mass. In other words, you can measure them only by forward motion, not by their weight. This is a nice illustration for the life of a disciple. Our lives as disciples are worthless unless they're in motion—learning and serving. The résumé is worthless, to stop and look back and say, "I did this and that." That's to convert discipleship into what the Boy Scouts used to joke about—a bladeless knife without a handle.

Maybe over the years you've bumped into believers who say something like this: "I don't want to study all this Bible stuff. I accepted Jesus, and I believe him. I'm good." Shirking continuous development is wrong-headed. Discipleship is sanctification, lived out. None of us live perfect lives with these holy demands (Matthew 5:20; Mark 10:26–27). The point is that to be a disciple means continuous forward spiritual motion. Jesus makes this same concept plain in John 8:31–32—"If you hold to my teaching, you are really my disciples. Then you will know the truth, and the truth will set you free." This is often termed *sanctification*, or growth in knowledge and actions and temperament in serving Christ.

No single word defines a perfect Christian. Disciples walked out on their faith and disappointed Jesus and screwed up along with Paul. Saints are unsaintly. Christians recant. Believers stop believing. When things get hot—as they did under the Roman persecutions—disciples may deny or run. Scripture even speaks of disciples who simply "no longer followed [Jesus]" (John 6:66). The thief crucified on the cross next to Jesus started out that morning as a scoffer, only to end as a disciple, blessed with the promise of sharing paradise that day with Jesus himself (Matthew 27; Mark 15; Luke 23:39–43).

A seeker with wealth and power was a follower of Jesus, and Mark tells us that Jesus "loved" this aristocrat—only to have that same follower walk off, disappointed with his encounter with Christ (Matthew 19:16–22; Mark 10:17–22; Luke 18:18–23).

John talked about those who were "among us" at first, following, but who left never to return (1 John 2:19).

One disciple, Judas, became a traitor (Luke 22). Meanwhile the disciple that Jesus called "the Rock" denied Jesus three times to the rabble-rousers—but then he morphed into the world-renowned apostle Peter (Matthew 26:69–75; Luke 22:54–62). Scoffer Saul stopped rocking the believers with real rocks, and becomes the earth-shattering apostle Paul (Acts 8:1–3; 9:1–28). We can even see that John and the other disciples, through most of the Gospel accounts, were not believers until the empty tomb became their Aha! moment. They're better described before the resurrection as groupies (Luke 24:11; John 6:64).

John 20 clinches the point about the disciples' change in belief. When they truly "saw and believed" (not meaning optically got it, but rather *episteusen*, to comprehend and see in their core beliefs) the empty tomb and the evacuated burial clothes, those disciples believed that Jesus was resurrected—that he was alive, after having come to save and call followers to himself. They believed Jesus was God (John 20:8). Disciples first, then believers. But nobody following Jesus was perfect. No matter what label they owned.

The "ship" ending in the word discipleship—what does that mean? It does not occur in Scripture at all. The word *disciple*? Yes. *Discipleship*? No. But the -ship is attached to several older English words to connote something useful here. *Ship*, as a suffix, points to the process of conforming more or developing in some specific way. The "ship" at the end is drawn from the old English word *scipe*, inferring improving upon or the development of something, like an apprentice.[106] Said another way, shaping something, as in citizenship, partnership, mentorship, apprenticeship. "Ship" points to sustaining something, and gaining more in that thing.

The practical disciple lives a life of being "discipleshipped" (I cobbled that word up). Discipleship through all of life. So there's no "arrived" in this life of discipleship, no earthly form of completed sanctification. Ongoing sanctification is always the process. That, too, must be part of the Christian culture—that believers never stop developing, never stop learning, always pursuing the holy for the rest of their life: "Forgetting what is behind and straining toward what is ahead, I press on toward the goal to win the prize for which God has called me heavenward in Christ Jesus" (Philippians 3:13–14).

And so, disciples integrate these things into their lives in following the risen Christ as his people:

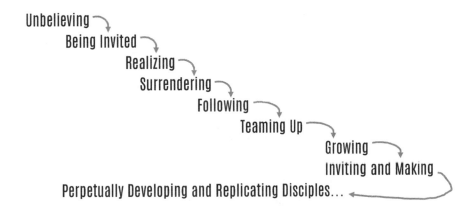

Unbelieving
 Being Invited
  Realizing
   Surrendering
    Following
     Teaming Up
      Growing
       Inviting and Making
Perpetually Developing and Replicating Disciples...

They're disciples who begin as unbelievers, but who evaluate, surrender, follow, team, and go. Living and walking with each other such that in all these spheres, in all these roles, the chances to share the hope within us are teamed and teeming with disciples in markets, academies, government, the arts, and the media.

Well, you've stuck it out this far getting a sense of the what is and the what ought to be. You deserve some practical steps to consider in deciding whether or not you'll take on the dilemma. With a disciple's attributes in hand, we've arrived at the trailhead out of the dilemma, the path forward for leaders.

If Christ is indeed Lord,
He must be Lord of all of life—in spiritual matters of course,
but just as much across the whole spectrum of life,
including intellectual matters and the areas of culture, law, and government.

Francis Schaeffer, *The Great Evangelical Disaster*

11

A Path Forward: The Mission and Culture

Geneﾠral Motors, Tesla, Ford and the other car companies don't build cars. Not one. Boeing does not build airplanes, and Apple does not manufacture iPads and iPhones. What those companies do (by way of their leaders) is articulate a specific mission, build a reinforcing culture to execute on that mission, and organize so people can make the things the companies want to produce. The leaders keep the mission front and center, and keep the community's culture reinforcing that mission. Their "disciples" go make more manufacturing disciples—the intent being to develop person-to-person capability and motivation.

Whether you're unwinding the dilemma for one or two people seeking to be disciples, or trying to restructure a mega church, some principles are common in the quest. To get an organization—whether another person, a church or a parachurch movement or even a small group—to be a discipling culture, three things must function: leadership, mission, and culture.

"If Christ is indeed Lord, He must be Lord of all of life—in spiritual matters of course, but just as much across the whole spectrum of life, including intellectual matters and the areas of culture, law, and government." Said Francis Schaeffer.[107] A willing and engaged leadership is the first necessity, and those leaders must intentionally promote the other two key functions in their organization—the mission and the culture, just as Christ taught disciplers to disciple. What specifically is leadership to do? First, we must understand mission. If your group uses terms like *vision* or *purpose* or *values*, and you wonder how they differ from a mission or culture—well, that's a good question. The terms do get mixed up and confused. Here's a way to think about them: Vision describes a future outcome, in broad terms. It describes how we'll know that we've completed a mission. As a metaphor, vision is the pinnacle of the very high mountain you want to climb.

Here's a biblical example of vision:

> I am the LORD, and I will bring you out from under the burdens of the Egyptians, and I will deliver you from slavery to them, and I will redeem you with an outstretched arm and with great acts of judgment. I will take you to be my people, and I will be your God, and you shall know that I am the LORD your God, who has brought you out from under the burdens of the Egyptians. I will bring you into the land that I swore to give to Abraham, to Isaac, and to Jacob. I will give it to you for a possession. I am the LORD. (Exodus 6:6–8 ESV)

That's big vision. Forward looking, game-changing, describing a future-specific amazing outcome.

Mission is the path to achieve that vision. God gave Moses a mission: Divest yourselves from Egypt, Inc. Relocate your corporate headquarters from the Nile to Canaan, and finance your exit with crowd-funding. And do not get wobbly when the Egyptian Chairman has a hostile reaction when you pitch the divestment deal (Exodus 3:16–22). That's a mission.

Purpose is usually a cleverly selected alt word lacking shape or form, but making up for all that by being vague. Sometimes purpose is used as vision. Sometimes it's a substitute for mission. Sometimes purpose is strategy. Likewise, the term *values* take on a life of its own, declaring a group to be this way or think that way, though rarely are values really applied in a day to day setting after the marketing offsite crafts them and loads them on their website.

For the sake of clarity, *mission* and *culture* will be the main terms used in this book.

Later we'll get very specific on what the mission of Christian community is and is not. Let's start here by focusing on the broader meaning of mission.

Mission is not a statement. It's not core values, nor is it supposed to be a management secret. So what is it? Mission is the method an organization uses to get to its vision. Everything an organization does or does not do should pass through the filter of the mission. The commonplace and the crisis—all are under subjection to the mission.

Most organizations publish a mission statement as an obligatory exercise, and they park it on a website or shelf, perhaps dusting it off for a look annually in some planning session, or perhaps never giving it the light of day again. In its proper place, however, mission is the *daily definition of performance for an organization*, and the standard bearer for its culture. Here's where the business world and the Christian community differ: Christians don't have to develop their mission. It's already sorted out. God already gave it to us. Before you blow a fuse, hear me out. Each individual Christian has differing strategies (talents, circumstances, motivations, aspirations) to accomplish the mission. But we all have the same mission. The same mission, prepackaged for us by Christ.

Culture is the lived-out manifestation of mission, in that culture is the way things are done. Culture represents the expectations, the guardrails, and the propulsion that will energize people, who then go execute the mission. Culture prompts its people to behave one way, and it discourages them from behaving otherwise. It motivates people to do certain things and avoid doing others. Think of the mission's values and the strategies coming to life. Culture draws a line in the sand to demand "This is who we are." Culture encourages people to be bold and take risks to accomplish the things of the mission, and to encourage others to do the same. Culture requires that its people pass on that culture to other people—the new people that come in.

Clear Examples, Good and Bad

Let's go deeper and look in on the Bible's examples of good and bad leaders, and of mission and cultures done well or not so well.

Be on the lookout for two kinds of leadership. One kind includes caretakers who sustain and support what they've inherited, be it good or bad. The second kind includes change agents who expect people to change from what has been, and to embrace the leader's expectations—in effect changing the old culture into the new.

There are plenty of examples like these throughout Scripture and history. Use the ones mentioned here to get a grasp of how important leadership, mission, and culture are in the life of a community of God.

A caretaker tolerating a bad culture—that was Jotham, who was also a good king of Judah, doing right in God's sight. But his impact on the perverse culture was nil.

> He did what was right in the eyes of the LORD, just as his father Uzziah had done, but unlike him he did not enter the temple of the LORD. The people, however, continued their corrupt practices. (2 Chronicles 27:2)

A bad change agent driving a bad culture would be Rehoboam, Solomon's son. He does *Breaking Bad*[108] early on in his reign, and his influence as king takes the culture of Israel down with him:

> After Rehoboam's position as king was established and he had become strong, he and *all Israel with him* abandoned the law of the LORD. (2 Chronicles 12:1)

Fortunately, we also have biblical examples of change agents who sought the Lord with all their hearts and changed their cultures too. One is Jehoiada, a priest:

> Jehoiada then made a covenant that he, the people and the king would be the LORD's people. All the people went to the temple of Baal and tore it down. They smashed the altars and idols and killed Mattan the priest of Baal in front of the altars. (2 Chronicles 23:16 17)

Another change agent is King Hezekiah. His leadership meant changing the culture with its pernicious and widespread practices of the Asherah poles and high place idolatries throughout Judah:

> The entire assembly of Judah rejoiced, along with the priests and Levites and all who had assembled from Israel, including the foreigners who had come from Israel and also those who resided in Judah. There was great joy in Jerusalem, for since the days of Solomon son of David king of Israel there had been nothing like this in Jerusalem. The priests and the Levites stood to bless the people, and God heard them, for their prayer reached heaven, his holy dwelling place. When all this had ended, the Israelites who were there went out to the towns of Judah, smashed the sacred stones and cut down the Asherah poles. They destroyed the high places and the altars throughout Judah and Benjamin and in Ephraim and Manasseh. (2 Chronicles 30:25–31:1)

There's nothing wrong with being a caretaker leader, if the community is right in its mission. But if it isn't, change is necessary, which is not caretaking. That can require not only winsome communication, but conflict, confrontation and gracious yet change-driven diplomacy. This kind of leadership isn't well understood by many in business nor in the Christian community. In my experience, people serve where their strengths exist—for example most church leaders excel in in communication, counseling, in sermons, teaching, setting up groups, hosting mission trips, putting on programs and events. In the business world all that is often categorized under continuing personnel education and development, something you want groups doing together. Things continued after individuals have been qualified and trained at doing what they do. But group continuing education is not personal mentoring, which is necessary in discipleship.

Equipping disciples is much more granular than those larger-scale activities and programs. The culture of discipling is one of personal relationships involving disciples, who are able and willing to serve outside the church operations, relating individually to believers and the people outside.

So we must think of culture change as altering the spiritual DNA of modern believers. DNA is the biological operating system that drives everything an organism does, how it functions, and how it interacts with its environment. For example, DNA calls the shots on red hair, brown eyes, and so on. Once the DNA is in place, the features and functions are internally driven and natural, not tacked-on external cosmetics.

We could alter the metaphor slightly and talk of digital DNA, like the iOS or Android operating software driving so many of our personal gadgets. Digital DNA, once burned into memory, has a specific function: to allow a human to interact with a phone, and to keep things in the phone running smoothly. Similarly, an organization's culture—its DNA—causes its people to behave in a certain way with each other, and in doing whatever they do individually, in good and bad times, in big and small settings, it runs as it was trained to run.

Some of the social DNA in a church can be seen as people gather on a Sunday to laugh, hug, talk, worship. Contrast that social DNA with the one that exists when you're in a tax audit at the IRS. Not so warm and fuzzy, eh? Organizational DNA is culture. Everything in the institution's system—from a worldview to particulars on daily operations and ethics—is driven by the DNA.

DNA is what leadership makes it, or allows it to become by default. This is an important point. Leaders must establish that DNA, and splice it into people's lives for it to take hold. You can't simply hand out a book saying, "Here's what we expect our culture to be," and hope for much from it.

In troubled companies, I often encounter an executive team or board wanting "the answers" to fix their problems. There's frequently an expectation that the right people have a canned package that will get things done. It's a fantasy—that there's a premixed instafix. In reality, the disciple dilemma has been compounded by much time, national and local social norms, and the individual Christian community with their unique people and their attitudes and skillsets and personalities and their own traditions.

In a lot of organizations, a culture is a default of time and circumstances, rather than intentional splicing into people's thinking and acting. Typically there are lectures, values, and vision—and posters and slogans and programs. But DNA is much deeper than surface stuff. To change a life requires time and personal relationship. That means someone walking alongside a disciple so they will understand the new culture and own it themselves. It becomes a disciple's DNA—their personal ownership of a way of thinking and acting, or else it won't last long.

An illustration: My wife will come to me and say, "I need you to vacuum and dust the den. And do a good job please—guests are coming tomorrow." I fall to her feet and pledge my immediate service. Then I go dust. Three or four minutes later, I'm back in my office working on this book draft as she walks in. "Did you dust and vacuum?" she asks. "I did," I reply, expecting overwhelming joy and praise for my exceptional work. "Well, if you did, you missed [significant list here], and you dorked up the [complete furniture inventory recited], so we're both going back in there to teach you to do your job right!" Her expectations were clear in her mind when she originally told me to do a good job. She knew what she wanted. I heard the words. I tried to employ my skills of setting very low standards and then failing to meet them. Clearly she had expectations that exceeded my standards. To get the culture spliced into my way of life, she graciously volunteers to stand over me and coach what and how I do my thing on the motes accumulating all over our materialism. And she helps me get better, to think ahead, to improve my game. She uses personal time and relationship to help me change my DNA of shoddy cleaning into something much more in line with her standards. I am being discipled through a close relationship built on love.

Trying to establish discipleship in a community can be much like that. Recently in a Colorado church, I listened to a sermon encouraging everyone there to be a disciple. It was a really good sermon, right in line with other solid preaching and books I've heard over the years: 1) You need to grow in spiritual maturity. 2) You need to become strong and capable in your faith. 3) You need to have relationships with other Christians. 4) You need to make disciples. 5) Go do that. Now, I'd agree that this is all directionally correct and good. We can point to Bible passages to support that exegetically. Yet this was where I began to realize that most efforts in discipling are like that checklist of five things to do. It's aspirational, and it's biblically correct. But it isn't relational, so that the programming, the DNA, can take hold in someone's individual life. A sermon is rarely going to get that done.

Leaders can easily be tempted to do discipleship top-down. A talk, a video, a study, a series, a group, and the people will get it. Except they won't. How do medical schools develop doctors in the complexities of the human body, diagnostics, and treatment options? Lectures and study are a part of that, but life-on-life discipling of doctors, and practicing life as doctors, is the critical part of making great practitioners, internists, surgeons, pathologists, and the like. Lectures, YouTube, and seminars are not the singular answer for doctors, nor for disciples. I want a surgeon inside my chest cavity who's done more than listen to lectures or watch a video. I want a dedicated learner who's worked beside a great cardiovascular mentor!

A mission to produce disciples means close relationship, tailored to individual development, working on strengths and weaknesses, just as in producing excellent doctors. It must be disciples raising up disciples and living closely alongside peers as disciples. There aren't enough leaders to do that well. No leader can mentor more than two or three people. The path forward is a community of disciples building disciples, relationally, closely, daily.

Getting down to practical things on culture change means leaders structuring the background of administration and metrics and management so that disciples can be predominant in the foreground, learning, practicing, participating and then making others like that. Even if it's only a few people, motivated to connect with one or two other people in daily living, in serving Christ transparently, honestly and openly. Culture change must begin somewhere within your community. Many may choose not to come along. It is rare to be able to invoke a mass change. You may have a very influential pastor or person in your church and many go right along. It's more likely to be slow, incremental, messy but multiplying change. It is likely that you, as a leader, will have to pair such disciples alongside each other in the early years. If there's any sense of a programmatic element to this, that's where it will be: leaders have to encourage people to team up, to mentor up, and how to keep that process going organically into the future will need a routine and constant shoring up. It is pairs (or perhaps trios) living through good and bad together, ups and downs, joys and sorrows. And doing those relationships in a way where those pairings also connect and relate with other people who don't at first understand any of this. And of course, disciples maturing and being sent out to do all that over again and again with others. How will you bring that kind of culture to life in your community?

Many people have lived all their lives as converts, believing that accepting Jesus as Savior, plus a bit of morality, makes all good and right. Stephen Neill, a twentieth-century Scottish Anglican missionary and Oxford scholar, wrote of this challenge:

> When the convert has come in from a wholly non-Christian background, he brings with him, however sincere he may be, a heathen imagination, a non-Christian set of standards that can only very gradually be reduced to order.[109]

Today we can see that Neill's "wholly non-Christian" background would be seen as a step up compared to modern Christian religion. The syncretism, the blending of so many mythologies, opinions, distortions, and social compromises, will seduce even faithful churchgoers today to buy in to bizarre and useless theological disorder. It's a disorder that relational discipling is specifically equipped to address. And it's specifically addressed through a mission and culture of biblical, relational, intimate discipling that leaders structure and execute on.

Leaders owe their people that kind of organization. And while teaching and encouragement can come from a pulpit, they must not only come from a pulpit, but rather come alive in relationships.

The disorder obviously comes when the external world lures conformity of thought and action inside Christian community with the current political, sexual, and social agendas of societies. But faulty and disorderly thinking comes also from the traditions and rejections of biblical community coming from inside the walls as well. Neither the external nor the internal faults can coexist alongside a discipling mission and culture.

Back to our questions: How do leaders establish such mission and such culture? This is where intentional design matters. The dilemma promotes membership and produces low-yield discipleship. This does not mean membership should go away. But it does mean designing an organization where membership takes a back seat to the mission of discipling, and that the things that are traditional measures of Christian community must become subservient to that preeminent mission of discipling.

The lesser traveled road for Christ's mission is the one in which leaders will design, implement, and operate the mission, and expect their people to come along on the journey. That kind of leadership and culture deployment has tremendous impact on people's responses to mission and culture. We cannot miss this point. Organizations either define and focus on Christ's mission of discipling, or the circumstances and complexities of life will wash out that mission, just as it did in the third and fourth centuries. Such corporate business chokes out the priorities. Then the mission falls, because organizations off-mission will prioritize themselves, and not the mission. Culture becomes the muscle memory of whatever priorities hold sway, whatever it may be.

How do leaders get started? It can seem strange at first. You may be used to having sufficient influence to just push it out there for everyone to hear and promise to pick up on. Or, you may think you have little or no leverage to get anyone to do anything at all. Practically, it will begin with you having your own grasp of what's off and on in discipleship among your people.

Then you have to have others. This isn't a solo event. It will require a lot of communication. Mission and culture development cannot be some Freemasonry secret society where only the elite know what's going on, or only the leaders have the grasp. Nor is it a popular opinion poll seeking group happiness, or mimicking the competitor moves that other churches are making.

Leaders often try to outsource discipling by throwing people together in plausible gatherings. Every organization, commercial or Christian, has to figure out how to get the DNA into their people, and that means close relationships, not lectures or town halls. In business, the proven failure route is that herd community we mentioned earlier, "just throw them together, and hope it sticks." The excellent businesses put like-minded people together in pairs or very small groups, so that newcomers can closely understand the "why" and see the "how" up close. The trick is, they've found a way to convince the people that this culture is the better way. And people buy in. Newcomers can observe and emulate other people further along who "get it." Not just a weekly coffee hour, but in daily relationships. That's relational discipling. That's mission focus. That's culture reinforcement.

Be mindful how you approach your duty. If your church is more than, say, six months old, pay close attention to the perils of abrupt mission change, lest there be war. And likewise, playing Moses—coming down from the mountain with the new ten cultural commandments chiseled out in HTML—is not a good method of change either. Change in these areas of mission and culture require winsome, humble, over-communicated interaction and servanthood by leadership.

Getting Started

Let's be realistic. A formulaic approach assumes everybody in each body of believers is the same. But they're not. Don't trust your perceptions. Get out of the leader's huddle and talk to people, especially ones you rarely talk with, or those you disagree with.

How many should you talk to? I don't know. Some groups could work with one or two influential people and have a comprehensive understanding of the challenges in a culture change. Others will need to canvass a lot of people to understand how their people see discipleship and how they would react to change if it were necessary. In either case, leaders need to see where culture is now—the muscle memory, so to speak, of behavior and obedience and pursuit of Christ, and where the emotional energy and objections are pointed in their people.

In business one of the most important parts of strategic planning is to get a grip on the environment the business operates in. Things like what the organization is good at, and what it's weak or even incompetent in doing. This is an internal look at the culture of a business. It takes work—there are no canned programs or seminars that prepackage answers in those sorts of things. You put experienced people together, energetic and influential people, roll up your sleeves and get to work finding out how to improve the business. Culture change in a Christian community is no different in getting at this kind of understanding. You have to ask good questions and ask them to the right people to see the culture and decide where to go from here. Below, I'm offering you a series of thinking projects for getting to know your people and culture better. Whatever else you do, don't assume you already know them well! Unless you've recently put in time doing work like the things listed below, you don't really know. As a leader, ask questions, then listen very well. Here are twelve examples of starting a journey in culture change toward discipleship:

1. *Know your organization.* Do any of the traditions we've described touch a nerve? If you think about the traditions, symptoms, and people issues in the disciple dilemma, what among them might exist here? Do your people think anything is amiss in the mission and health of your people—or, as in the Barna study, is all seemingly well? And is there energy and enthusiasm toward biblical discipleship—or programmatic, cause-based or works-based member discipleship? Is there apathy, or disdain? Asked another way, do significant numbers of people among you demonstrate Christ's model of one-on-few discipleship and development, or is it off their radar? How will your people react to a change in the relationships and community described in *The Disciple Dilemma*?

2. *Know the true mission, cold.* Be able to explain it so anybody hearing knows you're excited about it, and can explain simply why it matters and why it benefits them.

3. *Map out how power and influence really flow toward or away from your mission.* Who are the formal and informal leaders? How do decisions get made? How would these formal and informal leaders help or hinder a discipleship mission and culture? Who else should come along with you to ensure your success in this change journey?

4. *Pitch the deal.* Make a concise and clear case to a very few influence leaders about the disciple dilemma, the mission, the culture needed, and the ideas and strategies to get from here to there. The idea of "the deal pitch" is useful here. In investment banking, a popular presentation challenge is having a crisp thirty-second presentation, a five-minute talk, and a one-hour interactive version for full question and answer. The thirty-sec-

ond version is known as "the elevator speech"—the time you'd have with an influential person while riding between floors on an elevator.

5. *Be ready and grateful for objections and pushback.* What are the key questions and issues to be ready for? You will get them. Ranging from "This will never fly with these people" to "I am excited, how do I get to help?" Are all your formal leaders in favor of a discipling mission? How do you know? What do the informal leaders think about this? Who really needs to be convinced so that most people come along with this change?

6. *Deal with disagreements early on in the process.* If leaders are opposed or deeply divided over discussions around mission, culture, or strategy, what should you do to build strong consensus in leadership, before going more public with a change?

7. *Learn from the past.* Are there divisive issues or emotionally charged moments from the past that might be instructive here?

8. *Engage your people with real unity and determination of purpose.* Will your leaders demonstrate a united position to address the disciple dilemma? Can key leaders explain the changes ahead, and in such a way that people understand it? Do all the leaders agree enthusiastically with this work? Can secondary and informal leaders explain and endorse this? In the way leaders express their enthusiasm, does it feel like a mafia shakedown—or are people genuinely drawn in to the process?

9. *After the questions above have been scrimmaged among a few and consensus holds, interact with lots of groups and secondary leaders.* By this point you'll need to have brief and coherent answers to the questions you've already encountered. Here's one that you'll face: What's the best way to explain and illustrate the transition from group-structured discipling efforts to true relational discipling? How could you test out this kind of discipleship to spark interest and chatter? How can you avoid productionizing it?

10. *Invest in a gradual and winsome revelation about what's needed and what ought to be done.* You live in a personal autonomy society. Everyone has thoughts. Everyone wants things to go their way, and to have their personal influence shaping things. Even if your governance model for significant change issues like this led centrally, perhaps by groups like elders or

trustees, how will you offer, socialize, and decompress this kind of (often radical) change with your people so they feel included in the development and journey? How could you establish a high repetition learn-and-lead process to help the willing people embed this mission and journey as their own? This is likely the most crucial change issue for culture change.

11. *Plan the launch.* How will an initial cadre of biblically modeled disciples be launched? Discipling will ultimately come down to very small groupings, such as pairs or triplets perhaps. Do you already have a prototype for this somewhere? How will you replicate this initial venture into new relationships? Which influential people in your community will advocate this and help motivate change among others? Will discipling relationships be primarily vocational or missional in the early launch? Age-tiered or based on spiritual maturity? How will the mentors in these relationships coach and teach and live out making disciples? How will they educate up-and-coming disciples? How and when will they send their charges out? How does this relational discipleship become the culture of your individual people?

12. *Recognize that this culture journey will affect "normal."* People will sense the change that's underway. What was normal may be threatened. For example, how will disciples actually participate further in the official worship life of the church, versus the old ways? How does this culture shift affect deeply held brand, programs, staffing, and physical facilities? As a new mission rolls out, where is power lost or shuffled around among legacy members?

Think through—and write out—what you're learning from other people in these explorations. Stack the pluses and minuses in changing a mission and your culture from big to small. Start a second list that anticipates where issues will become emotional or tense, even if the issue itself isn't all that significant. Be sure to bring in a few dissenters, and graciously back-and-forth things. Do you understand dissenters well enough to explain their position? Would they agree that you understand them? Then bring in more dissenters. Keep your cool, learn how they think and why. Avoid the temptation to run to the congregation for a quick vote. Talk less. Listen much more. Walk the process slowly. When you've got all the assenters amped and articulate, and all the dissenters agree that you understand them, then town-hall the findings. Don't lecture. Listen.

How long will this journey to become a discipling culture take? Years, most likely. But over the months, things get better, faster. Momentum will build. Discipleship is community change, and community change is a long game. More akin to growing a pine tree than microwaving popcorn.

If you have, say, two hundred to five hundred members, you could reasonably spend six months getting the disciple dilemma assessed and developing a go-forward mission. That's just at the leadership end of things. We're not suggesting a flourishing disciple-making culture alive and well at the end of those six months. Rather, it will take six months to get a rough change plan ready to talk about. Six months assumes someone is good at setting objectives and keeping others on task in wrestling through the church's specific situation, in working the leadership dynamics, and in developing a clear presentation of what needs to occur and when. Tripling that timeline is not at all unrealistic for less rigorous efforts.

And remember that time is not the friend of conviction. Time kills deals. Kills intentional change. Time induces unwanted and unexpected changes. Start and don't languish.

The heavy lifting of going to the people begins when a rough plan is worthy of the light of day in front of influencers. With strong leadership support and a very crisp plan, another six months will likely be needed to bring these key stakeholders alongside your leaders. The influence people must come along to start warming up the waters, so to speak, for impending change. Opinions need to be aired. Conflicts resolved. Didn't-think-of-that will need to be sorted through. And surprises like a pandemic and internal problems can ambush progress as well.

After about a year, the mission may then be ready to start showcasing in teaching, preaching, and small-grouping these ideas with your secondary and informal leaders—the people with broader connections who can back you up and say, "We have to do this, and here's why." If you're faithful to keep moving this culture process downfield, if you have excellent exposition of Christ's model for life with intimate relational discipling, then somewhere around twelve to eighteen months, your first pioneering discipleship relations will emerge, and the multiplication journey is underway.

Be ready for fallout. Yet equally, be ready for discipling growth! Some people aren't going to be happy. Be prepared for that. Some will walk in saying they heard what you're up to and they want to buy in. Be ready for them too. *Some* here may mean one percent or ten percent or fifty percent of people coming or going.

Giving people lots of time to hear, understand, wrestle, object, fume, or grasp is so important. If you've been awake in the book up until now, you can appreciate that cultural friction is the heat generated from traditions being changed. It's friction from years of people expecting concierge religious services. From years of people content with low standards of discipleship, and unwilling to endure change. There'll be pushback from people thinking the traditions are right and good, just as they are. And there will be blowback from people who think they have no obligation to be present in discipling to win in spiritual accolades.

Some people will walk off. Be ready with your influence people to help. Meet and talk. Listen. Understand. Be humble. Don't argue. Show people—by listening, pausing, and thinking, graciously and lovingly— why being a disciple is better than being a spectator. Bring their friends in on the conversations. Help them, using their love languages and familiar means of understanding to realize discipling is what our gathered family in Christ must do. And that we want them to come along because they're important to us, and to the future generations of disciples.

You might experience ten walk-offs for every one walk-on. But in time, making disciples will drive multiplying gains.

This discipleship mission will deal with size as a symptom, not a marketing plan. Having a discipling mission and its complementing culture means disciples are giving up the spectator life, going and doing discipling in community, business, the arts, media, government, schools, and the world as surrendered followers of the Most-High God. This is exactly what disciples are supposed to do. Being salt and winsome light, inviting scoffers, skeptics, and spectators everywhere they go to come check this thing out.

It all begins with you leading them. It would be great if we could jot down a punch list to get this going. But there's not one. You're going to have to work for it.

First the leadership has to decide if the disciple dilemma is real or not. If so, is leadership prepared for the time and cost of change? That's when mission and culture has to be sorted out. Then comes the part about embedding that culture in your Christian community to serve that mission, live out that culture. That kind of change begins with two things: 1) the consensus of a few people committing to accept and pursue that mission, and 2) strategy—the whats and hows that bring the mission to life in the hearts of your people. That's all you need to do. Easy enough, right?

Perhaps you still think you need a playbook. Why can't we have a playbook? Think of it this way: Asking for a program or recipe to make disciples, with your group's unique issues and unique collection of people, is equivalent to asking, "How do we mass-produce an individualized custom dream house for every person in the United States that costs us little or nothing to build?" Do you see? You cannot make up such a checklist, because all gatherings and people are different. Culture is designed to bring them together, but you begin with many people, far apart. The only path forward is to know your people well, to bring them to the mission, and together to change the culture. And it will take time and effort and will cost leadership to get this going.

Personal discipling is not a program-driven outcome. It's personal growth that flourishes as leaders deploy mission, using their unique people, through a winsome culture of discipling.

Strategy and Issues

Let's talk about some likely headwinds you'll encounter:
- How do we explain the balance in our church community between welcoming anyone who wants to be here versus insisting on discipleship as we define it?

- What will we do with people who just want to attend? Nothing? Something? For how long?
- Will our community naturally (or deliberately) be uncomfortable for people who reject our disciple-making ethos?
- How do we transition from a group-centric or programmatic process to one-on-one or one-on-few discipling clusters? How do relationships come to be formed? How do we lead in matching up people? Who leads this? How do we deal with flame-outs in pairings?
- Be ready for surprises. How will the church deal with moral crises and problems in disciple clusters?
- Think about discipling structures. Does an effective discipleship culture mean a mentor in the development of every disciple? Do we expect pastors and staff to have a viable mentor in their lives? To have viable peer disciples in their lives? What constitutes "good" and "not good" in such a structure?
- How loose or tight are our standards for mentoring disciples? How long do we expect to spend in making a new disciple? Is anyone ever done being discipled?
- How will we equip people to be confident in making disciples? What happens if people refuse to go and make?
- Do we expect disciples to have the skills to engage with nonbelievers relationally? In connecting with people, how do we break through the social stereotype of disciples as sales calls, or people as a mere ministry project?
- In a discipling church, what roles should disciples play that are different from traditional staff-dominated programs?
- How do we mentor disciples—coaching and assisting them—to take the hope that is in them and confidently impact community, business, the arts, media, government, and schools?
- How do we pair up people in ways that integrate lives? Not weekly accountability interrogations, but real life and camaraderie as disciples tackle life together where God has placed both of them.

- As disciples make disciples, and new disciples develop, will you hold tightly to them as your own intellectual property? Or do you expect disciples to learn here, then go elsewhere to bring disciple-making to others?
- How do we manage the tension between close relationships in discipling and the size of a church?
- How will we know we're getting where our mission tells us to go with individuals? With our church?
- How will we equip and support staff and leadership to sustain this culture without being held to some false standard of performance or bureaucracy?

Questions like these—along with the far deeper and richer literature of discipleship handed down to us over the years—are useful strategic conversations. But leaders can rarely turn to a recipe book or program to right their organizations. It's no less true in discipling. In implementing a community of discipleship, don't fear the absence of a template. Embrace the richness of God's biblical roadmap, and follow the Holy Spirit's guidance along the journey. Use counsel and Scripture to help see your way forward to unwind any of the dilemma you encounter, and to develop a community of robust disciples.

We've emphasized here that leaders are charged with conceptualizing and publishing the DNA of their organization, which is mission, culture, and strategy. But that's only half of the job. For a leader, the fuller duty is to be among people, persuading, reasoning, and making the case for that new DNA. Leaders must live as examples, relationally, graciously. Then people will want to come along. They'll be touched by leaders who want to take them on a mission, and they'll want to endorse and conform to a culture. That means they then become the next generation of disciples, who attract more people and who make more disciples (2 Timothy 2:2).

Mission and culture, clearly delivered to the people, lived out in personal example and in persuasive interaction—that's leadership's true role in Christian community.

Some Christians have a concern with strategy, thinking it's another Wall Street technique that doesn't belong among believers. In fact, it's a biblical concept. Examples of biblical strategy—literally, God's planning—can be seen in Micah 4, Psalm 40, Nehemiah 2, and Jeremiah 51, where the Hebrew words literally mean "the way to get to a place," or "purpose, a thought device, creating outcomes." In other words, if the organization's strategy is biblically faithful, we should see discipling emerge among individuals like Peter, as we considered his life in the previous chapter.

That's what we want strategy to do. Strategies take us toward the mission and reinforce the right culture as desired outcomes on "the factory floor," to use manufacturing terminology. In this case, those factory floor outcomes are all about making disciples. The leaders own the responsibility of defining mission, culture, and strategy, and following through as leaders to ensure culture, through biblical strategy, comes alive in people, which results in the desired outcome—equipped and "going outbound" disciples. We want people to willingly and eagerly come along with us in that mission, culture, and strategy. Leaders need to provide the equipment, virtual or real, that ensures the forming of relationships. We need to equip people to expect, enjoy, and seek out those kinds of relationships. Then discipleship, as Christ designed it, will truly produce disciples.

Strategy exists to achieve a mission, yet it too thrives or dives because of a culture. Culture supports mission, motivates people to pursue mission. Mission drives real discipleship. People may well encounter the call of discipleship through the traditional things, like worship, fellowship, ministries, sermons and programs. Those are all truly useful tools for disciples. Yet those tools are not the effective cause for discipleship any more than a hammer causes house construction. Discipling can initiate in classes and sermons and simple community group events, but such group events are not the model we were given by Christ. Is a strategy different from a program? Here the answer is absolutely yes. There are no programs to make disciples—only disciples making disciples.

So here's a test question to see if you're still awake. How does a church or organization bring about the action steps we outlined in chapter 10 about Peter's discipling journey (Invited, Realizing, Surrendering, Following, Teaming)?

The answer: It doesn't. Those steps are people with people, as disciples. The organization and its leaders build the greenhouse for those steps to rise up, a discipleship greenhouse.

By the way, business often launches culture change from the inside out, which means small groups of people (not necessarily an entire organization) pilot the new way, to get started on a bigger cultural journey. Most corporations cannot simply tell their employees, "Everybody be different tomorrow!" and expect any meaningful results. It's no different in Christian community. There's so much inertia in the ways things have always been done that no memo, website, or lecture can reverse that. Instead, launch a small invasion force to beachhead what you want to accomplish in plain view of all. You'll be amazed to see how much traction can be gained by showing winsome success for others to emulate.

I want to repeat that this book is not a diatribe against size. Any size can have various strengths and advantages for a congregation, from talent to financial resources to ministries to significant influence in communities. But larger size creates relationship complexity, smaller size creates resource complexity, and complexity is very tough sledding for discipleship.

After a certain size threshold, the church's pastors can't know everybody. Tim Keller, the founding pastor of Redeemer Presbyterian, a megachurch in Manhattan, made this observation: "Generally speaking, when a church gets over a thousand people it becomes much more bureaucratic."[110] Keller's broader context was that at some point in church growth, leaders are drawn away from relational community and specialize into silos and compartments to oversee their parts of a big organization. This is disconnection from the very basis of discipleship—those people in the pews. That kind of size disconnection can be overcome in a culture, but it's tricky. And very easy to lose sight of relationship and discipleship in the bulk and bustle of a big church.

For some churches, size is a justifier to abandon the personal and close relationships as an operating system: "We're too big for that, let the small groups handle it." Several megachurch strategies have little to point to in biblical discipleship, but they do an excellent job tracking the number of small groups as a plausible alternate. Clear strategy, wrong mission. It can be just as difficult for small churches and house churches too, since time and distractions know no boundaries to diffuse and distract discipleship. Intentional design toward relationships based on small and tightly connected lives is the basis for a discipleship community. This design and sustainment of that interaction is the primary role, value, and calling of the leader, to drive the organization toward these relational ties in discipling people.

Discipleship as culture means (winsomely) a place where people see and agree that this is how discipleship should flourish—in personal relationships. The traditions insist that churches don't have time or enough staff or enough competent people in the pews to do all that. The result is that they don't. The traditional method is to have a few sermons on discipleship, market the small groups as the true way to make disciples develop, keep building staff, facilities, and programs, then wait for discipleship to slosh up.

In this chapter, we've asked you three questions:

- Are you as leaders together and all-in to change the discipling culture?
- Do your people understand and agree there is a dilemma?
- How will your community go about recovering person-to-person discipleship?

Change is never easy. Do we stay with the old ways and just tolerate the symptoms facing us, or take a big risk and start to make a difference? Just like discipleship, this change in a community could be costly to leaders. Just like discipleship, change is necessary for most Christian communities in discipling. Unlike discipleship, not everyone is called to be a change leader like you. So it's time for us to answer the question: "Why has God put me here, now?"

Discipleship is not just a ministry in the church.
It's the ministry of the church.
Eric Geiger

Many people are coming to Christ,
but the purpose is to present everyone mature before Christ.
If we train them to fish from the sea but don't prepare them to cook,
it is not good.
Ameen, "Gospel Light in Darfur"

12

The True Mission of a Christian Community

O ur focus doesn't get much clearer than statements like this one from by Eric Geiger: "Discipleship is not just a ministry in the church. It's *the* ministry of the church."[111]

When you meet "Lynn" you're struck by her joy, her peace and her quiet surrendered life to Christ. Yet her life story is more like something out of "Raiders of the Lost Ark". Lynn (not her real name) is a disciple maker, out where discipleship is toughest, out where most of us would whimper and run away. Lynn built long-term discipling relationships alongside people brought up as atheists, or passionate Muslims. You see, Lynn was an overseas missionary. Deep into communist Asia and Muslim Africa. Living in the hinterlands, far afield from the civilized urban assignments many married missionary couples and their families sought out. But even retired stateside today, Lynn isn't retired. She's still at it. She's an ESL coach. A seminary graduate, Lynn can be found teaching, or just as often, serving at her church's book store. She recorded videos to keep her discipling protégés underway during the pandemic lockdowns. A Bible study leader. A friend who walks beside friends, even when the friends don't know they're friends. Lynn and her roommate were prime examples of disciples supporting one another in hostile territory as wingmen/wing-women. Disciples shoring one another up to run the race every day, stand firm every day, to be there for each other when needed, and to endure in tough circumstances. The story becomes more interesting. Lynn's Asian roommate was a national—her life was at risk serving Christ in her very own country! But they did not shrink from the race. Lynn and her friends were pursuing the mission for all followers of Christ, as they mentored other believers, and were mentored by other believers. And they discipled nonbelievers. A lot of them walked off on her, or ratted her out. That's the way it is in real life. But she stayed at it, inviting people to meet Christ. Inviting other believers to greater maturity in their faith. And inviting people to "come and see" if they were nonbelievers. This kind of disci-pling does not get much press. One reason, of course, is that people in these hostile settings could die, or be expelled or imprisoned. But another reason is that many mission organizations don't measure discipling. They want converts. Conversions sell enthusiasm, raise support. Discipleship? Well, our Sunday morning enthusiasm gauges suggest that talking about discipleship with the congregation is only about 1.3 percent more inter-esting than watching paint dry on a wall. Like dry paint, discipleship is nice, colorful stories and all, but people don't want to get too stuck on it. After all, enthusiasm and headcount is the traditional way isn't it? But it's not Christ's way.

We've toured traditions, consequences, and challenges impeding dis-cipleship in Western Christianity. Now we turn to defining the specific mission of a Christian community. I want to try to convince you that the mission of a Christian community is different from the individual mission for the individual Christian. These are the crucial distinctions at the epi-center of the disciple dilemma: a community creates a discipling culture, while the individuals provide personal discipling.

In the business world, a commercial mission is a rickety thing. It relies on the whims and circumstances of a society, and it survives only as long as the passion or technology is an "in" thing. Kodak's mission was camera film. Remember film-based photography? Founded in 1888, Eastman Kodak was *the* name for photographic film, and a Wall Street darling through most of the twentieth century. But by the 1990s, Kodak's primary mission—producing photo-quality chemicals and film—was in its death throes. The digital photography era had arrived. Cell phone cameras would further erode Kodak's reason for being. Bankruptcy came in 2012. Twenty-three years from financially fantastic to fiduciary fatality. Things in the commercial markets can change that fast. And things can change that fast in a society based on whims and tastes. Think about social reversals in less than a decade toward sexuality, statues, history and even Dr. Suess.

Fortunately, the mission of Christ doesn't wobble from temporal feelings, fads, and fashions. And even though Christianity's single and ultimate mission may be worded differently from one gathering of believers to the next, it's a common and unchanging mission. Let the provocative notion of a single, common mission for all communities of Christ soak in a moment as we tee up some other issues.

How does a mission affect day-to-day operations? Ask most leaders how their mission drives the planning, design, organization, and decision-making for their group, and you usually get puzzled looks. You might think that if you have something that represents the utmost of importance for an institution, then every decision you make—the way you organize, the way you operate, everything you plan and do—would center on that. But that's not the norm in leadership thinking. Yet mission is that center point. Everything else dependent on mission.

To offer an illustration, you camp out overnight on a small knoll by a river. You wake up during the night with thunderstorms raging. When dawn arrives you crawl out of the tent to see the river rising and the knoll cut off as an island from the shoreline. You're trapped by the rising torrent all around you. The mission, obviously, is getting across the floodwaters to safety. That mission drives everything else you do. What to take. What to leave behind. Where to try to cross. When to cross. How to cross. How to maximize success. Mission focus should be no different in a business, or in your community of believers.

You might be tempted to presume that in planning and running an organization, savvy leaders will ask questions like "How does this decision fit into our mission?" or, "How does this action affect or enhance mission success?" But that wouldn't be the norm in most businesses. Mission is rarely part of decision-making. Usually, a mission is crafted, tediously, once upon a time in an offsite meeting somewhere, then entrusted to a dusty shelf to languish. Few mission statements see the light of day when leaders deal with the daily questions and myriad issues assaulting an organization. In other words, for most organizations the mission statement is a collection of sentimental words to be able to say you have it—a mission, a purpose. The real mission, what an organization actually exists for, is something else altogether.

Using mission-centric decision-making about a business or a Christian community can be a frustrating experience for leaders. The reason is that mission seems far afield from the mundane or urgent things that need to be dealt with right now. And because a mission and real life seem so detached from one another, so impractically distant, it's frustrating to try to have life and mission actually coexist. So, we park the mission on a shelf, then fight and wrestle with the usual stuff and surprises of daily life apart from our so-called mission.

Having a live and embedded mission—one that's widely understood, and that drives the ministries and administration—is key to discipleship. Because mission is what you actually do, not what you wrote down. It's what you actually use daily, for decision making, what sorts what you'll accomplish. That's the real mission you're on. If what you do is plan and act without the mission as the guardrails, then the mission becomes whatever burns hottest at any given time. True mission is the pivot point around the what and why that the organization exists. Everything else is subjugated (pivots around) the mission. What do you say? Is your organization about your stated mission, or is your stated mission an understated virtue signal? Let's say it another way.

A mission might be stated in a single sentence, or in lengthy paragraphs, or simply verbal. But it must convey the reason the organization exists. And it must tell us how to think about everything happening around it. There are clear and coherent missions, and there are fuzzy ones. Let's look at a few:

- *Space X:* SpaceX designs, manufactures, and launches the world's most advanced rockets and spacecraft.
- *The U.S. Marine Corp:* The U.S. Marines are forward deployed to win our nation's battles swiftly and aggressively in times of crisis.
- *Harvard University:* To educate the citizens and citizen-leaders for our society.

Space X has people, factories, policies to build and operate spaceships, but all those serve the mission. Harvard University has buildings, professors, students, seminars, books, classes, and occasionally a football team. Yet they all serve the mission. The Marines storm beaches, parachute from planes, guard embassies, recruit people, blow things up, scuba-dive, and fly jets and helicopters around and wish they could be as cool as the Air Force. (Ok, ok, Marines don't actually think about the Air Force like that...)

Each mission statement defines what an organization does, how it makes choices, and how it sorts out things. All those activities and assets and accomplishments for Space X, the Marines and Harvard are serving their mission. People often clutter up a mission with other things, like strategies and values, all of which have their place, but which are actually subsets, submitting to a mission. Sometimes mission statements aren't even mission statements. Some are wishy-washy word grab-bags. Or virtue brags. Bad missions attempt to say whatever resonates (today) with whatever their target audience wants now, instead of defining a purpose driving an organization. Here are some real-world examples of mission statements (excluding their names) that are not mission statements:

- (X) is a global, independent campaigning organization that uses peaceful protest and creative communication to expose global environmental problems and promote solutions that are essential to a green and peaceful future.

- (Y's) primary objective is to manufacture (widgets) that maximize long-term stockholder value, while adhering to the laws of the jurisdictions in which it operates and at all times observing the highest ethical standards.
- (Z) exists to help spiritual seekers become transformed believers, and demonstrate the love and compassion of Christ to the world, through humanitarian works and social engagement.

The problem with these three mission statements is that they're about *how* to do whatever it is they do. Which we can't clearly discern on their face. Some of this wording may be attempts to look good, some may be aspirational. But all these words fit in under a mission, as values or goals or the like, but they are not *the* mission. Strategic consultants in a mission do-over for these three organizations might suggests revamps like this:

- X exists to stop global pollution and wars.
- Y's mission is to make money producing widgets that do what widgets do.
- Z's mission is to make people want to be Christians, worldwide.

Now we get back to the common mission of disciples versus the organization's mission to flourish discipleship:

1. The mission is clearly stated by Christ for individuals, and also for his global Church, but the two are sides of a coin—not identical sides, but adjoined sides.
2. Everything else—preaching, social causes, ministries, going into the world—emerges from, thrives from, and succeeds by pursuing the two sides of that common mission.

Mission looking inward for the individual as it's defined by Christ is about surrender, sanctification, worship and service to God (Matthew 22:37–38). And the outward result of that mission is a following disciple, and making disciples (Matthew 28:19; John 13:34). How does that fit into Christian community? Here is where the individual mission and the community mission can be seen as two sides of the same coin. Let's begin with the organization.

Christian communities—whether churches or parachurch groups—are like greenhouses for discipleship. The role of the greenhouse? A place where what is sown flourishes. Such flourishing occurs no matter the external environment outside the greenhouse, because a greenhouse allows plants to thrive in winter or summer, through drought, floods, or otherwise.

Greenhouses don't make plants, and church/parachurch organizations don't make disciples. But the mission of Christian community is like a greenhouse: to allow the work of the people sowing and harvesting to flourish and grow. The greenhouse as an institution is not doing the planting. The organization is not doing the cultivating. The role of greenhouse leaders is not the plants themselves. Leaders oversee, support, and organize. There are people in the greenhouse who are sowers and waterers and tenders and harvesters for all that. Institutions are the structure, the tools, the nurturing greenhouse environment to flourish what's being grown. Leaders build environments (mission and culture) for disciples to connect with people, to be discipled, and to go out to make disciples.

A greenhouse can produce a variety of plants. A church can support a variety of people: vocationally diverse, diverse in giftedness, in various ages, diverse in ethnicities, diverse in affinity to travel, diverse in personalities and skills and so on. The job of the greenhouse leaders is to build and sustain an environment so people can come in and produce plants. Leaders support sowers, waterers, tenders, and harvesters on their mission to do what they each do in the greenhouse. And so it is with discipleship among God's many churches and organizations.

The mission of leaders is to ensure the structure (a.k.a. culture) exists that allows people to engage in real discipleship, to want to develop as disciples, and to go and make more disciples. There's no opting out as disciples, because a spiritual greenhouse by way of its nature (culture) motivates discipleship.

The disciples that emerge in that culture are spiritually strong, mature, able to handle life because they have been developed well in relationships and living side by side. Relationships exist not by the programs but by the relational momentum of the culture driving a passion to have relational discipling. Disciples are coached up and practiced to be living and serving in vocational, civic, and missional spheres alongside other vibrant disciples. Disciples in this culture gain confidence and willingness to engage in communities, ministries, business, government, the arts, media, the academies. Some even go to foreign nations, as various disciples are called to do. Disciples have diverse vocational gifts. They are evangelists, preachers, teachers, parents, politicians—and on it goes in their daily lives. All are disciples. All are living as disciples because leaders design, build, and sustain a mission and culture in that discipling greenhouse that makes for healthy disciples.

There will always be stylistic differences, theological variations, unique attributes, multiple sizes, and novel focus areas for different Christian communities. Yet there's one mission for all of them—to flourish discipling. And the other side of that coin—that each of us will be and will aim to make disciples.

Many approaches can be taken to serve a mission, based on the people, resources and circumstances available. A book describing such varieties of church mission style is *Discipleshift*[112]. The book outlines four different mission models used by churches today:

- *Educational:* The focus in this kind of church is knowledge and orthodoxy. Attracting new people, deploying people to mission service, and relationships are secondary efforts.
- *Attractional:* The objective here is attracting seekers to encounter Christ, in essence, *orthopathos*. Theology, mission service, and relationships are secondary.
- *Missional:* The aim in this style is deploying Christians to serve— *orthopraxis*. Theological development, attracting people, and deep relationships are secondary.

- *House:* The objective here is deep relationship and interaction with everyone. Theology, headcount growth, and sending people into mission service are secondary.

Each style can serve the mission of making disciples. And each style can fail miserably at discipling if the style itself becomes the mission. Which brings the primary solution to the disciple dilemma back to leaders: it's the role of leadership to define and implement a mission and culture, then stay focused on it.

The preparation for this book included a survey of small, medium, and large churches across North America—five hundred in all, including the top one hundred North American megachurches. This included sampling mission statements among many of those churches. The mission trends encountered were surprising in their consistency. For example, here are the ten most popular "wordcloud" phrases in church mission statements that we reviewed:

1. Preaching Jesus Christ to all the world (22 percent)
2. Being followers of Jesus (17 percent)
3. Being a community of God's people (13 percent)
4. Helping people believe (13 percent)
5. Showing love (11 percent)
6. A fellowship of like-minded people (10 percent)
7. Going out on mission trips with the gospel (10 percent)
8. Receiving the Holy Spirit (6 percent)
9. Teaching people about Christianity (4 percent)
10. Being free (4 percent)

Very few statements had just one focus phrase in their mission. Most had "multiple missions"—this plus that plus more. Trying to cover multiple fronts is a common flaw in mission statements, by the way. Not surprisingly, about half of these church mission statements focus on getting the gospel out. Surprisingly, only about 20 percent of the statements have anything to say about being a follower or disciple, usually mentioned as a subset of other priorities. Only two of the surveyed churches actually declared discipleship as their sole mission. That would be less than half a percent of the population survey. About fifty percent of these churches made it a point to call for justice, prospering, ministries, outreach, global missions, reconciliation, and so on into their mission statements.

So, not surprisingly, it seems many churches make evangelism their mission. While many contemporary and progressive churches might demur on this point, most Protestant communities agree that communicating the gospel is important, hoping that scoffers and skeptics might become curious and commit themselves to Jesus Christ. But to stop at "born again" is to abandon the crop just as the seed emerges, with the thorns choking and the hungry birds flying around. We cannot say evangelism, nor conversion is the ultimate goal for Christians relating with other people. We don't harvest at a sprouting. We must not fall into an evangelism trap where people "just" get saved. To bluntly challenge that old tradition, salvation is not the mission of the body of Christ. Making disciples is.

There are many important elements of ministry that have a rightful and prominent place in Christ's service. But we have to focus on the ultimate mission to make the other things sustainable. And we have to avoid putting the penultimate—the lesser things—ahead of the mission.

So here we are. After all the words of Jesus are brought to bear, his repeatedly blunt statements in the Gospels to "follow me" are shown to be the framework that everything in Christianity hangs on. It's the mission of the people of Christ: "Therefore *go and make disciples* of all nations, baptizing them in the name of the Father and of the Son and of the Holy Spirit, and teaching them to obey everything I have commanded you" (Matthew 28:19–20, emphasis added). This is Jesus's specific mission. The Great Commission.

Consider that all other causes and efforts depend on one thing: disciples. If other things are given a higher place in the stack, they dilute discipling. Interestingly, discipling as the mission amplifies all other things we cherish in serving Christ. Therefore, disciples must be the aimpoint—

must be the mission. Leadership's duty is then to make that mission plain to people, and to sustain it. Do you see? Get to it in discipleship and you get the rest of the things that are important aspects we think of in the churches and Christian community. Go for the other things first and put discipleship second and both collapse with time. And we are seeing that demise today.

By making discipleship its sole mission, your community will still gather and commune, and worship, honor, serve, and obey God. But spectatorship must die off. Membership, long a certificate of bona fides in lieu of discipleship in many churches, must be changed. The change means a commitment to discipleship ahead of all else. This mission will mean people developing as disciples, as Jesus defined disciples, and it must result in people actually wanting to be disciples. Everything else—causes of justice, reconciliation, ministry, music, mission trips, management, facilities, and all the other wonderful things a church must do—will properly flow from the mission of developing disciples, disciples who pursue the things of God with a whole heart.

Discipleship is the mission.

Repeating from the earlier chapters, it's so important that leaders not confuse programs and activities for discipleship. It's vital that people do not become lulled into thinking that being involved plus membership equals discipleship. It's paramount to organize so that discipleship is one-on-one, deep-life relationships, ongoing in the context of Christ's teaching and example. Discipleship as the mission is a game changer for a church, its community, its people, and the game changer for the world.

The implications in restoring the mission of biblical discipleship are huge, and they directly and favorably impact the many problems we've covered here. Discipleship is the counterforce to spiritual languishing, which the scholars call *acedia*. Discipleship is the counterforce to lack of commitment, lack of confidence, failure to endure, passivity, despair, inability to give a reason for the hope within.

Think also of the societal implications by way of Christ's disciples: unity in and between his people; lifting the oppressed; hope coming to life for friends, relatives, races, neighbors. In other words, show the love as disciples, then watch the world come knocking.

Think of disciples dying to their own agendas (in many parts of the world today physically dying as they live disciples' lives) and living in joyful, humble submission to their localities and among varied ethnicities. Ponder the impact of real disciples influencing the trajectory of business, the arts, media, government, universities, nations. Consider the game-changing implications from disciples who really want people to ask them about their weird behavior and strange beliefs. Disciples who are ready to answer. These disciples will be a powerful force, in the right sense of power, to address and attract a society of anger, power, fear, and loathing. Disciples of Christ do that with the saltiness that so many in Western Christianity have misplaced while seeking to be hip and relevant, or just comfortable.

And there's the universal solvent Christ spoke of, delivered by disciples: agape love. Regular people living humbly, talking confidently. And when asked, giving people their story. So that people will come and see for themselves, coming to a place where they encounter Christ.

Consider just one of those traits—unity. What a missing virtue in our world! It's irrational to hope that such unity will emerge in people outside the body of Christ through politics, causes, and counter-campaigns. Unity will not emerge socially until it shows its sacrificial reality inside the body of Christ, in the lives of disciples. Why? Unity without agape is just a temporal farce. Disciples know unity doesn't result from membership, nor from education or doctrines or dogma. Unity comes from disciples who have died to their own selves because Another's love—which they did not deserve—has reunited them to the Lord God Almighty.

Spectators stay in the seats in the coliseum, cheering for their own single brand and team. Unity comes as disciples step into the ring and kneel over the disenfranchised, the canceled, the infirm, oppressed, widowed, orphaned, and alien.

Unity among churches results from disciples, and not from niche church members, not from Christian Nationalism nor agendas seeking growth, prosperity, or globe-trotting. Unity seeks neither brands nor power. Where there's no common mission, there will be competition, as each church or denomination or movement claims to be the best or the only way, the sole truth, or the coolest life. And the remainder get caricatured as knock-offs or wannabes.

If the mission is discipleship, then things like size and uniqueness will naturally emerge to serve the mission. Mission in Christ does not thrive in business processes, market identity, or reactions to circumstantial challenges. It thrives by being on the offense, as disciple-makers. And when true disciples serve Christ, more disciples join the journey.

In true discipleship, there is unity. Real unity takes root across Christianity, then infects the broader society it dwells in. A disciple's unity is diverse unity. It does not seek specialized political or societal norms and fads to serve Christ. Disciples die to that kind of agenda. And this kind of discipling unity, found in a common mission, is not unnoticed by the passers-by.

Paul prayed this for the church at Ephesus:

> I keep asking that the God of our Lord Jesus Christ, the glorious Father, may give you the Spirit of wisdom and revelation, so that you may know him better. I pray that the eyes of your heart may be enlightened in order that you may know the hope to which he has called you, the riches of his glorious inheritance in his holy people. (Ephesians 1:17–18)

Leaders are to enable that mission that produces organizations where disciples rise up like this. Everything else that's of Christ will come forth when disciples do what they do: humbly seizing the day while shrewdly understanding the world, winsomely relating to people, staying committed to live or die in serving Christ.

I was listening to a sermon by a megachurch pastor recently. The pastor was speaking to adults in a Sunday worship service: "I like all of you, but I'm not interested in you, frankly. What I want to do is get to your kids. Get them saved. Get them into our university to make them solid believers. Because if we can get them in our school, we can get them going for God, and we can change the world." I disagree strongly. Program-them-and-they-will-succeed approaches are rare successes. Converted Christians with lots of facts are not disciples. They're knowledgeable people. But about sixty percent of those knowledgeable people will ditch the facts to hide in socially virtuous causes anyway. The remaining minority, thinking that facts are the solution got to that false answer by a sermon advertising facts instead of truth.

The duty of Christian leaders is not to make converts with killer arguments. The duty is to organize, encourage, and coach, so disciples will go make other disciples in the mold established by Christ. The plain and direct edict from Christ is for leaders to promote the mission. One where individual disciples understand that their destiny is to die first, serve second, love greatly, expect turbulence, and keep pressing ahead while making more disciples. It's a relationship life.

We aren't to avoid learning. The Bible directs us all as disciples to get understanding throughout life (Proverbs 4:5–9). And to walk through life together. Disciples together in real life. Not solo with witty answers. Serving with a whole heart in ministry, medicine, information technology, physics, history, the arts, engineering, business, civil and military service, banking, baking, and baby-rearing, alongside other disciples. And learning the heart-art of relating to people, sincerely and fully, so as to make disciples. So that more people will ask, follow, and check it all out.

As a business strategist, I can tell you something that's true for Christianity just as much as it is for corporations: If your leaders are not on a quest to make people personally absorb and own the real mission, no amount of training and education will ever be enough. Nor will there ever be enough time to do any better with the next generation as the last generation abandons what was not theirs anyway.

A mission is a singular thing, and all else is subservient to it. If discipleship is not the mission of Christian community, discipleship will not flourish, and something else will. Without disciples, the other attributes will not flourish long, as the non-disciples cut and run when things get tough.

Leaders are charged with owning and sustaining the mission of their organization. Mission has to be right, or the organization falters.

Time is not a friend in starting to right mission in a community. As was said before, most often, time is the enemy of conviction. Delay and extended pause have always been accomplices in organizational demise. The main instigator though, is a wrong mission, a distracted mission.

The clock is ticking. You're one of the leaders. This is your time as a servant of the Most-High God in leading people toward their mission. Toward their destiny. Here. Now. It's your duty.

Leaders must be able to spot roadblocks and clear them.
John White, *Excellence in Leadership*

Miss Dugan, will you send someone in here
who can distinguish right from wrong?
cartoon in *The New Yorker*

13

The Duty of Leaders

Corporate turnarounds are rarely without turmoil, never a slam-dunk outcome. In some situations, it's pandemonium at the outset. Morale is down, sales sliding, investors nervous, and maybe production is all hosed up. But there's another script. An all-too-common one. A situation where most folks inside the organization don't think anything is wrong. Morale is fine. The financial statements look okay. Customers seem happy. What's to worry? But in the distance, there's a problem. The bridge to long-term success is out. It could be product obsolescence, or a shift in the market, some global event, or even a pandemic. Yet few people on the company bus are noticing the chasm they're hurtling toward. What was a seemingly unending ride on the too cool road is the last mile. Bear Stearns, Enron, HealthSouth, and WorldCom were examples of this everything-is-great-then-it's-not tradition. The traditions that led to trouble in companies like that are little different from the traditions troubling discipleship today. Yet for most organizations the old ways and traditions mask the underlying effects, allowing the symptoms to keep replicating while few notice the effects around them. Sometimes the leaders came for the pay, the perks and power, and wrecked things. Sometimes good people inherited tough circumstances and it became bedlam. My best experiences in turnarounds have been working alongside other leaders who could come out of the trappings status and set their minds and strategy on righting things.

Walter Truett Anderson, an American political scientist and social psychologist speaks about leaders in modern society: "Today our leaders are stars, not heroes. Stars are surrounded by crowds, heroes walk alone. Stars consult focus groups. Heroes consult their conscience."[113] If Anderson got that right, then Mike and Dwala are heroes. Both seminary graduates, they could have taken a traditional path into mid-to-large denominational ministries in trendy cities, leading studies, preaching, teaching, and other pastoral stuff. But they didn't follow that path. They walked away from the glamor, off the traditional grid into discipling people in remote and difficult places. Places out in the hinterlands where even the country bishops we talked about in chapter 5 would fear to tread. Not only were Mike and Dwala personal disciplers, they were change agents for leaders in Christian community. Mike and Dwala were circuit-riding ministers where there were no circuit-riding ministers. Out where pastors' salaries could not be paid. Or would not be paid. Out where people viewed pastors as hired help to do the dirty work that hired help gets hired for: hospital trips, funerals, and preaching. Out where small churches were struggling to survive as their people died off, or just moved away. Out where changes like discipleship were not so welcome. You don't take this kind of role for the money and applause. Most pastors, if one was there at all, just preached and did their chores—the stuff hired help does. But Mike and Dwala didn't conform. Some folks didn't like them too much. Some of those came around. Others walked away. But Mike and Dwala lived alongside people, shared their family with people, got relational. They befriended and they coached. They taught Christ. You see, these two leaders, Mike and Dwala, are disciplers who just happen to be seminary graduates. It's not often glamorous, this kind of discipling. But it is the real world of doing Christ's business, going, meeting, making disciples of all races, styles, and types. The reason Mike and Dwala are heroes to me is that they did not try to go big—they went faithful. They went to their calling rather than traditional missions of growth or power. They were leaders changing communities, which allows leaders in those Christian communities to foster discipling, and believers to nurture relationships, the seedbed of discipling. That's what leaders do for discipleship.

A turnaround in the general Christian community for disciples is urgently needed. Leaders will need to take the driver's seat, to intentionally turn discipleship around. We literally, like the old New Yorker cartoon, need to find "someone in here who can tell the difference between right and wrong"[114], between ought and is, between today's now and the biblical mandate. Discipleship's mission must reroute from the traditions diverting Christian community away from Christ's route. As John White says of leaders, they must "spot roadblocks and clear them"[115] on the better route.

With any gathering of people, whether commercial or Christian, the key to being on the right road means following the right map, the right plan, one where mission, culture, and their strategy drive on the right route. Getting the map and following the route falls to leaders.

The obstacles (courtesy of the traditions) in our metaphorical road are these:

- radical individualism, where personal rights and desires eclipse surrender as disciples
- the false notion that groups, clericalism and concierge programs produce disciples
- the pursuit of metrics, management, brands, causes, growth, and conversionism

It's time for us to put some big bold words in the text, to say "Here's the crux of things going forward". **Culture is how your people think and act, by their own motivation, when you aren't around. That's your leadership challenge to shape. A biblical culture, based on Christ's mission, is the embedded passion of disciples to shake off the traditions, to surrender, to team up and live life together (one-on-very-few) living as disciples, making disciples in the middle of the watching world.**

Leaders are God's catalysts and caretakers of mission and its culture. In chapter 8 we cited a number of Old Testament leaders, good and bad for their impact on their culture and their people. The New Testament likewise gives us examples for leaders (e.g. 1 Corinthians 1:10; Galatians 1:6; 4:14; 1 Timothy 1:3; Titus 1:5; Hebrews 13:17; 1 Peter 5:1; Revelation 3:2). Where leadership defaults, degrades or demurs on taking that responsibility, deviations begin to emerge. Leadership deviations off mission are very destructive to discipleship.

Leaders exist to establish, embed, and continuously true up mission and culture. A mission without a culture is like a car without wheels—it may be a great car, but it's unable to fulfill its purpose. On the other hand, culture without a mission is a whimsy, and it will drift with circumstances and crises instead of holding to purpose. Both mission and culture are dependent on the stewardship of leaders to keep them focused and operating. Therefore, let's explore leadership's integrated use of mission, culture, and strategy, and warned away from their antithesis, which is traditionalism.

Getting impatient? Getting antsy to have the solution laid out, right now? Several pastors reading the early draft of this book told me, "I agree there's a problem, but, you aren't telling me what to do. I want to know what I'm supposed to do about all this." Some solutions were suggested to help with the puzzle:

- Reset the membership criteria…you have to do these (disciple-ish) things to belong
- Make current members participate in certain activities, or else
- Limit the size of a congregation to less than [fill in the blank]
- Increase the size of the congregation and resources to [fill in the blank]
- Up the number of leaders so the ratio of leaders to members is lower
- More education will set things right
- Mandatory pairings to force discipleship are what we need

It's tempting to want to do something tangible, right now. "Do this, solve that" is modern instant fix theory. We know we're missing something, so this plus that equals a win. But there's actually no formula common to any two culture changes. Think of it like this: If one person wants to go on a journey to Detroit starting in California, the route and requirements will be much different from someone else starting in New Jersey. The same route doesn't work for different groups in different places. Don't let the absence of a mythical panacea discourage you. Any biblical answer to the disciple dilemma in your Christian community integrates the unique understanding and employment of your people, place, and circumstances. It isn't tasks or training, it's culture change. There are likely few do-this-get-that options. Yet we *can* think about guiding principles for leaders in culture change, which, combined with your specific (local) circumstances, will get you on your way.

Now we could start at the less complex end of the spectrum, where you're relating to, maybe even leading, say, just one person. Maybe they're a skeptic, scoffer or a passionate servant of Christ. If that's the case, much of the organizational detail in this chapter won't do you much good. Yet. But it will surface soon enough.

One-on-one discipling is much more about relating day-in-day-out to an individual than creating culture and mission awareness for the many. But your time is coming. You're going to have to pass being a disciple on to that other one, then they on to others. If your mission doesn't transmit with the discipling relationship, then a tradition just snuck back in, a tradition of catch-and-release. Disciples have to transmit the mission and the cultural DNA to be disciples and make disciples or the old ways win. So it becomes problematic to opt-out of mission and culture in discipling, even in very small groupings.

Some basic principles for any leaders considering deep cultural change:
1. Leaders aligned in recasting what an organization or community's compelling mission is
2. Leaders investing the time and energy to deeply understand the environment and social dynamics of their people and the times

3. Reconstructing a culture that pulls people toward the mission
4. Bringing people into the process to learn more, to become invested in, and to plot the strategy (path) to keep culture on mission
5. Embedding and continuing to reinforce and sustain mission, culture, and strategy into the muscle memory of your people and organization

When an organization arrives at number 5, some actionable things will emerge, but not as the solution. They're part of the journey. It might be a very small core of believers teaming up to start a life-alongside discipling journey, or it might be a massive sea state change by nearly all in a congregation to break from solo Christianity and begin that deeper biblical followership. I don't know where you'll wind up as a community—but it has to begin with leaders designing the path, and living it out personally before a culture change can begin that sticks.

Here are some strategic questions I've used before with Christian organizations and with businesses in approaching change with people:

- How's your commitment? Are you as a leader all in?
  —Do you believe the dilemma is real and needs to change?
  —Are you willing to make a mission change?
  —Are you prepared for the cost of that change?
  —Are you prepared for how long the change will take?
- Are you prepared to clearly explain the problem?
  —How to explain the trends and symptoms underfoot in Christian communities?
  —Explaining the gap between what is, and what ought to be?
  —Unaddressed, where does the disciple dilemma take Christian community?
- Are you ready to make a concise and clear case for a new culture?
  —How to explain a compelling view of a "disciple's life," understandable to people using traits such as the ones outlined in chapter 11?

—Can you paint the picture in words that describes how you want your community to look in the years ahead, to reinforce discipleship and to sustain itself?

—How will your traditional activities and events be reconfigured as disciple-centric systems and programs? Said another way, how will your Christian community's life become a gateway toward discipling instead of a gate blocking it?

—What motivates people to be disciples in your community?

—What about the believers who refuse to come along?

—Why is this good for your community? The individual? The nation? The world?

—How will you team up people? How will you keep the community from reverting back to programs and staff-centrism?

- How effective is your communication?

—In pursuing this, what best serves your community in avoiding rumors and mythologies?

—Who needs to know first? Who are the influence leaders?

—How will you communicate this so people "get it" and can explain your thinking and your approach?

—How will you set up communications as two-way events versus one-way diktats?

- Are you ready for the objections?

—Who are the dissenters and informal leaders?

—Do you understand what your dissenters think, fear, and hope, and do you understand them so well that you can explain their view, so that they'll agree that you understand their point of view?

—How will you describe the new culture? What will be expected for participants? How will you grandfather in the uncooperative, or help them move on? For new arrivals, what will be the set expectations going forward?

—Who might be marginalized, or fear their status loss in this kind of change?

- Will you prove you believe in this discipling mission by personally living it out?
  —Will you live it as an individual, not simply as the leader architecting a change?
  —Will you constantly talk it up (in personal talk, not just sermons), so that people start completing your sentences? Will you do this again and again?
  —As a leader, will you step out of management and get into relating to people, explaining to many people what's up?
- How will the new normal phase in?
  —How will you ensure that everyone understands the new way?
  —How will you ensure that people generally don't feel exploited or coerced?
  —How long will the new expectations be simple aspirations? When will they become soft requirements? When will they become hard requirements?
  —What means will you faithfully apply to induce conformity to the culture?
  —What will you do about rebels?

Don't be intimidated. Great things come with a cost. Assess the dilemma. Prepare for the journey. Be able to talk through these kinds of issues graciously and compellingly. That's the beginning of a culture change. And if the disciple dilemma is to be addressed, change is necessary.

Real culture change pushes people, and it pressures people toward conformity. It can be intimidating if handled wrongly. Highly motivating if handled well. Think of the cancel culture today in keeping divergent opinions tamped down—that's an enforcement and shame culture model. On the motivational end, think of a pro sports team where players want to conform to the plan, to the process, and the commitments, because with it, they all win.

Culture is ultimately personal, and it's real life in real time. Culture affects my experience, my satisfaction, my authenticity, and my identity, right now.

Culture change is where the skirmishes will erupt. Culture change is where my personal life and your leadership either cooperate or crash.

A lot of organizations dictate the tone and content of their culture and demand conformity. Think of the military for example. In contrast, many organizations don't actually have a culture. They're captive to an outside force that directs their thinking and doing. The once autonomous city of Hong Kong is in such a place today, where Beijing tells the people of Hong Kong what they will say, do, think, like and believe—what their culture is to be. This is not the way for Christ's community.

All cultures have deep roots, and fear will emerge in disturbances. Any change attempted will take conviction, planning, tenacity, energy, and endurance to minimize panic or fear. And in Christian community it will require much grace and your own humble and meek displays of unity. Most leaders give up on culture change. It's long, draining, and risky work to bring a people around to a new way of thinking. For Moses, there was a forty-year struggle to change people. He died on that journey. Of the forty kings who succeeded David and Solomon in ruling over the Old Testament people of Israel, only sixteen were listed as "good" in the eyes of the Lord. Yet only three, arguably, were truly culture changers—Hezekiah, Josiah, and (with difficulty) Asa. It took William Wilberforce more than forty years—with many defeats and a lot of abuse in Parliament—to change a culture and get slavery abolished in the British Empire. He died just days after the change was voted. Change cost Lincoln his life even as his hope for that change was coming alive.

Is this struggle in discipleship worthy of that kind of price for you? That's the first step in changing a culture. You'll have to be in, regardless of the cost. Then others will follow.

In the military, soldiers are in a culture of commitment to their country and intolerance of insubordination, so they tend to go along with leadership's direction, whether they personally like it or not. In contrast, people in Christian communities tend to think of themselves more like a stockholder, or even board members—someone with vested rights and at least a voice in how things will go. Volunteers (members) often expect a chance to interact on big things before change is pronounced. Ironically, that's often true whether or not the members are highly involved. Youth, if inspired by charismatic leaders, may be more conforming and willing to accept dictated change. Most of us, though, not so much. People want to feel included in making big choices. Even in the most centralized forms of church governance, changes foisted on people can ruffle feelings and logjam progress. Some people, feeling surprised by new declarations, may fight. Others, feeling left out or ignored, may leave. Even the usual team players may scratch their heads and feel sidelined if lots of communication and gracious interaction is missing.

Relationships are key to discipleship, and in relationships, understanding what people think is vital to any culture change. Leaders must tread carefully in change, but they must tread. For people to buy in to change, it must come as a compelling case from leadership, a case that (most) people can believe in. And interestingly, relationship makes people believe in people. Belief begins there—in relationships.

To try to force quick change in the Western world of autonomy and individualism is to quickly invite failure. Culture change will depend on leaders who people trust, leaders who take the time and energy to reason with and relate to people. Of course, sermons and lectures and announcements will help, but those are more like the vitamins we've mentioned before. The core of culture change is from leaders in relationship, helping people to comprehend and to want to come along on the journey of a body of believers aimed at biblical discipleship. Relationships and credibility are key to culture change.

Are you willing to "eat your own dog food" as a leader? That's a metaphorical way of asking: Are you willing to conform to the system you're advocating? Change must have leaders living this new thing out as winsome examples among their people. Living it out in humility, conformance, love, and passion.

Dr. Calvin Miller—author, poet, artist, preacher—was one of my mentors as a college student. This book is dedicated to him and his wonderful wife, Barbara. Calvin took me with him to visit, to meet, to encounter and watch him disciple people. When we talked about life, stuff, and things, he would drop bread crumbs and a few bombshells on me. One of his recurring phrases was "Love and take care of your pastor —he has a really challenging life." Another one was "Keep the cookies on the low shelf," talking about relating to other disciples in ways they can grasp and understand the truth of Christ. That coaching always stuck with me in communicating with people. Keep the sights, sounds, and smells of change in a place where people can pick up on them as they come along with you.

In a culture change, people need a chance to understand and catch on to the good work you're advocating. Give them a whiff of the cookies; let them see the cookies and taste the cookies. Always keep a few discipling cookies on the shelf someone can reach.

Don't begin the journey alone. Yes, there are hero stories of someone going alone, and against all odds, bringing on a new way. But that's not the disciple's way. Who's alongside you? Who sees the dilemma for what it is, as you do? Discipleship is not a solo event. Who's willing to risk their political capital and time to work this alongside you? For me it was Ken "Sly" Fox. Sly is one of those Jedi Knight F-15 pilots, a "come along with me" leader, not ashamed of his faith, and really, really good in a dogfight. If you spent time around Sly you were going to hear mission, culture and Christ, again and again. Sly mentored me, made me stronger spiritually and professionally as a believer. Even though I was at best, a mediocre flyer, Sly risked his own reputation to give me a chance to develop. Thank you Sly!

"It's déjà vu all over again."[116] You have to repeat the mission and culture talks over and over until everyone thinks that it's déjà vu, all over again. Be patient, let people get familiar at their pace, and then keep repeating the new way forward over and over. Keep offering discipleship as a "we've been there before" event. And after all, you have been there before. Jesus Christ took us there first. Once the credibility and early interest about where things are headed starts to build among people, provide clear and achievable strategy steps for them to grasp, and to get some early wins on moving the culture. Strategy must motivate people to be part of the journey.

Change must come over time, a lot more time than you might think in order for people to catch up with your advanced thinking on this change. Most folks will not have had time to grasp the why or the what of everything you've long thought about and are now talking about. Change is scary; it suggests loss of control or influence. Many fret that change without their consent or control makes them irrelevant. Those kinds of perceptions could intimidate anyone. Help people feel involved and important. Help them to embrace change for what it is. Be gracious and patient to ensure that people have many opportunities and time to ingest the issues and ideas. Don't push ahead too far until people across the age, stage, viewpoints and strata of your church can tell you the story you told them, and get it right, and have a passion for it.

Know that you'll be tested in change. Culture must ultimately define boundaries and reinforce, positively and negatively, what is and isn't acceptable. Some will try to push these boundaries around, buck the system, dare you to act as you said you would. Culture doesn't have to be draconian, but it has to require conformity. Not as in mindless conformity—but in saying "this is what we're about"—making disciples who are surrendered and committed, and who'll go out to make more disciples. If that isn't going to work for someone, they need to realize that it will be awkward or even impossible to try to move the community off that agenda. The best communities are not fear-mongering brutes nor demanding taskmasters. They're loving, but insistent. Patient but firm. Clear and unequivocal.

Leaders in Christian community need to reclaim their shepherd's role and lose the celebrity, prosperity and guru trappings. I've seen this play out in business so many times. A CEO is leading the company, when success arrives. The CEO is no longer a coach and mentor but a celebrity. Not teaching people how to fish, but serving up unfathomable prepared dishes of wisdom. The pedestal is raised. The praise erupts. The books are published. Maybe even a TED Talk. Limited access and exposure with the regular people ensues. Gurus don't do curbside, right? Clerically, distancing is best, yes? No! Christian leaders, like CEOs, are coaches for their people. They're shepherds, to use a more biblical term, among their disciples.

Which brings to mind two discipling heroes of mine—Greg and Stacey Oliver, who founded and lead Awaken Recovery in Birmingham, Alabama. In their own words, hear how they confront the disciple dilemma with people battling sexual brokenness:

"This discipleship recovery journey is not formulaic, it's relational. This is the part of discipleship that seems to frustrate people and cause them to begin looking for the door. A discipleship approach to recovery means this is going to involve more than completing a workbook or checking off a certain number of meetings or counseling sessions. It's going to involve learning how to follow Jesus for the rest of our lives. We follow Him as He reveals to us healthy paths to healing, beliefs, actions, and everything else that's been hanging us up. What does this look like, specifically? Healthy recovery looks a lot like what Paul said in 1 Corinthians 11:1. "Follow my example, as I follow the example of Christ." Recovery community allows men and women to meet others who have been where they are. It allows them to hear stories of other people. As the Big Book of AA says, "Our stories disclose in a general way *what we were like, what happened, and what we are like now.*" What a great start for discipleship! We relate to those ahead of us because their stories sound like our stories. We listen to how they encountered God in their struggle, and the difference He made. We see what their lives look like after they committed to follow Jesus (and others ahead of them). And we decide to do the same thing. Before we know it, our lives are different and we now have the opportunity to have others after us benefit as followers. Discipleship!"

Relational leadership matters greatly, whether recovery or simple community. Another of my mentors, Conrad "Buster" Brown, is a winsome leader of a megachurch near Charleston, SC. Every time you're in that church, there's Buster, the senior pastor, out among the people, young and old, talking life, football trash, current events. He knows the names and birthdays of your kids. He spends time in small groups—groups of three and four young men, weekly, as a discipler. Not just tending to his inner-circle leaders, but relating and living among to the rest of the people. A beautiful example of a shepherd's heart.

Get out among your people! Not just casual Sunday morning hellos, but out there with them. That builds credibility for change, and even more importantly, it builds people who want to be and make disciples. If your organization is too large for you to to do that regularly don't panic. But do be sure everyone has leadership connections, no disciple lost, so to speak.

"In all your getting, get understanding." (Proverbs 4:7). This culture change thing works only if your people believe you get them, and that this change is theirs too, not an edict or fatwa. That will require personal capital on your part, relating sincerely and graciously with folks, to understand, to motivate, to share the experience. This cannot be done by administrative fiat. That doesn't work in business, and it won't fare any better in Christian communities. We're too stiff-necked to let you get away with change that easily. But once people really get the problem, really grasp the mission as their own, and believe in their leaders' sincerity and support, then the disciple dilemma begins to unravel.

Are you worried that God may not have placed you in this role? Do you feel insignificant in the mission, or under-equipped to give the effort and time required for the culture challenge? If you do, you're a member of the leadership club.

People are watching you. Realize that your life matters and has influence. I remember the leaders in my life. When they talked, I listened. Most of them would never have thought they were significant people. But they were significant to me. Flaws? Sure. But they were the leaders. I remember their faces, their words, their leverage in my life, thinking "That pastor invaded and changed my worldview on this." or "This lady is the CEO, and she helped me to rethink my ideas." or "Wow, he's one of the political leaders in our town and he said…"

Somewhere along the way, I must have had a leadership lobotomy. Because, when I became a CEO or served in Christian leadership, it never occurred to me that anyone thought much about what I said or did. (Ditto in fatherhood too.) But people *were* watching. And talking about you, though you might not hear the words.

You have no idea how much sway you have with your employees or your church folks. One day a personal mentor, who had nothing to gain from doling out compliments told me, "You have no idea how much influence you have in your role." I aw-shucks'd him for his kind words, while swelling up with the accolades from my guru, walking toward me. I don't, exactly, remember what happened next. The room went wobbly, the lights went out.

After I came to and picked myself up off the floor, he continued. "I never said you're an amazing person who ought to be admired. I said you don't realize how much influence your role carries with people." He went on: "Even cynics want leaders. They expect you to blaze the trail. They expect you to be fair, to be honest, and not to treat them like chattel. Relate to them. If you live with integrity and humility in your role, most will follow you. That's influence as a leader. The ones who don't buy in to the mission can leave."

You don't have to be a rock star to have influence on people. You don't have to be a West Point or Cambridge graduate to lead. Ordinary people have always been the bedrock of the global church, often to the dismay of the elite. But building a discipling community will require leaders who are convinced of their call to make things different. They're humble, gracious followers of Christ called to lead so the community's disciples can flourish making disciples.

As a leader your greatest contribution is in being the greenhouse manager—to be the enabler of multiplying rather than the one doing the addition. You're in that kind of leadership role now, for "such a time as this."

The phrase "such a time as this" jumps out of the book of Esther regarding the role of another leader, a woman leader: "If you remain silent at this time, relief and deliverance for the Jews will arise from another place, but you and your father's family will perish. And who knows but that you have come to your royal position *for such a time as this?*" (Esther 4:14, emphasis added).

You're called as a leader to help your people do justice, to love mercy, and to walk humbly with your God (Micah 6:8), true touchstones of Christian culture, the very stuff Christian leadership is to foster in disciples. This kind of leadership is an invigorating and motivating culture for disciples.

Where to start? Any change in a cultural context requires strong convictions, clear direction, deep humility, and a long-term commitment to talk things out with people, well before trying to foist those expectations or taking any votes. In business and Christian community, there will always be holdouts against change and leadership. Such dissent is normal. Dissent requires patience and true understanding, even if you don't agree with someone. They may be vile and ugly, devious, or just stubbornly resistant. Stay to the high ground. Be the leader. The common and often damaging leadership mistake is thinking everyone has to do what I want, not caring about people at all. Equally bad: whatever anyone wants is probably okay, just don't ruffle feathers. Or yet another big screwup: leaders assuming everybody knows what the leaders know, and that everyone understands and agrees with us, so just zoom ahead.

A culture change journey depends on knowing the times—the things pushing on and agitating and vexing people. For example, digital technology is constantly on in people's lives today, fomenting anger, fatigue and despair, especially around change. Every few moments, gadgets buzz, beep, and implore. Watch the docudrama *The Social Dilemma*. The real-life architects of social media lay out their "omagosh" realizations that they've created an addictive polarizing techno-solvent to attack community and society. Their information algorithms, much of them drawing on sensationalized and unverified information, concentrate and bait for FOMO (fear of missing out) as an engine of tribal xenophobia, which amps up anger, despair, and anxiousness instead of comfort and discipleship. These kinds of significant influencers in people's lives today mean change can feel like a very scary thing.

Mapping out the best way to proceed in the disciple dilemma is a complex task. That's because every organization has different issues, different people, and different societal dynamics in its space and place. However, we committed to be practical in this chapter, so let's unpack a few examples to use in a journey of culture change.

Thom Rainer and Eric Geiger in *Simple Church* advocate a way that leads a church through phases of awareness and consensus in a change journey. Their terms *clarity, movement, alignment,* and *focus*[117] formalize a mission change. The book is well written and has a clear and thoughtful process to follow. My layman's "but" is that the book offers a program— literally a punch-list to swing a community toward mass discipling, instead of the relational discipling issues discussed in this book.

Like other strategic planning or culture change models, trying to stick with a checklist can become a diversion all unto itself in the uniqueness of your church versus the author's experience. Be aware, for example, that Rainer and Geiger's *Simple Church* model assumes staff capability to seek, design, and execute change, much as a company might orchestrate a strategic plan. Church staffs are often not experienced in that kind of relational and grainy change process. And just as often, they're distracted by the administrative chores and traditions mentioned in earlier chapters. The outcome of a community reformation, without both lay and staff leaders having experience in this endeavor, will probably have low odds of success.

Lastly, in the *Simple Church* there seems to be little caution about the risks of top-down change, rather than a careful approach and the soak time needed for Western churches to go bottom-up (where the rest of the people take change on as their own). It is a good book, yet no one size or process fits all.

The disciple dilemma is worth the risk. The church in the West is shedding its voice and its saltiness at an accelerating rate today. Contemporary Christians are caricatured as unremarkable, dour-faced, and fearful introverts who think right in line with the scripts of the talking TV heads.

Leaders owe disciples better than this. Disciples owe everyone else better as the disciples Jesus told us to be.

Christians need four things for functional discipling to flourish: 1) leaders who get God's mission; 2) discipleship as the mission and its supporting culture; 3) a community absorbing that mission; and 4) people who are motivated by that mission, and participating in that culture.

The popular definition for insanity is doing the same thing over and over again while expecting different results. May your role as a leader reverse that: not doing the same (traditional) things and expectantly changing, becoming different, focused on a mission of discipleship, enabling a community to foster disciples making disciples. That is practical leadership.

It's time to land the plane. Our last chapter touches down on some closing thoughts about this time and the circumstances we find ourselves in. In short, like most other periods of history—in chaotic surroundings. We're about to hit some turbulence. Be sure your seat belt is snug and your tray table is in its upright and locked position.

Therefore we will not fear,
though the earth give way and the mountains fall into the heart of the sea,
though its waters roar and foam and the mountains quake with their surging.
Psalm 46:2–3

So often the contemporary church is a weak, ineffectual voice
with an uncertain sound.
Martin Luther King Jr., "Letter from a Birmingham Jail"

14

Leadership and Discipling in Tumultuous Times

S kim these headlines in the recent news cycles:
abortion, Afghanistan, Al Queda, Antifa, artificial intelligence, bankruptcy, Beirut, BLM, borders, Brexit, canceled, censorship, China, CHOP, climate emergency, coverups, Covid, debt ceiling, Delta variant, Dreamers, economy, election, fake news, fires, fossil fuels, floods, gender fluidity, hacked, Hong Kong, hurricanes, identity, immigration, inflation, infrastructure, injustice, Iran, ISIS, Israel, Jihad, LGBTQ, migrants, misogyny, North Korea, nukes, oppression, PPP, polarization, political corruption, poverty, protests, QAnon, quarantine, racism, recall, recession, recounts, revolution, riots, Russia, sanctions, sexual abuse, slavery, social distance, social justice, social media, statues, Syria, Taliban, Taper Tantrums, tariffs, terrorism, transgender, transhumanism, Uncle Tom, unemployed, vaccines, vote tampering, war, white privilege, and woke.

Anger, fear, or sadness may erupt about these things, but the theme is turmoil. Any one of these topics by itself carries massive implications for life and society. But these once-afar things trouble our own neighborhoods, divide friends, family and faith, not just other people out there in the world somewhere.

"So often the contemporary church is a weak, ineffectual voice with an uncertain sound." said Dr. Martin Luther King Jr.[118] Modernity has shackled much of the contemporary Church, like the people in Plato's cave. Chained inside a cave (trapped in our present), with a fire intended to warm us (science, myths, politics, rumors, religions), we see shadows on the wall (the "news") which amps up fears, speculation and distrust, causing even the believers to lean in toward despair and panic. People are inclined to think these flickerings are all there ever was, and all that will ever be. It all seems hopeless. We stay riveted on the wall, on the flickers. We do not peer outside the cave, where we can easily see the true heritage God provided for his disciples, and the future he destined for us, despite any headlines.

Christian community must restore biblical discipleship. Only Christ's disciples—not casual participants—true disciples, can have hope amidst earthly turmoil. It is the disciples' mission to help people hear of the better way, outside the cave, about the ultimate hope. Only as disciples will death-to-self result in life for others amidst a world of turmoil. And only by leaders intentionally addressing the disciple dilemma—even amidst the turmoil—will biblical disciples consistently rise up, see outside the cave, and rekindle true hope for people.

Alongside other passages in both Testaments, Psalm 46 makes plain that disciples are expected to serve steadfastly during these kinds of things, and despite these kinds of things:

> God is our refuge and strength, an ever-present help in trouble.
> Therefore we will not fear, though the earth give way
> and the mountains fall into the heart of the sea,
> though its waters roar and foam and the mountains quake
> with their surging.
> There is a river whose streams make glad the city of God,
> the holy place where the Most High dwells.

God is within her, she will not fall; God will help her at
break of day.
Nations are in uproar, kingdoms fall; he lifts his voice, the
earth melts.
The Lord Almighty is with us; the God of Jacob is our for-
tress.
Come and see what the Lord has done, the desolations he
has brought on the earth.
He makes wars cease to the ends of the earth.
He breaks the bow and shatters the spear; he burns the
shields with fire.
He says, "Be still, and know that I am God;
I will be exalted among the nations, I will be exalted in the
earth."
The Lord Almighty is with us; the God of Jacob is our for-
tress.

Disciples are not casual spectators relying on a membership or participation in institutional brands. Disciples are not people who by praying
ritual words are deluded into thinking themselves complete in Christ.
Disciples cannot stand being muted in their hope, or opting in and out of
being saved or thinking social causes or politics are the New Testament's
nirvana.

The phrase *follower of Jesus* is not a fad or brag or hobby. It is surrender—people as bondservants (*doulos*), each one. People willing to die to
personal agendas, pursuing God with all their heart, mind, and strength
(Deuteronomy 4:29; 10:12; Hebrews 8:10). People living out life together,
continuously developing in Christ. Living in very close relationships, and
yes, in gatherings too, such as church. This is the biblical context of a disciple. Submitted in good order to God's direction, rather than modernity's
got-to-be-me. Teamed, not lone-wolves. These disciples are paradoxically,
both sons and daughters to God, and bondservants, free to be servants,

bound as heirs, sons and daughters of God. Disciples, whose price on the auction block of enslavement to self/spirits/society was paid by Another.

That's the discipleship culture that leaders owe their people and their world. Then and only then can the people in your charge begin to experience the lift from a community in true mission for Christ.

How would the Old Testament people assimilate this whole-heart calling as individuals, tribes, and a nation devoted to God's kingdom? The answer is leaders. And mostly in the midst of horrid turmoil and barbaric situations. Not a program launch, not a sermon series, but leaders pursuing the mission of God, teaching people the shema (Deuteronomy 6:4-9), to embed and sustain a "remember and practice" culture. A culture that only emerges by way of leaders.

The relational design imparted by leaders was obvious in Scripture— leaders passing downstream to clans, then to families, then to individuals. Not one leader doing such discipling to all people, rather, leaders creating well, delegating effectively that culture of the shema. All deeply relational in ever smaller groupings, such that one-on-one or one-on-few was the culture.

To be sure, these Old Testament folk were more willing to follow authoritative leadership than the radically autonomous rebels in our generations. (Yes, boomers, this means you too.) A disciple must surrender that rebellion. The process God established back then is just as pertinent as it is now. Some ideas just seem built to last, don't they?

Leaders must be the designers and administrators in the greenhouse, so that the disciplers can be about raising up disciples, who remain faithful to their call, no matter how intimidating the Roman arenas may seem to be, or how Jacobin the politics and university policies are, or how angry and micro-offended the woke warriors and their histrionics may be. The expectation then and now is that leaders design the greenhouse to produce wholehearted, humble, just, merciful followers in Christ, following without fear and despair, teamed and active in society. We are to be disciples living lives with a singular purpose: to draw other people to follow Christ.

The temptation is to work the symptoms. Strategy is tough sledding. Working on the root causes instead of the symptoms can be vexing for leaders. It can feel like watching crops grow instead of microwaving things. Working the root causes can feel like you're focused on the wrong things, because things aren't changing fast enough, or the turbulence you encounter messing with long-standing and beloved traditions. But leaders are the only ones that will get past the symptoms to the roots, to the dilemma. It will not be easy to stick to the long game. The traditional play, you see, is in quick fixes. Or pass the buck. Or avoid conflicts, and bemoan the symptoms, play with the symptoms, instead of attacking root causes.

Short-term fixes strip the credibility gears of onlookers, as yet another solution comes down from the mountain, and everyone knows it won't last or succeed. So leadership must lead change going after the root causes, which is very different from the fashionable pablum of prosperity, brand-centrism, and conversionism Christianity. Leadership must transcend secular trends and practice a better way in Christian community:

- *The mission of Christ does not change*, no matter what's trying to take over the lead.
- *Intentional culture emerges from that mission*, and culture is not redefined nor distorted by hysteria, fear, intolerance, charges of bigotry, or new attempts to use very old arguments to lure people away from their Hope, or frighten disciples into silence.
- *Living with God's peace and being present* is what people want to see in you as a leader. And they want to hear from you. You owe them your own certainty of a peace, which is possible only by being alive in Christ. A peace that points people to true north—back to the Lord and his mission. As a leader, don't get snookered into thinking uneasiness disqualifies you. Uneasiness and peace can coexist in leading. But a leader must have peace, as Christ meant peace, in the midst of turmoil.
- *Understand the times*, as the men of Issachar did. For those of us less gifted than Issachar's people in seeing through walls, we must be at prayer, calling out for the Holy Spirit to fill us, which

is God's guaranteed presence as we lead. And we must have the iron-sharpening counsel of others.

- *Use insightful people tools, to better understand the environment around you, to understand your people, and to find the best path to execute on the mission.* For example, SWOT is a granular and contemporary version of Luke 14:28. SWOT stands for *strengths, weaknesses, opportunities,* and *threats.* Strengths are things we can control, things that we do well. Contrast strengths to weaknesses, attributes or things we are in charge of, yet must be improved. Opportunities and threats involve things we can't control—whether things in our favor, or things that impede or negate our mission. In strategy and planning, a SWOT analysis can help us think through the fast-changing environment we're in to keep us effective and on mission.

"Never let a good crisis go to waste."[119] Leaders, this may be your time—now more than ever—for you to address a cultural crisis, for changing a traditions-laden culture. Know the true mission. Get on that mission. Stay on that mission! Be able to explain well and winsomely how the culture will conform the church to that mission.

Leaders in times of turmoil must (re)construct mission and culture, then live as examples in it. Leaders are disciples living life as Christ told disciples to live as well as leaders of the strategic changes we speak of here. In turmoil, leaders must be intimately connected with their people, not necessarily as their personal discipler, but as encouragers of relationships, connecting people with people—getting the pulse, knowing what's up, staying the course, staying the mission. Remember that people are watching you. Live as you were called to live. And lead in that place you occupy. If your church is too big for your leaders to connect with everyone, consider strategic changes to do something about that.

If a Christian community is riddled with bad traditions, or broken in some ways, lead in repentance and humility. But change things. Leaders must give disciples a way forward, a strategy that subjugates turmoil, a way for spectators and skeptics and scoffers to encounter the glory and *agape* of Christ. Leaders owe their disciples of all stripes and styles and beliefs an organization supporting disciples, making disciples, as Christ taught.

It was turmoil when Christ said to all of us, "And surely I am with you always, to the very end of the age" (Matthew 28:20). He said "with you always" to empower the mission he'd just given them, and us: "Therefore go and make disciples of all nations, baptizing them in the name of the Father and of the Son and of the Holy Spirit, and teaching them to obey everything I have commanded you" (Matthew 28:19–20).

Leaders, may it be so for you—to lead us, to enable us to better pursue Christ's mission as his disciples!

CONCLUSION

What am I supposed to do? What are the next steps and the method? What struck me on this journey through the disciple dilemma is how many of us have become acclimated to a tool or a process to fix anything out of whack in our organizations. And how unaware we can be as leaders, of the forces affecting disciples. My takeaway from my study of all this: It is leadership's crucial and strategic responsibility to restore a discipleship very different from modernity's version.

It bears mentioning that wrong conclusions of guilt or despair, perceptions that you or I have not done things right regarding discipleship, and now it is too late are our reality. The point of the book is to consider if we need to courageously re-evaluate where things stand, then to begin to act. Re-evaluations like that were fountainheads of the Reformation, the awakenings and numerous missionary callings. Christianity is not a rear-view mirror angst trapped in traditional practices. Christianity is a forward following based on the historical death, resurrection, grace and mercy of the Most-High God demanding we go out there and disciple.

Don't look for a recipe to fix things. Evaluate who you and your community are in giftings, personalities, geography, resources and then go. Biblical discipleship is art, not science. Relationship, not production. Christ did not provide a discipling checklist built on institutional assets nor traditions. He gave us the example of one-on-few discipling, of deeply relational life alongside others in order to meet Christ, know Christ, surrender, and then to follow with all our hearts the true living God. Our hope is not in traditions, nor attributes of an institution—not in size or programs or branding. Our hope, as the New Testament intended the word *hope*—is in the certainty of Christ's resurrection and redemption for us. This redemption demands our full and complete surrender to serve him and follow him, even if it costs us everything in our mortal life, including our mortal life. This is a disciple. It is not possible to really understand redemption and do anything otherwise. Of course disciples will screw it up, and repeatedly. But under grace disciples stand back up, and persevere again. The world deserves disciples like that speaking into societies. And into Christian communities. This where you come in.

What is expected of you? Re-establish an atmosphere and the essential mechanics suited to your community, so that disciples make disciples. In other words, teach the delegation of relational, replicating and intimate biblical discipleship. Administration, management, metrics are secondary things for you. Necessary things perhaps, but they cannot distract you from this holy delegation of discipleship. If you refuse to delegate, you will saturate and discipling will flounder. If you refuse to delegate your leadership teams will emulate that. As a leader, you own the rights of the cultural road, the signposts and guardrails on the journey for disciples. Make it count for discipling few who invite and disciple few, and watch that biblical model grow.

As a leader, you must decide whether discipling is worthy of a redirect away from the lower roads of the traditions and onto the higher road of discipleship. As a leader of people with that certain hope, you have the obligation of strategically directing people to a fuller discipleship, precisely as Jesus meant the word disciple. No longer converts, as Islam or Marxism meant converts, but disciples who have begun to abandon their autonomous life, a life that will only end in death anyway. Jim Elliot's words ring out: "He is no fool who gives what he cannot keep to gain that which he cannot lose."[120] This discipleship is a deal of unfathomable worth. One where the best this life has to offer is unworthy of the real return on investment that Paul described: "Our present sufferings are not worth comparing with the glory that will be revealed in us" (Romans 8:18). That's what disciples live for, and what biblical disciples offer the world.

Christianity in the West has been infiltrated. The traditions of cheap grace and powerful religious institutions are producing ever-more sclerotic followers, trapped in a concierge Christianity where we actually believe a prayer, membership and a few activities will cover the bill. And such a compromised disciple believes that we can keep silent in the streets and offices, or justify walking away entirely, since our version of a religion is really no different from any other religion, ultimately.

"We must do something! So speak up!" These are the words of Israel in Judges 19 as they came to realize morality and commitment were long gone from the fabric of their culture, and they were now a bankrupt people, following pantheon gods, doing whatever any individual deemed right for themself. Somebody had to speak up. Somebody had to set things right. The somebody were going to have to be the leaders. Most leaders in our Bibles are ordinary, compromised, flawed and timid souls just wanting to live life. Until God called them out as leaders.

Discipleship needs you leading. It needs men and women in leadership, to enable others to be disciples, to run the race as disciples, to invite more disciples. Disciples unhindered, throwing off the traditional baggage. God expects you to lead us away from the dissipation of traditions of failure. God expects you, as a leader, to redirect your community back to the true mission. To establish a supporting culture to that true mission. To teach people how to follow Jesus as Jesus taught us.

What am I asking of you?

1. Decide whether or not you think something is amiss in modern discipleship. If it's not, send me your reasoning, why you believe all is well and I'll refund your book purchase.
2. Decide what you're willing to do about the disciple dilemma. You, personally, as a leader.
3. Be able to winsomely explain the situation facing discipleship today.
4. Bring other leaders alongside you, and start a culture change.

5. Be ready for turbulence and blowback. Don't give up.
6. Start a turnaround for your Christian community.
7. If you're feeling unsure of what "start a turnaround" means, reach out to us at www.thediscipledilemma.com

You need to be a disciple too, as you lead. Walk alongside other peers as disciples. Live as disciples are to live. Invite people into your life. Disciple believers and unbelievers alike. Stand out from society's ways, be weird enough, in love and life, to draw questions. Be ready when people (eventually) ask you for the hope within you. Do not conform to the fashionable passions of the angry, the offended, and the tribal social warriors out there.

This is your time, leaders. The dilemma is real and only you can address it. So lead. Go and lead to remake a community that will shake off the bad traditions, so that we then, as disciples, actually go and make Christ's disciples.

"Go therefore and make disciples of all nations, baptizing them in the name of the Father and of the Son and of the Holy Spirit, teaching them to observe all that I have commanded you. And behold, I am with you always, to the end of the age." Jesus, Matthew 28:19-20 (ESV)

ABOUT THE AUTHOR

Dennis Allen has served as the Chief Executive Officer in both national and international business spanning distribution, manufacturing and technology across electronics, software, building materials, environmental services and oil & gas. He has been a member and served in leadership in mega, mid-sized and startup churches as an elder, deacon, teacher, board member and speaker, with emphasis on strategy, discipleship and planning. Dennis was combat rated in the US Air Force as an F-15 fighter pilot, mission commander and instructor pilot prior to his business career. He has a B.S. in Industrial Management from the University of Alabama, an MBA from Xavier University in Cincinnati, OH, and is an alumnus of the Oxford Centre for Christian Apologetics in Oxford, United Kingdom. Dennis and his wife Karen live in Reston, VA.

You can reach Dennis at www.discipledilemma.com.

ENDNOTES

1   As quoted in "Imagine There's No Clergy" by William Shea and David Cloutier, *Commonweal*, January 20, 2018.

2   James Carville, "It's the Economy Stupid", as quoted by Jerry Jasinowski, Huffington Post, November 5, 2015

3   Carl Wilson, *With Christ in the School of Discipleship*, Zondervan, 1978, 19

4   "Making Kingdom Disciples", Tony Evans, YouTube.com, @00.14.10

5   Joseph Liu, "Many Americans Say Other Religions Can Lead to Eternal Life," Pew Research Center: Religion & Public Life, December 18, 2008

6   "What America Really Believes," Baylor Religion Surveys, 2007

7   "Sharing Faith Is Increasingly Optional to Christians," Barna Research, May 15, 2018

8   "Church and Religious Charitable Giving Statistics," NP Source (website), accessed August 14, 2021

9   Melinda Denton & Richard Flory, *Back Pocket God*, (Oxford University Press, 2020), 228

10 "In U.S., Decline of Christianity Continues at Rapid Pace," Pew Research Center: Religion & Public Life; October 17, 2019

11 "Religion and Beliefs," Humanists UK, Freedom of religion or belief » Humanists UK

12 *The State of Discipleship: A Barna Report.*

13 Barna Research Group, "American Bible Knowledge Is in the Ballpark but Often Off Base," July 12, 2000, as cited by Ken Boa, "The Reliability of the Bible (Decision Magazine Article)," January 1, 2000

14 "New Research on the State of Discipleship," Barna Research.

15 "Americans Divided on the Importance of Church," Barna, March 24, 2014

16 "Millennials in Adulthood", (Pew Research, March 7, 2014); General Social Survey 2016, (NORC, University of Chicago, 2017) "In US decline of Christianity Continues at a Rapid Pace, (Pew Research, October 17, 2019)

17 Michael Lipka, "A Closer Look at America's Rapidly Growing Religious 'Nones,'" (Pew Research, May 13, 2015), "Fact Tank, A Closer Look at America's Rapidly Growing Religious Nones"; (Pew research, May 13, 2015)

18 Jeffrey Jones, "US Church Membership Down Sharply in Two Decades," (Gallup, April 18, 2019).

19 Dean Kelley, *Why Conservative Churches Are Growing: A Study in Sociology of Religion with a new Preface,* Mercer University Press, 1996, 1.

20 William Wilberforce, *A practical view of the prevailing religious system of professed Christians: in the higher and middle classes in this country, contrasted with real Christianity, (New York: Crockee and Brewster), 1829, p76*

21 Rod Dreher, *The Benedict Option: A Strategy for Christians in a Post-Christian Nation* (New York: Penguin Random House, 2017).

22 R.R. Reno, *Return of the Strong Gods* (Washington, DC: Regnery Gateway, 2019).

23 Jonathan Wilson-Hartgrove, *Reconstructing the Gospel* (Downers Grove: IVP Books, n.d.).

24 Sherry A. Weddell, *Forming Intentional Disciples: The Path to Knowing and Following Jesus* (Huntington, IN: Our Sunday Visitor, 2012), 16.

25 Os Guinness, *The Magna Carta of Humanity, Sinai's Revolutionary Faith and the Future of Freedom,* (IVP, Downers Grove, IL, 2021), 20

26 Denton & Flory, (as cited above), 144-149; Religious News Service, 2018; Public Religion Research Institute (PRRI), 2017; Statista, 2017; Pew Research Center, 2014 (as cited above); "Rhett's Spiritual Deconstruction," (YouTube, February 9, 2020)

27 Missio Nexus, "2021 Missions Data Summary"

28 Patrick Erskine, "Hey Men! You Need to Go on a Mission Trip," (P2C. com, January 24, 2017)

29 Jean Hopfensperger, "Fewer Ministers, Heavier Burdens," (*Star Tribune,* August 19, 2018)

30 John S. Dickerson, *The Great Evangelical Recession* (Baker Books, 2013), 22.

31 David Kinnaman, "The Porn Phenomenon," (Barna Research, February 5, 2016)

32 Denton and Flory at 227 (As cited above)

33 Denton/Flory at 228 (As cited above)

34 Sarah Eekhoff Zylstra, "What Millennials Really Think about Evangelism," The Gospel Coalition, February 28, 2019, https://www.thegospelcoalition. org/article/millennials-really-think-evangelism/; Kate Shellnutt, "Half of Millennial Christians Say It's Wrong to Evangelize," (Barna as cited in *Christianity Today*, February 6, 2019)

35 "George Barna on Trends in the Culture," Truth and Liberty Coalition (Truth and Liberty, August 14, 2021)

36 *The State of Discipleship: A Barna Report Produced in Partnership with the Navigators* (Barna Group, 2015).

37 "New Research on the State of Discipleship," Barna Research , December 1, 2015

38 Travis Mitchell, "Choosing a New Church or House of Worship," (Pew Research Center, August 23, 2016)

39 Hugh Hewitt, *The Embarrassed Believer* (Nashville: Word Publishing, 1998), 2.

40 T. C. Lethbridge, *The Buried Gods* (London: Routledge, 1975), 136; William A. Chaney, "Paganism to Christianity in Anglo-Saxon England," in *Harvard Theological Review* 53, no. 3 (July 1960): 198.

41 Doris L. Bergen, *Twisted Cross: The German Christian Movement in the Third Reich* (Chapel Hill, NC: University of North Carolina Press, 1996), 4.

42 "Discipleship ≠ Following Christ Your Way", The Gospel Coalition, Sam Allberry, Podcast, June 7, 2019

43 New Abbey policy, churchclarity.org, accessed August 14, 2021, (as of August 14, 2021), http://www.newabbey.org/who-we-are

44 Richard Dawkins, *River Out of Eden: A Darwinian View of Life* (New York: Basic Books, 1995), 133.

45 Matthew 16.24-26; Luke 14.26

46 Theodoret of Cyrrhus, *Historia Religiosa*, AD fifth century.

47 Herbert Thurston, "St. Simeon Stylites the Elder," *The Catholic Encyclope-*

dia, vol, 13 (1912).

48 Ramsay MacMullen, *Christianizing the Roman Empire (AD 100-400)* (New Haven: Yale University Press, 1984), 2–7.

49 Fred Sanders, *The Deep Things of God, How the Trinity Changes Everything*, (2nd ed., Crossway, Wheaton, IL, 2017), 97

50 Dietrich Bonhoeffer, *The Cost of Discipleship*, Simon & Schuster, 1995, 51

51 "Top Jobs That Hate Their Boss," Payscale, (as of August 14, 2021), https://www.payscale.com/data-packages/employee-loyalty/least-loyal-employees.

52 Denton/Flory at 233-234 (as cited above)

53 Bill Hull, *The Complete Book of Discipleship: On Being and Making Followers of Christ* (Navpress, 2009), 262.

54 William Wilberforce, in a speech before the House of Commons in 1791, as quoted in *Once Blind, The Life of John Newton*, 2008 by Kay M. Strom, Authentic Books, Bletchley, p 255

55 Darren Carlson and Elliot Clark, "The 3 Words That Changed Missions Strategy—and Why We Might Be Wrong," *Gospel Coalition*, September 11, 2019, https://www.thegospelcoalition.org/article/misleading-words-missions-strategy-unreached-people-groups/.

56 John S. Dickerson, *The Great Evangelical Recession*, (As cited above), 22

57 As quoted in Elisabeth Elliot, *Shadow of the Almighty: The Life and Testament of Jim Elliot* (New York: Harper One, 1958), 15.

58 John Piper, "Should Christians Say That Their Aim Is to Convert Others to Faith in Christ?" *Desiring God*, October 22, 2009

59 *The State of Discipleship: A Barna Report.*

60 Harry Blamires, *The Christian* Mind, S.P.C.K., 1963, 3

61 *Sheep Among Wolves, Volume Two: The Devil Is Gonna Hang*, 2019 film produced by FAI Studios.

62 Federal Aviation Administration Accident Report: NTSB on Payne Stewart aircraft accident

63 Attributed to Abraham Lincoln by Robert G. Ingersoll, *True Greatness Exemplified in Abraham Lincoln*, Unity, Mar. 1, 1883, no.1.

64 Fred Lunenburg, "Power and Leadership: An Influence Process," *International Journal of Management, Business and Administration* 15 (November

2012): 1.

65 Dom Gregory Dix, *The Shape of the Liturgy*, third ed. (London: Continuum, 2007; first published 1945), 304.

66 "AFA Boycott Helps Drop Kmart Profits, Force Closing of 110 Stores," *AFA Journal*, November–December 1994.

67 Warren Shoulberg, "How Many Sears and Kmarts Will Be Left By 2021's End?" *Forbes* , January 5, 2021.

68 Stanley Bailey, "Crystal Cathedral Founder Robert Schuller Achieved His Vision, But Couldn't Sustain It," *Orange County Register*, April 6, 2015.

69 Denton/Flory at 231 (as cited above)

70 John Piper, "Can a Woman Preach if Elders Affirm It?" (YouTube, Desiring God, April 13, 2017); N. T. Wright "Why women should be church leaders and preachers," (YouTube, September 25, 2019)

71 Martin Luther King Jr., "A Knock at Midnight" Sermon, June, 1963

72 Kimberly Ross, "The Christian Nationalism Experiment Failed,", *Washington Examiner*, January 14, 2021.

73 John Adams, "A letter to the Massachusetts Militia," October 11, 1798.

74 Sam Allberry, How Do Churches End Up with Domineering Bullies for Pastors?, The Gospel Coalition, January 21, 2019

75 Elena Giannakopoulou, "A Canonical Approach to Holy Canon 89 of St. Basil the Great," *The Ecumenical Legacy of the Cappadocians*, Nicu Dumitrascu, ed. (Palgrave: MacMillan, 2016), 118–37.

76 Bruno Boute, *Academic Interests and Catholic Confessionalisation*, vol. 35, *Education and Society in the Middle Ages* (Boston and Leiden [Netherlands]: Brill, 2010), 64.

77 Gary Macy, *Treasures from the Storeroom: Medieval Religion and the Eucharist* (Collegeville, Minnesota: Liturgical Press, 1999), 173.

78 Sean O'Conaill, "Christendom Compromised Christianity—and Gave Birth to Secularism," *Lumen Gentium* 37 (website), December 9, 2014,

79 Justin Taylor, "60 Years Ago Today Dawson Trotman, the Founder of Navigators, Drowned While Saving a Girl's Life: An Interview," (Gospel Coalition, June 18, 2016)

80 See Todd Engstrom, "The Insufficiency of Small Groups for Discipleship," (Gospel Coalition, August 19, 2013)

81 J. Heinrich Arnold, *Discipleship*, (The Bruderhof Foundation. Inc., Farmington, PA, 2012), 18

82 Such as Kate Kelly, *Street Fighters: The Last 72 Hours of Bear Stearns, the Toughest Firm on Wall Street* (New York: Penguin, 2009).

83 Elliott Nesch, *Church of Tares: Purpose Driven, Seeker Sensitive, Church Growth & New World Order*, (YouTube at timeline 1:50:35, Holy Bible Prophecy, September 28, 2014).

84 "World's First Megachurch?", Warren Bird, Leadership Network

85 The Hartford Institute, 2020 Megachurch Report

86 William Cowper, "Retirement" (1787), lines 615–16.

87 Dr. John, "In The Right Place", Right Place Wrong Line, Atco Records, 1973

88 W. H. Kent, "Indulgences," vol. VII, *The Catholic Encyclopedia* (New York: Robert Appleton Co., 1910), 783–8.

89 Ray Cavanaugh, "Peddling Purgatory Relief: Johann Tetzel," (*National Catholic Reporter Online*, October 31, 2017)

90 Natasha Rausch et al., "Charting GE's Historic Rise and Tortured Downfall," Bloomberg, January 30, 2019

91 "Country Data Profile," International Monetary Fund Datamapper, (as of August 14, 2021)

92 GE's 1990 Annual Report, letter from the Chairman

93 Paraphrase of G.K. Chesterton, *The Thing: Why I Am Catholic*, Dodd Mead & Company, 1930, Ch 4

94 Geoff Colvin, "What the Hell Happened at GE?" (*Fortune*, May 24, 2018)

95 Hull, *The Complete Book of Discipleship*, 294–98.

96 *The State of Discipleship: A Barna Report*, 10.

97 *The State of Discipleship: (As cited above)*, 10.

98 Peter Berger, *The Noise of Solemn Assemblies*, (Doubleday, New York, 1961), 120

99 Steve Turner, "Creed," in *Up to Date: Poems, 1968-1982* (Belleville, Michigan: Lion, 1985), 138–39.

100 Address by the Archbishop of York to the Church of England, Diocesan Synod of Chelmsford, March 2017

101 Justin Taylor, "85 Years Ago Today: J. R. R. Tolkien Convinces C. S. Lewis That Christ Is the True Myth", The Gospel Coalition, September 20. 2016

102 Dietrich Bonhoeffer, *The Cost of Discipleship*, (First Macmillans Paperback edition, New York, 1963), 49

103 Jason Fischer, "The Scale of Paul's Tentmaking Enterprise" (an academic paper posted at MidAmerica Baptist Theological Seminary)

104 "Do Latter-Day Saints Believe That Men and Women Can Become Gods?" in *Latter-Day Christianity: 10 Basic Issues*, edited by Robert L. Millet, Noel B. Reynolds, and Larry E. Dahl (Neal A. Maxwwell Institute for Religious Scholarship, 1998).

105 Faith Foundry, www.faithfoundry.org

106 Chris Shirley, "Discipleship," *Southwestern Journal of Theology*50, no. 2 (Spring 2008): 211.

107 Francis Schaeffer, *The Great Evangelical Disaster*, (Crossway Books, 1984), Preface

108 Breaking Bad (TV Series 2008–2013), from a Southern colloquialism to "raise hell"

109 Stephen Neill, *The Unfinished Task* (Edinburgh Books, 1955), 45.

110 "How to Bring the Gospel to Post-Christian America," (YouTube, Carey Nieuwhof interview with Tim Keller, May 11, 2020)

111 Rainer & Geiger, *Simple Church,* (B&H Books, Nashville, 2006), 68

112 Jim Putnam and Bobby Harrington, *Discipleshift: Five Steps That Help Your Church to Make Disciples Who Make Disciples* (Grand Rapids, Michigan: Zondervan, 2013), 25–28.

113 Walter Truett Anderson, as quoted by Tim Keller in "Hero of Heroes", Gospel in Life sermon podcast, February 3, 2013

114 New Yorker, "Miss Dugan" cartoon, March 24, 1975

115 John White, *Excellence in Leadership*, (Inter-Varsity Press, 1986), 62

116 Usually credited to Yogi Berra

117 Thom S. Rainer and Eric Geiger, *Simple Church: Returning to God's Process for Making Disciples* (Nashville: B&H Books, 2011), 68.

118 Martin Luther King Jr., "Letter from a Birmingham Jail", April 16, 1963

119 A phrase, or variants, attributed indeterminately to Machiavelli, Sir Winston Churchill and Rahm Emmanuel.

120 Elizabeth Elliott, *Shadow of the Almighty*, (Hendrickson Publishers, Peabody, MA, 1958), 11

A free ebook edition is available with the purchase of this book.

To claim your free ebook edition:

1. Visit MorganJamesBOGO.com
2. Sign your name CLEARLY in the space
3. Complete the form and submit a photo of the entire copyright page
4. You or your friend can download the ebook to your preferred device

Morgan James BOGO™

A **FREE** ebook edition is available for you or a friend with the purchase of this print book.

CLEARLY SIGN YOUR NAME ABOVE

Instructions to claim your free ebook edition:
1. Visit MorganJamesBOGO.com
2. Sign your name CLEARLY in the space above
3. Complete the form and submit a photo of this entire page
4. You or your friend can download the ebook to your preferred device

Print & Digital Together Forever.

Snap a photo

Free ebook

Read anywhere

Printed in the USA
CPSIA information can be obtained
at www.ICGtesting.com
JSHW022210140824
68134JS00018B/974

9 781631 957826